L. E. (Lucius Eugene) Chittenden

Personal Reminiscences, 1840-1890

Including Some Not Hitherto Published of Lincoln and the War

L. E. (Lucius Eugene) Chittenden

Personal Reminiscences, 1840-1890
Including Some Not Hitherto Published of Lincoln and the War

ISBN/EAN: 9783337010034

Printed in Europe, USA, Canada, Australia, Japan

Cover: Foto ©ninafisch / pixelio.de

More available books at **www.hansebooks.com**

Personal Reminiscences

1840—1890

INCLUDING SOME NOT HITHERTO PUBLISHED OF LINCOLN AND THE WAR

BY

L. E. CHITTENDEN

AUTHOR OF "RECOLLECTIONS OF PRESIDENT LINCOLN AND HIS ADMINISTRATION."

NEW YORK
RICHMOND, CROSCUP & CO.
1893

To
EDWARD J. PHELPS,
LAWYER, STATESMAN, AND FELLOW-VERMONTER,

AS A

MEMORIAL OF A FRIENDSHIP

WHICH BEGAN WHEN WE CAME TO THE BAR,

WHICH HAS SURVIVED A BUSINESS COPARTNERSHIP

AND MANY "TRIALS,"

WHICH GROWS CLOSER WITH THE PASSING YEARS, AND

PROMISES TO BE INHERITED BY OUR CHILDREN,

I Dedicate this Volume.

THE AUTHOR.

PREFACE.

If the opinion of a large body of correspondents is reliable, the reading-public have derived some pleasure from my "Recollections of President Lincoln and his Administration." The chief attraction of that book must lie in its great central figure. If, as these correspondents claim, it has other merits, I think they are comprised in the fact that the subjects are personal, and each is treated separately in a chapter of no great length. It was also my purpose to describe persons and events without exaggeration or prejudice, just as they appeared to me at the time.

The present volume is written in the same spirit and on the same plan. While it lacks the great central attraction of the "Recollections," I sincerely hope that each subject will be found to possess an interest or to point a moral which will justify its publication.

I have an impression that truth is just as attractive in a book as it is in the ordinary transactions of life. If there is any false statement of fact herein, it has escaped my notice and has been unintentionally made. No chronological or other order of subjects has been attempted. Observations upon birds follow remarks upon the financial policy of Secretary Chase without any infringement of my design. Each chapter except the "Study" is substantially complete in itself, and must stand or fall upon its own merits. I offer no excuses, I do not attempt to forestall criticism. If any chapter is unworthy of a place in the literature of the time, I have simply made an error of judgment and must bear the penalty.

I shall feel greatly disappointed if there is a sentence in it which shall pain any reader or lead him to wish that the volume had not been written. It is more local than I could wish, but that is perhaps unavoidable.

The "Study" which closes the book is not within its original scope. It is an attempt to show what the qualities were which made Mr. Lincoln great—which as a political leader, an orator, a writer of English prose, a statesman, a military strategist, a friend and benefactor of humanity, so elevated and made him the foremost man of his time. If I have succeeded only partially, I have shown to my young countrymen how they may emulate his noble purposes and perpetuate his fame, that—

> "While the races of mankind endure,
> So shall his great example stand
> Colossal, glorious, seen in every land
> To keep the soldier firm, the statesman pure."

L. E. CHITTENDEN.

NEW YORK, Feb. 1, 1893.

CONTENTS.

CHAPTER	PAGE
I.—THE EARLIEST FREE SOIL ORGANIZATION—THE ORIGIN OF THE REPUBLICAN PARTY,	1
II.—THE VAN BURENS—THE NEW YORK BARN-BURNERS,	11
III.—THE EARLY BENCH AND BAR OF VERMONT,	18
IV.—A LESSON IN BANKING,	26
V.—THE THIRD HOUSE JOURNAL—HOW WE REFORMED LEGISLATION IN 1850,	33
VI.—WOODEN SIDE JUDGES OF THE COUNTY COURTS,	43
VII.—THE VERMONT FLOODWOOD OR RIGHT ARM OF HER DEFENCE,	47
VIII.—A GRATEFUL CLIENT,	53
IX.—HYPNOTISM—SPIRITUAL AND OTHER ISMS,	70
X.—"THE BEAUTIFUL AMERICAN NUN,"	79
XI.—SECRETARY CHASE AND HIS FINANCIAL POLICY,	90
XII.—SOME NOTES ABOUT BIRDS—A LESSON IN ENGINEERING,	101
XIII.—JUDGE LYNCH—AN INCIDENT OF EARLY PACIFIC RAILROAD TRAVEL,	114
XIV.—JUDGE LYNCH, CONTINUED—AN EXPERIENCE IN A WESTERN MINING-CAMP,	126
XV.—ADIRONDACK DAYS—UNTRIED COMPANIONS IN THE WILDERNESS—THEIR PERILS AND EXPERIENCES,	139
XVI.—THE STORY OF MITCHELL SABATTIS,	151
XVII.—THE ADIRONDACK REGION—A WARNING TO THE DESTROYER—A PLEA FOR THE PERISHING.	159

CONTENTS.

CHAPTER	PAGE
XVIII.—November Days on Lake Champlain—The Story of Hiram Bramble, ...	169
XIX.—Duck-Shooting in East Creek, . . .	175
XX.—A Cold Morning on Bullwagga Bay, .	182
XXI.—Quacks and Quackery, ...	186
XXII.—Essex Junction, ...	198
XXIII.—The Humor and Mischief of the Junior Bar—Our Annual Bar Festival, . . .	205
XXIV.—Owls, Falcons, and Eagles, . .	221
XXV.—Novel Experiences in Official Life, .	228
XXVI.—The Death of Lincoln, ...	236
XXVII.—Savannah in Winter and in War, . .	246
XXVIII.—Teaching School on Hog Island—Its Advantages and Pleasant Memories, . .	269
XXIX.—The Book Chase—Non-Existence of Unique Copies—A Hunt for "Sanders' Indian Wars" and "The Contrast," the First American Play—Stolen Engravings and Drawings, ...	279
XXX.—Some Men whom I knew in Washington during the Civil War, ...	303
XXXI.—Law as a Progressive Science—Is Progress Always an Advance?—Circumstantial Evidence—The Boorn Case, . .	328
XXXII.—Abraham Lincoln: A Study—His Origin and Early Life, ...	340
XXXIII.—Abraham Lincoln (Continued): His Failures—The Farm Laborer; the Flat-Boatman; the Fighter; the Merchant; the Surveyor, ...	349
XXXIV.—Abraham Lincoln (Continued): His Successes—The Lawyer; the Advocate; the Popular Man, ...	356
XXXV.—Abraham Lincoln (Continued): The Orator; the Candidate; the Man of the People, ...	367

CONTENTS.

CHAPTER		PAGE
XXXVI.	—ABRAHAM LINCOLN (CONTINUED) : HIS ELECTION ; HIS PREPARATION AND HIS PROMISES,	379
XXXVII.	—ABRAHAM LINCOLN (CONTINUED) : THE DIPLOMATIST ; THE MILITARY STRATEGIST ; THE MASTER OF ENGLISH PROSE ; THE STATESMAN ; THE GREAT PRESIDENT, ...	394
XXXVIII.	—ABRAHAM LINCOLN (CONTINUED) : THE MAN FULL OF FAITH AND POWER, . . .	409

PERSONAL REMINISCENCES.

CHAPTER I.

THE EARLIEST FREE SOIL ORGANIZATION—THE ORIGIN OF THE REPUBLICAN PARTY.

IT is April, 1848. The Mexican War is ended. Shall the territory which we made the war to acquire —vast enough in itself for a republic—remain free, or shall it be surrendered to the domination of the slave power? This had been the burning question. We had hoped it was settled by the Wilmot Proviso, which declared that neither slavery nor involuntary servitude, except for crime, should ever exist there. We were now to learn that, touching the peculiar institution, nothing was to be regarded as settled, unless it was settled in the Southern way. The slave power had secured control of the Democratic party. In the name of that party it had hinted at a programme which involved the abrogation of the Wilmot Proviso, and between its lines could be read faint indications of measures which did not mature until six years later. Of these, "Squatter Sovereignty" was the most obvious. This doctrine declared that the people ought to settle the status of a State as between freedom and slavery, after it was admitted into the Federal Union. But "Squatter

Sovereignty" involved the repeal of the Missouri Compromise of 1820, which declared that slavery should not exist north of latitude 36° 30'; for how could the people decide in favor of slavery if it were already excluded by an irrepealable law? There were also occasional suggestions from the South of a stringent law for the capture and return of fugitives from slavery, and of the principles established afterward in the Dred Scott case, as additional planks in the Democratic platform.

It was not a favorable time for the slave power to assert new claims, especially in Vermont. While the Liberty party had never attained great numerical strength there, and its leaders were generally regarded as dangerous extremists, there were many good Democrats as well as Whigs who could not but respect such men as William Lloyd Garrison, James G. Birney, and Gerritt Smith, however much they might differ from them as to the means by which their purposes were to be accomplished. Their differences were of degree rather than principle. The New Englanders generally would have said: "Let slavery be content with its present possessions—we will not concern ourselves with it where it has been established by law. But freedom is the natural right and normal condition of the human race. Not one square inch of territory, now free, shall ever be darkened by the pall of slavery with our consent, nor without overcoming all the lawful resistance we can interpose." The Abolitionists, however, insisted that slavery had no rights and that it ought to be everywhere abolished.

In fact, slavery itself was cordially detested by the people of the Green Mountains. They inherited their love of freedom from their ancestors. Like Abraham Lincoln in his younger days, the thought of slavery made them uncomfortable. There had been a very warm spot in their hearts for the hunted fugitive ever since Revolutionary days, when Capt. Ebenezer Allen, "conscientious that it is not right in the sight of God to keep slaves," gave to Dinah Mattis and her infant, slaves captured from the enemy, their deed of emancipation; and Judge Harrington decided against the title of the slave-master, because he could not show a deed from the original proprietor— Almighty God! From the day when the name of the State was first adopted, no slave had been taken away from Vermont against his will. The fugitive who set foot upon her soil was from that moment safe if he was not free. Her North and South roads were underground railroads, and there were few houses upon them where the escaped slave was not provided with rest, food, and clothing, and assisted on his way. There were Democrats who would send their teams to carry the fugitives northward, while they themselves walked to a convention to shout for Douglas, and resolve that slavery must not be interfered with in the States where it existed by law.

Just about this time the Democratic party of the North gave way, and intimated its willingness to make the concessions which the Southern wing of the party began openly to demand. Chief among these was the rejection of the Wilmot Proviso, and acceptance of the doctrine of "Squatter Sovereignty." The proximity of Missouri and Arkansas would enable their temporary emigrants to decide that slavery should be lawful in Kansas and Nebraska; and the obstructions being removed from California and New Mexico, any one with half an eye could see that the Missouri Compromise would be swept away, and the whole region west of the "Father of the Waters" would become slave territory.

To such concessions there were many Northern Democrats who objected, and some who answered "No! Never!" Just then the Democratic State Convention was called to meet at Montpelier, and the leading Democratic newspaper, published at the State capital, announced that the convention would incorporate the new doctrines into the Democratic platform. The paper spoke as one having authority, declaring that the Wilmot Proviso was a violation of the Federal Constitution.

I was one of the recalcitrant Democrats and a delegate from Burlington to that convention. On the day it met I should complete my twenty-fourth year. I had been practising at the bar somewhat over three years and was (in my own opinion) a much greater constitutional lawyer than I have at any time since been considered by myself or other competent judges. I felt perfectly qualified to discuss the constitutional question involved in the Proviso. The more I examined the authorities the clearer the question seemed, until I arrived at the condition of mind where I regarded this new demand as a piece of cool impudence on the part of the pro-slavery Democracy.

I found that other delegates to the convention were of the same temper. One of them was Charles D. Kasson, a lawyer of Burlington and an elder brother of John A. Kasson, afterward of Iowa. The elder Kasson was as solid, reliable, and generous a citizen and friend as ever existed. He was removed

THE FIRST FREE SOIL PARTY.   5

by death only a few years later, and his loss was felt not only by the circle of his personal friends, but by the community.

With Kasson I promptly decided that if the convention committed itself in favor of Squatter Sovereignty and against the Wilmot Proviso, we would leave it and raise the standard of FREE SOIL. We corresponded with other delegates and invited them to join us in the revolt. Many of the younger Democrats were, like ourselves, indignant at the new dictation. But when it came to the question of leaving the party they (nearly) "all with one consent began to make excuse." We found only four who where willing to unite in heroic measures. These were Edward D. Barber, of Middlebury, Charles I. Walker and Charles K. Field, of Windham, and A. J. Rowell, of Orleans County. Barber was a great-hearted man, full of fun and frolic, but with a soul stirred to its depths by any story of cruelty or oppression. He was a born anti-slavery man. Walker was an able lawyer, who shortly after removed to Detroit, where he soon became the leader of the bar. Field was a lawyer of great natural ability, full of a grim humor and with a tongue as sharp and caustic as that of John Randolph. Rowell was like Zaccheus, little of stature, but great in push and energy. The qualities of the sixth party to the agreement were as may hereafter appear.

The six members referred to had a conference in Montpelier the evening before the convention. We agreed to go into the convention after we had notified the State Committee of our purpose to withdraw if the design of adding the new planks to the platform were persisted in. Possibly because I was the youngest, to me was assigned the duty of delivering our valedictory and leading the revolt.

We called upon the State Committee in the morning and were treated with contempt. At ten o'clock the convention was called to order. From the temporary and permanent organization and the Committee on Resolutions we were, as we had anticipated, excluded. The last-named committee met in a corner of the hall; the resolutions which had been prepared by authority were immediately reported to the convention. They were anti-Proviso and pro-Squatter Sovereignty in their most objectionable form.

I arose to make my first, my last, and my only speech in a Democratic convention. I began with the statement that the resolutions made the Democratic party of Vermont say that our free republic had not the power to maintain its own freedom; that if it was a violation of the Constitution to preserve the freedom of the territory acquired from Mexico, it was an equal violation of that instrument to exclude slavery from the northwest territory. That I would not venture to question the conclusions of the great constitutional lawyers of the Committee on Resolutions, but I would read a section or two from a law book of some authority which was diametrically opposed to the conclusions of the committee. The book was called Kent's Commentaries, was written by a lawyer of some authority in his day, and I read from it, not to resist the resolutions, but to show in what wholesale and ignorant blunders the committee had detected John Marshall, Story, and James Kent. I then read an extract from a letter of Mr. Madison to another member of the convention that framed the Constitution, thereby showing that the makers of that instrument did not know what they were about, for they supposed that the absolute control of the territories had been vested in Congress. This satire produced an uneasy feeling in the convention. Throwing it aside, I now, with all the earnestness of which I was master, exclaimed, "You who assert the power of leadership are making it impossible for a Vermonter who respects himself to remain in the Democratic party. Your resolutions prostitute that party to the service of the slave power. Our ancestors fought two states and a kingdom, through cold and poverty and hunger, for almost twenty years, to secure a place where Vermont was the equal of any State in the Federal Union. Your resolutions are unworthy of their descendants. Pass them, and with my associates I leave this hall for the time being and the Democratic party forever, unless it is redeemed from its present vassalage and restored to its former principles and dignity."

When I took my seat there was for some moments an oppressive silence, followed at last by what appeared to be a burst of genuine applause.

But an ancient Democrat, whose mind was impervious to argument, then arose and observed that as "the boy had spoke his piece, we might as well proceed to the business of the convention." No one else spoke. There was a subdued affirmative vote and a sharp "No" from the six to the resolutions. We did not challenge the vote, the chairman declared the resolutions carried, and the opposition party of six walked out of the convention. There was an effort to raise a hiss. It failed, and we took our departure in a profound and unbroken silence.

We crossed the street to the Pavilion Hotel, entered the room we had occupied, and closed the door. Barber was requested to take the chair and Rowell to act as secretary. Field arose, saying that he had a motion to make which he had committed to writing. It was brief but comprehensive. "I move," he read, "that we organize a new party to be called the 'FREE SOIL PARTY;' that its platform shall be uncompromising resistance to the extension of slavery or the slave power; that we select a State Committee of five persons; that we establish a weekly newspaper to be published in Burlington and called the *Free Soil Courier;* that we assess ourselves for money enough to pay for publishing four numbers; that we name its editors; that the first number be issued as early as it can be prepared, and that it contain our address to the people of Vermont."

There was no discussion, for the motion was drawn after our consultation of the previous evening. It was passed at once *nem. con.*, and the first Free Soil party formed in this republic, and out of the loins of which came the most effective political organization witnessed by the nineteenth century—the grand old Republican party—was organized.

Field was then appointed to write the address. Edward A. Stansbury, an active, young anti-slavery Whig, was in the hotel. He was sent for, came, and, after our action was explained, agreed to join us and to become the temporary editor of the *Courier*. We then subscribed fifty dollars each to the publication fund, and adjourned in time for an early dinner. Before the arrival of the daily stage for Burlington (for Vermont had no railroads then) Field had completed his address to the people. It was read, amended, and adopted. I was named as chairman and Stansbury as a member of the State Committee, and we were authorized to name the three remaining members—two from the old Whig and one from the Democratic party.

As I write after the lapse of forty-five years, the scenes of that day come back to me with vivid distinctness. Except myself all the actors have gone over to the great majority. For a few moments I call back Barber, his round, moon-like face beaming with delight as he croons the death-song of the Democratic party which he is composing. Stansbury, his sharp eyes sparkling through his gold-rimmed spectacles, is hunting for some one whom he may "pitch into," always preferring a "Hunker." Rowell, expert with the pen, is making a list of our probable recruits to whom the *Courier* is to be sent. Field, saturnine and solemn, declares that, as he contemplates the wreck of the Democracy, he for the first time understands the sensations of Marius surrounded by the ruins of Carthage. He would prefer a nice, fresh ruin with an agreeable odor, he declares, for those of the Democracy have a stale and graveyard kind of smell; while Walker recommends to Henry Stevens, of Barnet, that as those ruins are already desiccated, he should gather them up and deposit them in his receptacle for things lost upon earth. Even now there is a sensation of fun about the whole affair, for we were all then enjoying life in the freshness and vigor of that youth which, alas! never returns.

We never paid our subscriptions to the *Free Soil Courier*. On the first day of August Stansbury brought out the first number. It was so racy that the old hand-press upon which it was printed was kept running until it was wanted for the second number. Subscriptions for the twelve numbers to be issued before the November elections came in so rapidly that the enterprise was a paying one from the start.

I am aware that it is the prevailing opinion that there were no organizations of the Free Soil party in the New England States until after the Buffalo convention, held in August, 1848. Even Henry Wilson, who is usually accurate, fell into that error. Our organization had been in active operation for six weeks before the Buffalo convention was called.

CHAPTER II.

THE VAN BURENS—THE NEW YORK BARN-BURNERS.

IN June, 1848, the feud between the Barn-Burners and the Hunkers of New York was at fever heat. The *Evening Post* was the organ, "Prince" John Van Buren the recognized leader of the Barn-Burners. One of the first and most encouraging evidences that our movement begun at Montpelier was attracting attention was a letter from William C. Bryant, then chief editor of the *Evening Post*, urging us to persevere and either nominate a State ticket or adopt the candidates of the Liberty party. We had already determined to adopt those candidates, for they were men of worth and ability.

During the last week in June I received a letter from John Van Buren urging me to come to Albany on the 1st of July. On reaching that city, I was, on the morning of July 2d, introduced to a party of gentlemen, some of whom I think have been members of about every political party which has since been formed. I cannot now recall the names of all of them. "Prince" John Van Buren was by common consent the leader. I remember also N. S. Benton, at one time Secretary of State, Judge James, of Ogdensburgh, and Cassidy, afterward editor of the Albany *Atlas*, at first a Free Soil sheet, but afterward transferred with its editor to the *Argus*, an ultra-Hunker journal. There too I first met William Curtis Noyes, and formed a friendship interrupted only by his death. He appeared to be a genuine lover of freedom, a sharp fighter, and a determined, but fair and honorable opponent of the slave power. Among the party there was also another young lawyer from New York City. He was said to be an immense card—a man of extraordinary brilliancy and adroitness. He had just written some excoriation of the Hunkers which had given him great *éclat*. His name was *Samuel J. Tilden*. He was understood to breathe no atmosphere that was not saturated with hatred of the Hunker Democracy.

It was very apparent at the first meeting that the object of these gentlemen was to defeat General Cass rather than to restrict slavery. Cass had received the Democratic nomination for the Presidency and was supported by the Hunker wing of the New York Democracy. The Barn-Burners had bolted his nomination, and had decided to hold another convention and nominate ex-President Van Buren on a Free Soil platform. The purpose of the meeting at Albany was to frame the call and fix the time for that convention, and the grave question for decision was whether the call should be made broad enough to invite such men as Charles Sumner and Charles Francis Adams, who had never been either Democrats or Abolitionists.

The question seemed to be one of policy. If these men were excluded, the convention would be held by the Barn-Burners only. This party had little strength outside the State of New York—not enough, it was feared, to defeat General Cass if it was exerted for a third candidate. On the other hand, the Barn-Burners were loyal to the Constitution and would not affiliate with men who believed in disregarding its provisions as the Abolitionists were quite prepared to do. Tilden seemed to be the leader of those who favored a restricted call, Mr. Noyes of the Liberals, while John Van Buren had not yet declared himself either way.

For two days the debate went on. Toward evening it became acrimonious, but the inimitable humor of Prince John and the excellent dinners he gave us at a private residence on Capitol Hill restored harmony. We had reached cigars at the dinner on the 3d of July, when, as if the idea had just struck him, the Prince exclaimed: "Let us adjourn this debate and go to the theatre! To-morrow morning we will drive down to Lindenwald and spend the Fourth with father. He shall give us a good dinner and help us to a settlement of this question."

The proposal met with universal favor. I had all the curiosity of youth for a near view of the ex-President, which I may here say was the more interesting since it was the only one I ever had. I did not feel much interest in the question, for its decision either way would not modify our action. But there were others who thought that it was prudent, in a matter of so much importance, to avail themselves of the wisdom and experience of the sage of Kinderhook.

Early the next morning Prince John called at my hotel, himself driving a pair of horses and a light Concord wagon. He insisted that I should carry my portmanteau, as we might pass the night elsewhere than in Albany.

That drive was as delightful as the subsequent

visit, and both were memorable. The road, along which we bowled at a speed of nearly ten miles an hour, was shaded almost the entire distance from the rays of the summer sun, and so lively and amusing was my companion that I was unconscious of the lapse of time, nor can I now tell the length of the drive. His mind seemed preoccupied by General Cass. I learned how sharp hits were made in public speeches, for he was to make an address somewhere about General Cass, and for a part of the drive he was employed in casting and recasting the figures of speech to be used in the delineation of his person and character. Brilliant as he was, I discovered that the best of his apparently impromptu expressions were the fruit of very careful preparation.

I was disappointed in the linden trees that gave their name to the country home of the venerable ex-President. We would have called them in Vermont rather inferior bass-woods. But with the hearty welcome which shone from the sunny face of the active, sprightly man who met us at his gate and threw his arms around the neck of his stalwart son, I was charmed and delighted. How plain of speech are the eye and the arm! There was all the fervor of boyhood in the meeting of this distinguished son with an honored father. It told of a mutual love, warm, cheering, and unbroken, from the cradle of the one to the waiting tomb of the other. Some might have deemed them careless of each other's sensibilities. All that day they hurled their shafts of wit at each other, but the closest observer could discover no instant in which the Attorney-General of New York forgot the respect due to his honored father and the ex-President of the United States.

In addition to his guests from Albany, several of his neighbors called upon Mr. Van Buren, and the day passed in political and general conversation in his pleasant grounds. I had an experience of that marvellous influence which our host was reported to exercise over those with whom he came in contact. His first inquiry of me was concerning a Vermonter for whom I had a high esteem.

"William C. Bradley and I entered Congress together," he said, "and Mr. Bradley but for his deafness would have been the more successful man. He had no superior intellectually, and was the peer of any member of either House."

He spoke of Judges Phelps and Collamer and also of Judge Chipman in terms so complimentary that I was proud of Vermont and charmed with Mr. Van Buren. Although our host was probably informed of the occasion of our visit, the day passed without any reference to it. After a delightful dinner the cloth was removed, and then Prince John made a brief but entirely fair statement of the point of difference. William Curtis Noyes, who was a master of the art of concise statement, gave the reasons on one side, and Mr. Tilden on the other. There was a very mischievous twinkle in the eyes of the ex-President as he said:

"I am delighted with your success, Mr. Tilden. I was not aware before that the Barn-Burners were so strong."

"I have said nothing about our strength, Mr. Van Buren!" replied Mr. Tilden.

"True; you have only implied it," answered our host. "You must be very strong if you are already picking and choosing from the recruits who offer

themselves for enlistment. I had supposed that we
wanted every man who was opposed to the extension
of slavery. Would it not be well first of all to defeat
General Cass, and show the pro-slavery party that
they shall not invade free soil? To that end, is not
the vote of Gerritt Smith just as weighty as that of
Judge Martin Grover?"

A brief silence followed, broken at length by Mr.
Tilden.

"I had half converted myself," he said. "Mr. Van
Buren is to be our candidate. His opinion is obvious. Unless some gentleman wishes to discuss the
subject farther, I move the adoption of the call for a
national *Free Soil* Convention presented by Mr.
Noyes, and that the convention be held at Buffalo on
the 9th day of August."

There were several seconds, and the motion was
unanimously adopted. Our mission was ended. Subsequent events are now historical. The convention
was held, Mr. Van Buren was nominated and after
a sharp campaign General Cass was defeated and
General Taylor elected.

I recall one of the incidents of our dinner at Lindenwald which serves to illustrate the unconventional
relations which existed between the ex-President and
his son. The plate set before me for one of the
courses was most exquisitely decorated, and with the
gaucherie of an inexperienced curiosity I could not
resist the temptation to turn it over and look for the
maker's mark.

"Is not that a beautiful piece of china?" inquired
the Prince. "It has a history. It belongs to a dinner set made at Sèvres for the King of Italy before
the fall of Napoleon. I discovered it in Paris, and

although it was expensive, I purchased it and presented it to my father. Ought he not to be grateful for such a magnificent present?"

"Indeed I am grateful," said the ex-President, "perhaps more grateful for this than for another present you made me about the same time."

"Another present! What was it? I do not remember it," said his son.

"It was a bill of exchange for acceptance for more than the cost of the china!" replied the elder.

"Yes! yes!" said the Prince. "I intended that the entire transaction should represent a beautiful case of filial and paternal affection. I presented you with the china—that was filial. You paid for it—that was paternal. Could anything be more complete?"

We slept at Lindenwald. The next morning I breakfasted with the ex-President and his son. Our wagon was at the gate. Holding my hand in his, the venerable host said kindly: "Young man, you have chosen a good part. Persevere to the end, which you may see, but I shall not. The recent aggressions of the slave power may destroy the old parties, but they will perpetuate the republic. You have enlisted under the banner of *Free Soil*. Carry it forward to victory. The contest may be long. I foresee that it will not be ended by the present campaign. Slavery cannot long exist under restrictions. It must expand or perish. The great Northwest, by the consent of the South, has been consecrated to Freedom. Her rights must be maintained at any cost. To your generation is committed the high duty of maintaining them and of making our beloved country, permanently and truly, 'The land of the free and the home of the brave.'"

CHAPTER III.

THE EARLY BENCH AND BAR OF VERMONT.

It is one of the prerogatives of age to believe that the world is progressing backward. Without asserting this privilege I will set down, from old note-books and from memory, some incidents of the early bench and bar of Vermont, and leave my readers to make their application.

My early professional life was passed before such judges as SAMUEL PRENTISS, of the Circuit Court of the United States for the District of Vermont, a court ocasionally dignified by the presence on the bench of SAMUEL NELSON, of the Supreme Court of the United States. Some of the judges who then served the State for salaries of seven hundred and fifty dollars per year were Stephen Royce, Charles K. Williams, Samuel S. Phelps, Jacob Collamer, Milo L. Bennett, and Isaac F. Redfield. Later came the two Pierponts, Robert and John. There was not one of these who would not have honored a seat on the bench of the highest court in the land. And they had other than judicial qualifications. In the opinion of Mr. Webster, Samuel S. Phelps was the best lawyer in the Senate of the United States of his time. "Jack" Pierpont, as we affectionately called him, was not only a lawyer and a judge, but he knew and loved every game-bird and was the best wing shot in a close cover the State ever produced. I cannot help thinking sometimes that this old race of lawyers no longer exists.

Lawyers of the present day will put on a look of wise incredulity when they read the statement which I here record. When I left the State and its bar in 1861 I had never heard so much as a whisper against the impartiality or integrity of a Vermont judge. At that time we should have looked upon a lawyer as an unworthy brother if he had not implicit confidence in the bench. We used to find fault with their decisions; we availed ourselves of our privileges as defined by Judge Grover, of the New York Supreme Court. We could and did appeal from the decisions, or go down to the hotel and complain about the court, and sometimes we did both. But no lawyer suspected or intimated that the decisions were influenced by fear, favor, or affection, or that they did not comprise the impartial judgment of the court upon the facts and law. I might here refer to some of the reflex influences of such judges upon the bar, but I will merely say that they made the first twenty years of my practice a time to look back upon as the most delightful of a long professional life.

There were some of the earlier Vermont judges of whom my knowledge was legendary. One of these was Elias Keyes, a singular compound of law, good sense, and sarcasm. That eminent scholar and statesman, George P. Marsh, gave me the following account of one of Judge Keyes' sentences which he had received from Hon. Charles Marsh, his father. A disconsolate-looking tramp was convicted before Judge Keyes of the larceny of the boots of United States Senator Dudley Chase from before the door of his room at the tavern in Windsor.

He was convicted and called up for sentence.

"You are a poor creature," said the judge. "You ought to have known better than to steal. Only rich men can take things without paying for them. And then you must steal in the great town of Windsor, and the boots of a great man like Senator Chase, the greatest man anywhere around. If you wanted to steal, why didn't you steal in some little town in New Hampshire, and the boots of some man who wasn't of any consequence? And then you must steal from him when he was on his way to Washington, and, perhaps, the only boots he had. You might have compelled him to wait until some shoemaker made him another pair, and shoemakers never keep their promises. And perhaps by the delay some important treaty might have failed of ratification because he was not present in the Senate. The country might have been involved in a bloody war with Great Britain or some other power because of your stealing these boots. Now, you reckless creature, you see what awful consequences might have followed your crime. What have you got to say why you should not be sentenced to State prison for the term of your natural life for stealing Senator Chase's boots?"

"I have got to say that you seem to know a derned deal more about stealin' boots nor what I do!" piped the prisoner.

"That is a sound observation," said the judge, "and I will only give you one month in the county jail, not so much for stealing as for your ignorance in not knowing better than to steal the boots of a great man like Senator Dudley Chase."

Another original and strong character in the early

judicial history of Vermont was Theophilus Harrington. He was elected Chief Justice of the Rutland County Court in 1800, and when the system was changed in 1803 he was elected a judge of the Supreme Court and held that position until his death in 1813. He was a farmer, who never studied law until 1802, when he was admitted to the bar of the court of which he was Chief Justice.

It was Judge Harrington who decided against the slave-owner who had arrested his slave in Vermont, because he could not show title from the "original proprietor." The grantees named in the New Hampshire grants were called original proprietors, and when a lot-owner could show a chain of title which commenced with a deed from the proprietor to whom his lot was assigned in the division of the town, his title could only be defeated by an adverse possession or a subsequent deed. The slave-master supposed he had made a good title to the fugitive. Judge Harrington held otherwise. "But," pleaded the owner, "I show a deed from the owner of the mother of the slave."

"Your title may be good in Virginia," said the judge. "It is worthless here unless you show from the *original proprietor.*"

"Who, then, is the original proprietor?" asked the master, "if not the owner as whose slave he was born?"

"The Almighty, sir!" sternly answered the judge. "He or his grantee can have an order from this court to return a man to slavery. None other can!"

I take the following notes from the letter written me in 1860 by Obadiah Noble, a lawyer of Tinmouth, then in his eighty-fourth year: "Judge Harrington would express more in fewer words than any man I ever heard speak. He took no minutes of the evidence, yet he would repeat all that was material in a long trial with perfect accuracy. After a clear and perfectly fair charge to the jury, he would often say: 'If justice controls your verdict you will not miss the general principles of the law.'

"I remember a case in which Daniel Chipman was counsel, in which he produced a deposition of a witness who, he said, was one of the most reputable men in Troy. 'I am sorry for Troy, then,' said the judge, 'for if the angel Gabriel had signed that deposition I would not believe his testimony.'

"I once heard him explain the statute of limitations or adverse possession in this way: 'When the first settlers came here a day's work would buy an acre of land, and men were not particular about their line-fences. They often varied from the true line to get a more convenient place for the fence. But when two owners made a crooked fence which gave one more land than his share and let it stand for fifteen years, that fence could not be straightened without the consent of both owners.'

"On the trial of an action of ejectment for a farm, the defendant offered a deed of the premises from the plaintiff, to which Daniel Chipman objected because it had no seal. 'But your client sold the land, was paid for it, and signed the deed, did he not?' asked the judge. 'That makes no difference,' said Chipman; 'the deed has no seal and cannot be admitted in evidence.' 'Is there anything else the matter with the deed?' asked the judge. Chipman 'did not know as there was.' 'Mr. Clerk,' said the judge, 'give me a wafer and a three-cornered piece of paper.' The clerk obeyed, and the judge deliberately made and affixed the seal. 'There! Brother Chipman,' said the judge. 'The deed is all right now. It may be put in evidence. A man is not going to be cheated out of his farm in this court because his deed lacks a wafer, when there is a whole box of wafers on the clerk's desk!' 'The court will give me an exception?' asked the counsel. 'The court will do no such thing,' said the judge, and he did not.

"On another trial where counsel was examining a witness, Judge Harrington looked at him very intently and broke in with the question, 'Did you not once live in Rhode Island?' The witness answered that he did. 'Leave the stand, sir!' thundered the judge. Then turning to the lawyer he demanded what excuse he had for offering such a witness. The counsel claimed that he was an important witness, and that his client was entitled to his evidence. 'No, sir,' said the judge, 'that fellow don't open his mouth in this court. He is a knave, a scoundrel, who was convicted in Rhode Island for horse-stealing.' The counsel insisted that his conviction should be shown by the record. 'I tell you that I know the fact myself. I should not know it better with a dozen records. Go on with the case!'"

With all his peculiarities, the good sense and rugged integrity of Judge Harrington made him very acceptable to the bar as well as to the people. One other anecdote of his career must suffice:

He was vehemently opposed to the importation of Spanish merino sheep. On one occasion when he was at the State capital, a farmer who had at great expense imported a small flock of these sheep, and had them on exhibition there, had a long argument with Judge Harrington, in which he claimed that it was a benefit to the farmer to improve the grade of wool. He succeeded in inducing the judge to see the sheep, believing that his prejudices could thereby be overcome. The judge looked at the sheep, felt the fineness of their wool, and said nothing. "Do you not see," said the importer, "that this wool is worth a third more per pound than that of the coarse-wooled Canada sheep?" "That may be," said the judge, "but if improvement of wool is your object, why don't you go into the business of cultivating the negro? You could raise just as good wool and save the cost of dyeing!"

My note-books contain a large quantity of material which has given me a high esteem for these early settlers of my native State. Judge Harrington was by no means a solitary example of a judge of the highest court who had no legal education, but who discharged judicial duties to the entire satisfaction of his fellow-citizens. They were strong men, those early settlers, almost without exception, men whose education was limited to reading, writing, and the four simple rules of arithmetic. The sharp struggle of their fathers for existence in a new country, the necessity of utilizing the labor of their sons, made this restricted education, acquired by a few weeks' attendance at the log school-house, a necessity. Yet there were men among them who could frame a good constitution, but who could not write a grammatical sentence. There were civil engineers, military experts, diplomatists, and statesmen in the old Committee of Safety. Many farmers administered the law from the bench. Their strong common sense, inflexible integrity, and devotion to the principles of liberty perhaps qualified them for the judicial office better at the time than three years' service in an attorney's office or lectures at the law-schools. The precedents they established have seldom been departed from by their successors, some of whom have all the advantages that study and education could give to great natural abilities trained by long and intelligent experience.

CHAPTER IV.

A Lesson in Banking.

The ownership of a few shares of stock and my neutrality in a controversy among the stockholders made me the president of a bank at a very early age. I was fortunate enough to retain the office until I entered the Treasury in the spring of 1861. Our bank redeemed its notes at the Suffolk Bank in Boston, and I became rather intimately acquainted with Mr. J. Amory Davis, the president of that venerable conservative institution.

In the "fifties" the profits of a country bank were made upon the sale of drafts upon the cities for a premium, or from the interest upon securities on which they issued their own bank-notes—in other words upon their circulation. For every outstanding bank-note the bank was supposed to hold some interest-earning security. This was in substance the same as the interest upon the circulation. Our bank with a capital of $150,000 was permitted by law to carry three dollars for one, or a limit of $450,000. But in order to maintain the credit of our bank, it was necessary to redeem our notes in coin in Boston as well as at the counter of the bank. In old times, before the Suffolk system, it was easy to carry a circulation. Now, with the expresses, railroads, and improved means of transportation, our notes went to Boston as if drawn by a magnet. We were fortunate

A LESSON IN BANKING. 27

if our circulation averaged thirty days—that is, every bank-note paid out was redeemed in Boston once in about thirty days. If our whole circulation was, say, $400,000, we must place in the Suffolk Bank as much as $400,000 every thirty days.

Either because he commiserated my young inexperience or because he took a fancy to me, Mr. Davis gave me a large amount of useful advice and instruction in bank management. One day when we were alone in his room he said to me:

"Would you like to know one way of distinguishing a rascal from an honest man when both are strangers?"

"I certainly would," I replied.

"I do not promise to give you any infallible rule," he continued. "The mind often acts upon impulse and without any apparent cause. If what I am about to tell you shall save your bank from even one loss, it will be worth remembering. You should observe any stranger and form an impression about him as soon as he enters your bank or your room. It will be well to sit in your chair, facing the entrance. If a man enters with his head erect, looking straight before him, and walks to the desk or window and states his business without hesitation or circumlocution, he will usually turn out to be an honest man. But if he halts upon the threshold and looks to the right and to the left, scanning every person present as if he feared recognition—if he sidles up to the window edgewise, he is a man to be watched. If he is asked to be seated and turns to look at the chair as if he was afraid he might sit on something, it is almost certain that he is a bad man. You will notice other acts which I cannot describe from which you will draw inferences. One rule I would strongly recommend. If your first impression is against a stranger, do not change it except upon very strong evidence; it is better as a rule to have nothing to do with him. There may not seem to be much value in what I am telling you, but I think its value will grow upon you."

I thanked Mr. Davis for his advice and remarked that his experience must be valuable to me. He was certainly right in one respect. It has grown upon me. The moment I see a stranger I cannot refrain from forming an opinion about his character.

Years afterward, one day when I was writing at my table in the directors' room, the card of a gentleman who wished to see me was handed me. As I said "Show him in," I raised my head and saw standing upon the threshold a man of clerical, even venerable aspect, apparently about sixty years old. He was well dressed, with well-blacked boots, dark gloves, a new silk hat and white cravat. His hair was oiled and plastered to his head. The moment I saw him the whole lesson of the Suffolk president flashed across my memory. "I will have nothing to do with you," I thought, though I could scarcely tell why, for except a sweeping glance which embraced every one in the room there was nothing suspicious in his appearance.

He came forward and presented two letters of introduction, one from my friend, *the president of the Suffolk Bank*, the other from Blake Brothers, our uncurrent money brokers in Boston. They were in similar terms. They knew the gentleman personally and well; he was a member of the old firm of lumbermen in Thomaston, Me., F—— & Co., with

A LESSON IN BANKING.   29

whom the writers had long done business. F—— & Co. had recently sold out their lumber interests in Maine for $260,000. They had purchased a quarry about fifty miles from Chicago, where they employed four hundred men in quarrying and dressing stone. We might find it profitable to do business with them. There was no doubt about their wealth, we could rely implicitly upon their statements, and the writers "were very respectfully, etc., etc."

As I finished reading the second letter, the person asked if he could leave a package in our vault for a few hours. I said yes—called the teller, to whom he handed a package, in shape like bank-notes, marked $10,000 in the well-known writing of the cashier of a bank about thirty miles away. This disposed of, my gentleman opened his business.

"He had come to us," he said, "because our notes were well known and in general circulation in the town where their quarry was situated." This was true, for we discounted $5,000 per month for a customer in business there. They had been paying their laborers in Maine currency, but they lost time in going to Chicago to exchange it; sometimes got drunk and lost the money. Our notes they would keep by them until paid out for living expenses. It would be better for the men—much better for their employers (this was rather far-fetched, but it would pass at a pinch). He wanted to arrange with us ultimately for $10,000 per month if we liked the business and the length of the circulation was satisfactory. This they would make at least sixty days. For this money they would give us drafts on Boston on thirty days' time. To start the business they would give us sight drafts on Boston for the first $10,000.

We corresponded daily with the Suffolk Bank and with Blake Brothers. I knew their paper, its engraved headings and handwriting as well as our own. I had not the slightest doubt about the genuineness of the letters, or that the person was just what he claimed to be. A more attractive proposition to a country bank could not be made. He had covered every point. The thirty-day drafts would mature before the notes could come in for redemption and so the drafts would redeem them. In fact, the offer was too attractive. It was all profit for the bank. It was too good.

And yet when he laid down his engraved sight drafts on Boston accepted by the "old, wealthy Maine lumbermen," said he supposed I would like to think the matter over and he would call in an hour or two for our decision, I told him he need not take that trouble, for we declined his offer. At first he seemed dazed, he "couldn't understand it. The Suffolk Bank recommended him to come to us; said we woud like the business. Why did we decline? Did we doubt his word?" I answered that the Suffolk Bank did not guarantee our discounts; we were under no obligation to give our reasons.

He persisted that it was important that he should know our reasons and have an opportunity of answering them, and I yielded so far as to give him two reasons. "Your proposition is too good," I said. "On such paper you could have got all the currency you wanted without coming to Vermont. The Suffolk Bank would have given it to you. My second reason is that we do not care to do business with strangers."

He now began to be persistent and somewhat impudent. Would I not submit his proposals to our board? I said: "No. The decision is final and will not be reconsidered." He then in an injured tone demanded his package. It was handed to him. He declared that he considered that he had been insulted, and stalked out of the bank into the street.

Where did he go? What became of him? He was never seen or heard of afterward. If he had been annihilated his disappearance could not have been more perfect. The pursuit began next day. It was intelligent and thorough. It was continued through many months at a cost of more than thirty thousand dollars. It was utterly fruitless.

"You have been defrauded. The pretended letters are forgeries. No such persons known to us." Such was the unwelcome message sent to six banks as soon as their letters, written on the day of his disappearance, were opened by the Suffolk Bank and Blake Brothers.

The officers of the defrauded banks were so mortified by the success of the fraud that it was a long time before the details transpired. It then appeared that the scheme had been most carefully matured. The paper was identical with the letter-paper of the Suffolk Bank and of Blake Brothers & Co. It was made by the same mill. The engraved headings and the writing had been most skilfully imitated. The places where the notes of each bank circulated at the West were ascertained and a story devised suited to each bank. There were four conspirators, each of which dealt with two banks. My visitor had succeeded with one before he called on me. Five of the others succeeded, one only failed. The fruits of the fraud gathered in a single day were sixty thousand dollars.

Months elapsed before the notes began to come in for redemption. They came from Quebec, Toronto, St. Louis, New Orleans, in so small amounts and so scattered as to give no clew to the fraud.

It would be idle for me to claim that our bank escaped through any superior sagacity of my own. When the fraud was exposed I attempted to analyze my sensations to ascertain why I did not give him $10,000 in our notes for a sight draft on Boston which both our correspondents said was good. I decided that the suspicion that the transaction was too profitable would have been destroyed by the story which fell so naturally from the rascal's oily tongue, and that the lesson of the venerable city president in this instance saved our bank from the loss of ten thousand dollars.

CHAPTER V.

THE THIRD HOUSE JOURNAL—HOW WE REFORMED LEGISLATION IN 1850.

THE first half of the nineteenth century touches its close. Legislation is in full blast. There are few general laws; railroads, banks, bridges, turnpikes, cemeteries, almost every corporation is created by a special charter. Much of the legislation is absurd, more of it dangerous. Existing corporations found it necessary to be represented by counsel at the State capital during the whole session. There were thus brought together many lawyers who had little to do but to watch the daily journal and the interests of their corporation clients.

We had come to be known as the "Third House." We met daily in the State Library and lampooned everybody who deserved our attention, especially the members of the two *lower* houses. More effective work for our clients was accomplished by the satirical items which we made for the newspapers than by our legitimate work before the committees.

At the beginning of the session of 1850, it was suggested that we ought to have a permanent organization, elect a speaker, and appoint our standing committees. The suggestion met with favor and was adopted. The proceedings of the first day's session were published in the first number of the *Third House Journal*. This proved to be a success, and demand for it was so great that Gen. E. P. Walton assumed the expense of future numbers.

Like all printed papers which have only a transitory interest, these copies amused for the moment, went into the waste-basket and were forgotten. Twenty years later I found a single number in a long-disused portfolio, and its perusal induced me to attempt to collect all the numbers. The most diligent search failed to disclose another number. It was not until 1874 that Henry Stevens, of London, submitted to me on approval a package of Vermont material in which were all the numbers of the *Third House Journal* for 1850 and 1851. I fastened upon them, had them bound, and they are now before me. They are valuable because they are unique. There is not another copy in existence. They are very precious to me for another reason. I have just been reading aloud from them, and my eyes grow moist when I reflect that of that circle of genial fellows, almost a score in number, only three survive to testify to a friendship which has subsisted unbroken for more than forty years.

Forty years ago corporations were created by special acts of the legislature. Anybody could petition for one, and, if not opposed, the act usually passed. New corporations thus authorized were often ruinous to those already established. In such cases the old corporation found it necessary to be represented by counsel during the whole session. The contests before the committees were sometimes very angry. As the committees did not sit during the session of the House and Senate, that time was usually employed by the lawyers in the preparation of their cases. The most effective way to defeat an application was to turn it into ridicule. The proceedings of the Third House, now to be described, therefore had a definite purpose—that of defeating improper and unnecessary grants of charters for corporations. That purpose was successfully executed.

So many of the members of the "Third House" became distinguished in legislative, judicial, and diplomatic life that I am not inclined to give their names. It is shown by the record that on Monday, the 4th of November, 1850, the House was called to order by its youngest member and proceeded to the choice of a speaker. Three candidates were nominated, each of whom certified that he was neither a railroad attorney, a director in a turnpike company, nor a stockholder in a bank. After several ballots, one of them was elected and proceeded to deliver his salutatory in the approved form. Of himself, he said, he could do nothing, but being a son of Patience as well as a son of Temperance, with the assistance of the members he expected to rise superior to great emergencies. He should himself perform all the functions of the Third House unless prevented by impertinent interference. That everything might be done decently and in order, he would proceed to appoint the standing committees for the session. Among them were:

A Committee on *Useless Information*, with power to collect and preserve "things lost upon earth."

A Committee to devise *additional taxes* upon banks, colleges, female seminaries, Methodist chapels, two-story school-houses, lunatic asylums, and such like aristocratic institutions.

A Committee on *Log-Rolling*, with power to report upon the expediency and propriety of banking without specie, trading without capital, and lobbying without pay.

A Committee on *Aggravation*, with power to keep our "Southern brethren" in a stew on the subject of slavery, by resolution or otherwise.

A Committee on *Hocus-Pocus* and *Artful Dodging,* Twisting, Turning, Wire-Working, and Ground and Lofty Tumbling in connection with railroads and bridges.

A Committee on *Amiability of Temper*, Sweetness of Disposition, Purity of Expression, Uniform Propriety and Decorum in social intercourse.

Without an acquaintance with the persons appointed on these committees no one could appreciate their humor. As each committee was announced, the crowded room was filled with a roar of applause, which reached a climax when the last one was filled by three of the most nervous, irritable, and uncomfortable individuals that I have ever known in Vermont or elsewhere.

Banks were then created by special charter. There were too many banks already, but every village and hamlet became possessed with the idea that a bank was necessary to *develop its resources*. Every improvement or evidence of growth was described and presented with the petition for a bank to the legislature. The result was that some banks were chartered that could never be organized, and others were authorized for which there was no apology.

Another evil which claimed the attention of the Third House was the growing custom of the legislature to visit, in a body, any section of the State supposed to be affected by new legislation. Railroads were in process of construction, and the country members were always willing to accept a free ride upon the railroad. Banks, railroads, and other corporations occupied three-fourths of the time of the legislature.

On the first day of the session of the Third House, a petition was presented for the incorporation of the "Moosalamoo Bank" in the mountain hamlet of Ripton. The petition declared:

"That the public interests of the town of Ripton emphatically demand an immediate charter of a bank at that place, to be open during the summer months, to meet the growing wants of a young, an elastic, and a thriving community. A turnpike already penetrates the heart of the village, two sawmills are in the full tide of successful experiment within its limits, a shingle factory has shot up in its midst, and ere the gorgeous colors of another autumn shall have cast their glories upon the mountains, a *blacksmith* shop will occupy the spot lately sacred to the wilderness and the savage. No doubt can be entertained by any reasonable man that a vast capital could be permanently loaned to the people of Ripton, and that the resources of the country—the spruce, the hemlock, the charcoal, the partridge, and the trout—can never be successfully developed without the aid of a banking institution.

"Your petitioners therefore pray your honorable body to appoint some day for an excursion, to visit the proposed location, at the expense of the State; and that thereafterward a bank may be incorporated, with a capital of five hundred dollars, divided into five hundred shares of one dollar each—the bank to be open three months in each year, with power to deal in fish-hooks, powder and shot, Monongahela whiskey, and to do a general exchange business in the various descriptions of charcoal and spruce-gum."

The Moosalamoo Bank promoters met with the usual experience of the public-spirited patriots who go to the legislature after a good thing. Only two days after their petition was presented, certain residents of the kingdom of Tupton, on the shores of Lake

Dunmore, presented a remonstrance which threatened
the defeat of the enterprise. They

... "looked upon the effort to obtain a charter for a bank at
Ripton as an unwarrantable attack upon vested rights of your
remonstrants, who reside on the borders of Lake Moosalamoo,
vulgarly called Lake Dunmore. To grant the prayer of the
petition would be to steal our name. Besides, the wants and
the necessities which require a bank are tenfold greater at
Moosalamoo City, in the kingdom of Tupton, than at Ripton.
We have a most extensive glass factory establishment there,
consisting of buildings which cost $10,000, which ought to be
employed to some good purpose instead of being a tax upon
the owners. As many as forty banks could be kept in those
buildings. There is a blacksmith shop *already erected*, a good
building for a store, an extensive tavern establishment, a
good haunt for muskrat, and quite a plenty of cards and other
small game. The flourishing village of Sodom is about one
mile distant, where are carried on all sorts of business, un-
profitable solely for want of bank accommodations. Not far
away is *Satan's Kingdom*, where four coal-pits are burning
and may go out for want of bank accommodations. It is only
four miles to Jerusalem, a new and thriving village, and if it
should be decided to rebuild the Temple there, banking facilities of one million dollars will be required before it is completed.

"There are at present no banks nearer than the decaying
villages of Middlebury and Brandon. Finally, there is no way
of getting to Ripton except over the turnpike, which has been
so completely swept away by a freshet that its remains could
not be found with a search-warrant. The trout and spruce-
gum interest is as extensive here as at Ripton and the Monongahela fluid better and more abundant; we want the bank
more than they do at Ripton."

This remonstrance was followed by others, new
petitions were presented, and a debate resulted which
was as acrimonious as the rules of the Third House
permitted. It was continued to the end of the session,
when it was found that there was no member who

could make up his mind which way to vote. It was finally decided to postpone the subject to the next session, two of the members intimating that they had learned that there was some good woodcock ground in that vicinity, and that they proposed to visit it, taking that opportunity to test the Monongahela, during the vacation.

After an exhaustive research these members decided in favor of Ripton. Under their direction a new charter was prepared and presented at the opening of the session of 1851. It would have passed unanimously had not the ridicule proved too sharp for the two lower houses. Not only were all pending applications rejected, but no bank has since been chartered by the legislature of the Green Mountain State. This was the charter:

MAGNA CHARTA OF THE MOOSALAMOO BANK.

"*Whereas*, The Third House at their last session, in tender and sagacious consideration of the growing wants of the Kedentry and of the utter incapacity of the two lower Houses of the legislature of this State on all subjects in general and on most subjects in particular, did by implication· and 'with force and arms' direct at Montpelier aforesaid the two of its members most noted for wisdom and virtue to set out, locate, and propound for the benefit of the people and the assistance of the financial operations of the Third House, a certain *Grand, Mutual, Disinterested, Reserved-Guaranty-Capital-Liability Institution*, to be known by the name of the *Moosalamoo Bank*, and described and bounded as follows, to wit: Commencing at a hole in the ground a little way north of a white oak staddle on the principal trout-stream in the town of Ripton, four miles above the uppermost human habitation in said town; running thence southerly, from the summit of the highest range of the Green Mountains, to a stake and stones standing at the foot of Rattlesnake Point; thence in a right line across Lake Dunmore to the northeast corner of a shadbush standing near the Devil's Den in Lower Sodom; thence in a circumambient direction, in a slope movement, down upon, to and including the bar of Pray's Tavern in Moosalamoo City; and thence by the most convenient route to the north line of Ripton Flats, near the bar of Fred Smith's Tavern, and the Baconian Mineral Spring which irrigates the pasture lands of the Honorable George Chipman; thence easterly in the said last-mentioned line to the place of beginning: containing all that part of creation, more or less, together with all the waters, vegetation, spruce-gum, fish, including eels and bull-pouts, animals, human and otherwise, and other appurtenances thereto belonging—the said bank being established upon the rotary principle; the headquarters being at Moosalamoo City, with power to adjourn to any part of the aforesaid territory as occasion may require.

OFFICERS.

"The officers of this eleemosynary corporation shall be, first: A governor, who shall be at least twenty-five years old, more or less, of as good moral character as the times will admit; a member in good standing of the only true political party and church; a good judge of fun, with at least four senses, viz.: An eye for a horse—an ear for music—a nose for gunpowder—and a taste for good liquor; a married man, owning at least one dog; attached to the principles of the Constitution of the United States and the Resolutions of '98. To guard against imposition, any candidate for the above office shall, before the election, justify as to qualification before the commissioners in the same manner as is provided for bail on mesne process.

"Second: There shall be at least fourteen deputy-governors, who shall be native Americans, addicted to such virtues as a majority of the commissioners shall approve. It shall be the duty of the senior deputy-governor to preside over the deliberations of the board, provided he can justify, at such times only as the exigencies of business may require, when the governor, in the opinion of two-thirds of the stockholders present, shall become so far '*beguiled*,' '*disguised*,' '*fatigued*,' or '*discouraged*' as to be inadequate to the discharge of his official functions.

"Third: There shall be as many directors as may be thought

THE MOOSALAMOO BANK. 41

best. Each director shall have been a Plattsburgh Volunteer, or a member in fair standing of some flood-wood company, or a side judge of some county court, or a hop-inspector, or a secretary of some moral performance, or the proprietor of some patent right. He shall believe in a good time coming; the Bloomer costume; the Fourth of July; the infallibility of the Third House, and the 'Manifest Destiny.' He shall be a consistent advocate of Freedom of Speech, Rambouillet Sheep, Political Temperance, Woman's Rights, Bank Reform, Black Hawk and Gifford Morgan Horses, Morus Multicaulis, and the Universal Brotherhood of Man.

"Fourth: There shall be a cashier, who shall consist of at least one man of an amiable disposition and genial temperament, with a pocketful of rocks and a hatful of bricks. He shall write or play, as the case may be, a fair hand, be cognizant of the French language, accustomed to female society, and well disposed to the good order and happiness of the same.

"Fifth: There shall be a committee of three of the most venerable, wise, sagacious, and prudent stockholders, most noted for wisdom and virtue, whose duty it shall be to taste and smell for the institution, and their sessions shall be secret.

REGULAE GENERALES.

"All the financial business of the Third House shall be transacted through this institution: the debentures of the members, the bounty on sap and putty, the expenses of the militia system, of the construction, painting, and repair of the wooden side judges, and of such excursions as may be made by the Third House, and the expenses of the Montpelier Hotel Company shall be paid at the counter in the circulating notes of the bank; and any other business thought proper, when met.

"All subscriptions to the capital stock shall be payable in trout, spruce-gum, lumber, game-birds, charcoal, powder and shot, fish-hooks, Monongahela whiskey, or other liquids to the acceptance of the tasters and smellers; and in drafts on the North American Dog Association, indorsed by Col. Brick, on the call of the commissioners and at the option of the subscribers; provided, that before signing each person shall deposit with the commissioners, for the use of the stockholders, one pint of such fluid as shall be approved by the tasters and smellers, and shall take the following oath or affirmation, viz.:

"You do solemnly swear or affirm, as the case may be, that you do subscribe for shares in the Moosalamoo Bank in good faith in the feasibility of the measure and in the hope of fat dividends; with the intent on your part to retain all you may get, and get what you can for your own use and benefit of the stockholders generally, and not under any agreement, understanding, or expectation that your subscription shall inure to the benefit of any third person or at his expense (save in the way of refreshments), and that you will improve the dividends to the advancement of sound national principles and the supremacy of the Third House.

"Long may you wave."

The foregoing charter will become known to future generations, if historians do justice to the Third House, not only as the most comprehensive, but as positively the *last* special bank charter presented to the Vermont legislature. As a measure of State economy it ought to have secured a large measure of popular gratitude to the members of the "Third House." But republics are notoriously ungrateful, and instead of approving our patriotic labors the members of the lower houses denounced us as a set of pestiferous scamps who lay awake nights to invent new schemes for ridiculing our superiors.

CHAPTER VI.

WOODEN SIDE JUDGES OF THE COUNTY COURTS.

THE "side judges" also had the attention of the Third House. This was a purely ornamental office bestowed upon two citizens in each county, who would look wise and say nothing. The change proposed would have been promptly adopted, but for the opposition of an ex-side judge from Grand Isle, the smallest county in the State, who insisted that these officers were sometimes consulted by the judges of the Supreme, who always presided in the County Courts. He said that when Judge Samuel S. Phelps was on the bench and one of the lawyers had argued a dry ejectment case to the jury for eight hours, Judge Phelps had actually consulted him—that although it was in a whisper, the judge distinctly asked, "Don't he make your back ache?" to which he, the side judge, answered that he'd "be darned if he didn't!" There were some who did not believe this statement, and those who did thought it should not defeat an improvement which, after the first outlay, would save the State expense, and had other advantages. Accordingly, early in the session a resolution was introduced and referred to the "Committee on Useless Information" of the following tenor:

"*Resolved,* That it is expedient that the present system of electing side County Court judges ought to be abolished, and that, in future, such judges should be manufactured of cast-iron, wood, or putty, and be set up in the several court-houses for immediate use."

The committee, after, as they said, giving to the subject their "careful and prayerful attention," reported

"that the institution of wooden side judges for the present perishable creatures of flesh and blood would eminently subserve the great *butt-ends* of public justice. They will render the court *permanent*. Their decisions will be *uniform*. They will be *punctual*. They could not be *browbeaten* by insolent language. They would be *insensible* to the sophistry and artful appeals of demagogues. They would be *incorruptible*. The measure will promote *cheapness* and *economy*.

"The committee had been much assisted by the learned author of the Astronomical Calculations for Walton's Register, a gentleman of transcendent abilities, who in a mathematical problem in the rule of three had demonstrated that the present side judges cost the people $75 per hundred, while better meat has been selling in the butchers' stalls for three cents per pound.

"The committee had been in doubt about the kind of wood to be used. Some were in favor of spruce because it could be easily kept in check and possessed gum-ption and would *stick* to its opinions. But it was objected that spruce was *ever-green* and cross-grained. Some wanted bass-wood because it was easily *impressed* and exceedingly *sappy*, and the court would never be a *heavy* court. Others favored bird's-eye maple, for it would keep an open eye upon mischievous lawyers. But maple had to be rejected because it was inclined to be *rotten-hearted*.

"After conferring with the Committee on Hocus Pocus, all differences had been compromised, and the committee recommended the construction of wooden side judges as follows, viz. :

"The heads of ebony, with heavy, lowering brows, so that wicked lawyers would always be under the frown of the court, the highly polished faces thereof acting like a mirror casting reflections upon the bar for its sharp practices. The eyes to be of the most effulgent punk-wood obtainable ; the bodies

WOODEN SIDE JUDGES. 45

of spruce, so that the court may be kept in check, possess gumption and stick to its decisions; the heart of black locust, for it never rots; the bowels of cork, for by reason of its lightness and elasticity they would be more easily moved by the appeals of the unfortunate; the backbone and legs of well-seasoned hickory, without joints, so that the court may not be bent to the purposes of unprincipled lawyers; the arms of iron-wood, to remind the people of the protection of the strong arm of the law; the feet of *lignum vitæ*, so that the people can say that their judges have *solid understandings*.

"The committee also recommend that the Rutland sculptor be employed to make 150 plaster casts of that number of the best-dressed members of the Lower House most noted for their beauty and sobriety; and that 150 wooden images be manufactured as hereinbefore provided, which shall be faithful copies of said plaster casts—28 of which shall be distributed to the several counties in the State, two to each county, to be used as side judges; that any attempt to usurp their places be punished as high-treason; that three be donated to the city of Vergennes, the only city in the State and the smallest in the world; that fifty be delivered to the president of the Historical Society, and that he be requested to deposit them in his receptacle of 'things lost upon earth,' to evidence the spirit of the age and mark an era in judicial history; that the balance of said images be given to the Resident Agent of *International Exchanges*, to be by him immediately forwarded by express to the most illustrious of the crowned heads of Europe."

The logic of this report was irresistible. Its recommendations were all adopted with very little opposition. But the "perishable creatures of flesh and blood" are still in use; their wooden substitutes have never been sculptured. They would have been constructed in 1851, as the committee afterward reported, but for an unfortunate complication. There were two hundred and forty members of the Lower House, and every one of them insisted that he ought to be a model. They would not yield to any compromise or consent that the fortunate one hundred and fifty should be ascertained by lot. The Senators also complained that they were excluded from the competition and unfairly deprived of an opportunity to transmit their portraits to posterity at the expense of the State; and so it fell out that, as in many other instances, human progress was delayed and a great improvement defeated by selfish personal interests.

CHAPTER VII.

THE VERMONT FLOODWOOD OR RIGHT ARM OF HER DEFENCE.

SEVENTEEN regiments of infantry and one of cavalry; four companies of sharpshooters; three batteries and one company of artillery; six hundred officers contributed to the naval and military organizations outside the State; 5,287 lives, or 6.8 per cent of her sons engaged—these were some of the contributions of Vermont with her small population to the preservation of the Union between 1861 and 1865. It has been said that the Vermonters did not lose a stand of colors during the war. Technically this statement is true. But Vermont cannot afford to have her record clouded even by a distorted statement. The surrender of Harper's Ferry in September, 1862, through treachery or incompetency, comprised the Ninth Vermont. While the gallant Stannard and his men, enraged that they were not permitted to hew their way out, were breaking their swords and destroying their guns, two privates divided the colors and wore them on their persons. One of them was taken sick and went into a hospital, where they were taken from him. The other kept his portion concealed six months until he was exchanged. This is the only instance in which the enemy ever obtained even a part of a Vermont flag!

In 1851 the military resources of Vermont were

only spoken of with ridicule and contempt. I doubt whether she had even the skeleton of one uniformed company. Her fighting material had fallen into such a state of innocuous desuetude that it comprised only one person who wore a uniform. He was the adjutant and inspector-general, who as a private would have been a model of conceit, but who swelled with his official dignity like a cock-sparrow on a mullein-stalk. The official report for that year was as ridiculous as could well be imagined, and it was so stuffed and padded with military terms as to be incomprehensible to the average reader.

Such a subject, such a document, and such an officer formed a toothsome morsel for the Third House. I was the chairman of the Committee on Floodwood. My associates were a poet of Democratic principles and a Plattsburgh Volunteer who in 1814 stayed his steps at the wharf in Burlington because for the militia to go outside the State was a violation of the Federal Constitution! His personal appearance strongly suggested that of a walrus, and he added greatly to our amusement by an honest belief that we were in "dead earnest" in our efforts to excite the military ardor of the Green Mountain boys.

My committee did not permit the grass to grow under its feet. It promptly reported that existing laws relating to the militia were "unconstooshunal" (this was the word of the Plattsburgh Volunteer) and in utter disregard of the precepts of the Father of his Country and the great Apostle of Democracy, namely, G. Washington and T. Jefferson. So much was obvious from the masterly, eloquent, and lucid report of the adjutant-general, which covered so much ground that there was none left for the committee to stand upon. We therefore reported "An Act for the resurrection of the Vermont Floodwood, and to create certain salaried officers therein named." This act in its first section provided:

"That it shall be the duty of every male citizen above the age of sixteen years forthwith to provide himself with a red feather or plume, at least three feet long, together with such other ornaments as the taste or ability of the individual may suggest, with some offensive weapon, not dangerous to be handled, a priming wire and brush, for the purpose of doing duty in the floodwood of this State. Provided that in lieu of these ornaments and equipments any person may provide himself with any musical instrument whereon he may be able to play.

"SECTION 2.—It shall be the duty of every such male citizen to repair, armed, equipped, and ornamented as provided in the first section, at the break of day on Tuesday and Thursday of each week, to the yard of the dwelling-house of the town clerk of the town where he resides, for floodwood purposes and general training, and to spend said days until sundown in such services.

"SECTION 3.—There shall be at least two officers to every private in the Vermont floodwood, provided that any person with curled hair and black whiskers shall be ex-whiskerando an officer of as high a grade as lieutenant-general.

"SECTION 4.—It shall be the duty of the adjutant and inspector-general immediately to set out from his place of abode, armed and equipped as the law directs, preceded by drum-major, drummer, fifer, and corporal, armed with some weapon of war, and proceed into each school district to consult with the boys as to the best method of encouraging a spirit of martial ardor, and to make permanent arrangements with the school master or mistress, as the case may be, as to the best way to get up a spirit of military enthusiasm and induce the pupils of each school to attend all June and other trainings in such towns.

"SECTION 5.—There shall be immediately appointed one hundred and fifty assistant adjutant-generals—men noted for personal beauty, to be chosen by a female committee of three of mature age, to be named by the governor; which officers shall assist the present adjutant-general in the discharge of his arduous duties and hold up the general interests of the floodwood. These officers, if already married, or if they shall marry within sixty days after their appointment, shall hold office for life with an annual salary of $1,500 each per annum."

This act was laid on the table and published in the *Third House Journal*. It brought the disgraceful condition of the militia to the attention of the State and excited a universal demand for its reformation. A well-framed act to that end was promptly introduced into the Senate. Those who had opposed similar acts on the score of expense were set upon by the newspapers and lashed into silence. The new act simply provided that the State should furnish arms to uniformed companies, and pay the men a *per diem* for a few days' drill in each year. The consequence was that uniformed companies were organized in the larger towns and their ranks kept full. So that when at last Sumter fell and the summons came, it was answered by the formation of the First Vermont Regiment, ready at Rutland to be mustered into the service on the 8th of May, 1861.

It may be thought that I am giving too much space to a subject so unimportant as the Third House. But its influence upon legislation was powerful and permament. Once the lower Houses were rash enough to complain of the librarian for permitting such "pestilent fellows" to show up their follies in the State Library. This complaint made great fun for us. We forthwith published our solemn protest against the interference of their spies with our dignified sessions, and gave notice that if they provoked us farther we would appeal to the people to abolish the lower Houses altogether, so that "the places that once knew them should know them no more forever," and they "shall cease to have a local habitation and a name;" and the dark chambers where they met and played "fantastic tricks before high Heaven, under the delusion that they were clothed with a little brief authority," "shall be given over to desolation, and only the hooting of the owl be heard within their walls;" "and the satyr shall dance there, and the great owl and the pelican, and the gier-eagle shall nest and the cormorant shall brood there, when those members have been driven forth into exile and outer darkness by the voices of an indignant people."

After this they let us alone, and we continued to make their action as ridiculous as possible. Almost every project we touched we destroyed. They had planned an excursion to Rouse's Point, where a railroad bridge across the lake was advocated and opposed on the most absurd grounds. We at once arranged to "excurse to Pocatapaug Flats, where it was feared that a proposed bridge would raise the water ten miles above, four feet higher than at the bridge, whereby the navigation of Lake Pemigewasset in New Hampshire would be obstructed," and the legislature took no more excursions. They passed a stringent act against the use of strong liquors except for "mechanical, medicinal, and chemical purposes." Our Committee on Useless Information produced sundry vouchers for the year 1788, containing "rhum, cyder, and flip" for the legislature, approved by Governor Thomas Chittenden, and we compromised the opposition by enacting that the term "mechanical" in the act should include the raising of barns and like cases, "medicinal" should cover cases of thirst and the like, and "chemical" cases where the fluid was employed as an aid to digestion. Two railroads on competing lines leading to Boston had almost reached Lake Champlain at Burlington. One of them by a combination with another leading northward would reach the lake at Rouse's Point. The other sought for a parallel charter to reach the same point. A fierce contest resulted—one endeavoring to defeat the application for a bridge so that its competitor could not cross; the other to defeat the charter so that its competitor could not reach the lake. The arguments of both parties were equally absurd and altogether ignored the public interest. It was this contest which called for the Committee on Hocus-Pocus, Log-Rolling, Wire-Working, etc. This committee was made up of the presidents of the two competing roads and the one leading from Burlington north. That committee made a solemn and comprehensive report on the abstruse subject of log-rolling, which caused the very proper grant of both charters as the public interest demanded.

CHAPTER VIII.

A Grateful Client.

It was before the invention of the telegraph, when Vermont had no railroads and the Green Mountains were supposed to present an insurmountable barrier to their construction. One afternoon, when the teller of the oldest, soundest, and most conservative bank in Burlington was about to seal up his daily package of current bills for transmission to the common redeemer of country banks, the Suffolk Bank in Boston, there entered the bank a youth, apparently inexperienced and very unsophisticated, who with a bashful air asked if he could leave a little money in the bank for a few days. He was travelling, he said, to see the country. His father advised him, when he intended to stay in any place for a few days, always to leave his money in a bank. Burlington was a beautiful town. He would stay here a few days and would like to do what his father recommended. The teller, who thought the young man should be encouraged in well-doing, said he would take his money on deposit.

The youth then proceeded to extract a number of pins from the breast-pocket of his coat, from which he drew a sealed envelope, which he opened, exposing a pocket-book of ancient construction, in which lay fifteen new and crisp bank-notes each for $100, apparently issued by the " Shoe and Leather Bank of

Boston." The teller cast his eye upon them. He recognized the genuine appearance of the bills. They were just what the bank wanted. They would increase the credit of the bank with the Suffolk just at a time when circulation was coming in and they were having some trouble to take care of it. He asked the name of the depositor, entered his deposit upon a book, handed it to the careful boy, added his deposit to the package, and increased his remittance by that amount. Just then the expressman called, received the package, and the transaction was closed.

As soon as the bank opened the next morning the young man was its first customer. He had received a letter announcing the dangerous illness of his mother and must return home at once. He regretted it, for he had never seen so beautiful a town as Burlington, and he wanted to stay there a week or ten days. But he would have to leave at once and had called for his money. The teller counted out fifteen hundred dollars in bills of his bank and was about to enter the credit on the deposit-book, when the boy protested. He "wanted the same bills he had deposited! He knew all about those bills," he said. "He knew nothing about those which the teller offered him!" The teller explained to him that his notes had been sent to Boston, that the notes of his bank were just as good. The boy was finally half-satisfied, deposited the bills in his breast-pocket, pinned it up, and courteously took his leave.

In due course of mail the teller and his bank learned that the careful boy's deposit was worth just *fifteen dollars*, every one of the one-hundred-dollar bills having been neatly altered from a genuine bill for one dollar!

A GRATEFUL CLIENT. 55

Now the bank had a comfortable surplus upon which $1,500 would make but little impression. But the mortification of the bank officers, swindled by such an apparent greenhorn, was intolerable. They made every effort to suppress the incident, but it became public, and the ridicule of the newspapers and the comments of their brother bank officers were very hard to bear. The bank spared neither time nor money in its efforts to bring the guilty parties to justice. There were no Pinkertons then, but there were private detectives. These were employed, large rewards were offered, several arrests were made, but they were unable to lay hands upon the inexperienced traveller. Among the private detectives employed was one who afterward became somewhat notorious, under the name of Marcus Cicero Stanley.

Some two years after the event the newspapers announced that the criminal had been captured. The teller had identified him in a crowd of prisoners in the "Tombs," in New York City, and after a vigorous resistance by legal obstructions he had been brought to Burlington under a requisition from the governor.

"The young man who is charged with passing the altered bank-notes wishes to see you," said the sheriff to me one morning in court some days after the prisoner's arrival.

"I want business," I answered, "but not quite enough to go to the jail after it and undertake the defence of a counterfeiter."

"He may not be a counterfeiter," said the sheriff. "At all events, I have become interested in the young man, and I will bring him to your office if you will hear his story."

I assented to the request of the sheriff. He came to my office with a young man who did not look like a counterfeiter. He was apparently about twenty years old; was neatly dressed; had rather a feminine expression and the address of a gentleman familiar with the usages of good society. When the sheriff had presented him he drew from his finger a ring containing a single diamond, which he offered to me. "There," he said, "is the only thing of value I possess. In the 'Tombs' in New York I fell into the hands of shysters who got all my money, nearly all my clothing, even to my linen, and when they had stripped me of everything they could sell or pawn they abandoned me. This ring was in a pocket-book or they would have had that. I am brought here among strangers, destitute. But I am innocent, and if you will defend me I will pay you if I live."

"Have you any proof of your innocence?" I asked.

"Only this," he said. "As I was leaving the police court in the Tombs the clerk handed me this." He showed me a letter dated in the police court, of the following import:

"I doubt whether this young man is guilty of the crime charged. I *know* that he was not identified by the teller, among the Tombs prisoners, until he was pointed out by Stanley after the teller had selected another man.

"S. H. STUART, *Clerk.*"

He then told me his story. "I do not remember my father or mother," he said. "The first thing I do remember is living in the streets of New York, sleeping in a box or anywhere I could find shelter. Then I was an errand-boy in a policy-shop in the Bowery, where I swept the office, ran errands, slept under the stairs, was kicked and cuffed by everybody. After some years I saved a little money and ran away. I worked my way to St. Louis, where I got employment as a cabin-boy on a Mississippi steamboat. The captain was kind to me, and when his boat was laid up I went to a night-school, where I learned to read and write. I was on that boat more than three years. I was waiter, steward, bar-tender, and finally clerk or second officer. I saved money and tried to be a gentleman. The captain died and I decided to go to California. I had six hundred dollars and a trunk filled with good clothes. I came to New York, bought my ticket by the way of the Isthmus. Then I was arrested by Stanley; you know the rest. I was never nearer this town than Albany until I was brought here charged with this crime."

"Did you know Stanley in New York?" I asked.

"Yes—as a boy would know a lottery sharp who made the office his headquarters."

"Was there any hearing in your case in New York?"

"I do not know what you would call it. While my money lasted I was brought into court almost daily. When that was gone I was sent here at once."

"Then you do not know what evidence was produced against you?"

"No. I was told that one of the bank officers undertook to identify me at the Tombs. We prisoners were all brought into a room together. I was told that the teller first selected a man who was serving a three-days' sentence for intoxication. And I have heard that one of Stanley's friends says that I told him how neatly I deceived the teller. That was a lie, but Stanley would rather prefer a lie."

I told the young man, who said his name was

Thomas B. Wilson, that his story gave scarcely a shadow of available evidence in his favor. The statement of the teller made a *prima-facie* case. If that was confirmed by a confession, testified to even by an accomplice, I did not see any way of meeting it. If he attempted to prove that he was on the Mississippi at the time, his captain was dead, and if alive, we could not use his deposition in a criminal case. It might be better for him to plead guilty and so get a lighter sentence.

"I am not guilty," he said. "I will never plead guilty if I am sentenced for life and know that by pleading guilty I could get off with one year in the State prison. I have no claim on you, an entire stranger, but don't you see it is my last chance? I ask you to defend me on my promise. If you will, I will never leave this town until I have paid you and have convinced decent people that I am neither a counterfeiter nor a fraud."

This looked a little like bravado, and yet I could not avoid some prepossession in his favor. I said that his trial would not come on for some weeks; that I would consider his request and let him know within a few days whether I would appear in his behalf.

I corresponded with a firm in St. Louis which he said was the agent of the steamboat on which he was employed. They answered that they remembered such a man, but could not say that they knew him as early as the date of the crime. The clerk of the "Tombs" police court answered that the pretended identification took place in his presence; that there was nothing in it; that the teller first selected another prisoner, and only named Wilson after he had been pointed out by Stanley. This proof, however, could not avail him unless the clerk would appear at the trial.

A man unjustly accused should never despair. There is a human magnetism that may save him. As the time for the trial approached the sheriff became a firm believer in Wilson's innocence and proposed to pay the expenses of Stuart, the police-court clerk, if he would attend the trial and I would defend Wilson. The bank in the mean time had caused Wilson's arrest in a civil action to recover the money. Under these circumstances I consented to appear for him. He had in the mean time been employed by the sheriff as clerk in a hotel kept by him in a building connected with the jail, and had made himself very popular with its country patrons.

Still the prospects of his trial were very discouraging. The presiding judge of the court, although he intended to be impartial, always presumed that a person charged with crime was guilty until his innocence was proved; the statutes did not then permit the prisoner to testify; the bank officers were influential citizens who took a deep interest in securing Wilson's conviction, and the able counsel for the bank were permitted to conduct the prosecution. They made the trial dramatic. After giving a history of the crime and of his identification of the prisoner in the "Tombs," the teller was asked:

"Where is the person now who gave you those altered bills?" The teller waited until the attention of the crowded audience was fixed upon the prisoner; then pointing to him he replied with emphasis:

"There sits the man. I am as certain of it as I am that I am a witness!"

Hopeless as the prospect appeared, I cross-examined

the teller fairly but very closely. In the dim twilight of the court-room, with the respondent sitting half concealed behind me, I made him describe the counterfeiter as he was when he passed the notes. He did not suspect my purpose and described the green, awkward country lout with the skill of a painter. He imitated his nasal voice, his dialect, his motions, until the jury had before them the very image of the man. The lights were then brought in, and Wilson was asked to stand up in front of the jury and near the witness. He was a handsome, well-dressed young gentleman, as different from the person of the counterfeiter just described by the witness as could be imagined. His demeanor was unstudied and perfectly natural. The confidence of conscious innocence seemed to be expressed by his countenance. Anybody could see that his appearance did not correspond to that of the criminal as it rested in the memory of the witness in the slightest degree; anybody could understand that if he were guilty no reliance could be placed upon human judgment of the exterior of men accused of crime.

"Mr. G.," I asked, "do you consider yourself an experienced judge of men?"

"I ought to be," he said, "after an experience of thirty years."

"You have testified that you identified Wilson among a number of other prisoners in the 'Tombs.' Please point out to the jury what you saw in him that led you to think he was the awkward, green countryman who passed these notes."

I have cross-examined many witnesses. I remember no question to any of them which produced such an effect. He hesitated, seemed making an effort to speak, and was silent. Waiting until I thought the due effect was produced on the jury, I said:

"Never mind! we can all appreciate your difficulty. Now please answer me this. Did you not first select another man in the 'Tombs' as the criminal?"

He hesitated again and half admitted that he did.

I said I had no more questions. I was young at the bar, but I had learned when to stop in the cross-examination of a hostile witness. The skilful counsel for the bank, by suggestions and otherwise, made him try to repair the damage. The attempt was unavailing. He left the stand, and I knew that a fatal blow had been struck to the case of the prosecution.

I gave the case another shock when I called Stuart, the clerk of the Tombs police court, to prove that the teller first selected another man. He was an elderly man of dignified presence, and was treated by the court and the counsel for the bank as if he had volunteered to protect a criminal. His evidence was excluded on the ground that the teller admitted what I offered to prove by him, but the moral effect of his presence was in our favor.

I will not prolong the account. There was a powerful argument by the leading counsel of the bank, a terrific charge against him by the judge, but to the delight of the audience, manifested by ringing cheers, the jury acquitted the prisoner.

As Wilson could not furnish bail, I moved the trial of the civil action in favor of the bank. The bank submitted to a judgment in the prisoner's favor, and as it had the right to do, entered a review from it and so postponed the final trial until the next term, a delay of six months.

Wilson knew that the bank would have the evidence to secure a verdict at the next trial, if money would procure it. The officers treated his acquittal as a personal defeat, and it gave them excessive annoyance. He had some advantages. The sheriff trusted and employed him, so that he was under no restraint. We could use depositions in the civil case. Those of the police clerk, the warden of the prison, and of the person first identified by the teller were taken. By correspondence Wilson found two merchants in St. Louis who gave their depositions that their books showed that Wilson was one of their customers continuously for a year before and a year after the crime was committed, thus proving his *alibi*. This was all the preparation of which his case admitted.

A day or two before the term, while Wilson was in consultation with me in my office, my clerk presented the card of two gentlemen who wished to see me. The card bore the name of "*Mr. Marcus Cicero Stanley and friend.*" I showed it to Wilson. "Let them come in," he said. "Let us ascertain what the scoundrels want." They were admitted. Stanley proved to be a small, muscular fellow, with red hair and whiskers. He had the restless eyes and hard face of a knave, while his companion had the downcast look, well-oiled hair, and furtive bearing of a typical thief. "How do you do, Tom?" said Stanley with friendly cordiality. Wilson made no response. "What do you want, gentlemen?" I demanded.

Their mission was characteristic. Stanley said the bank had not treated them well. They had come from New York at its request to testify against Wil-

A GRATEFUL CLIENT. 63

son. The bank would only pay them some small amount, which they named. If Wilson would give them one hundred dollars, they would leave the State and not appear against him. Wilson, I saw, was almost bursting with indignation.

"What do you know against Wilson?" I demanded.

Stanley said he had seen the altered notes, and knew when Wilson and the friend here present started from New York to "shove them" on the country banks in Vermont. He was absent a few days and came back very "flush" with money. Wilson and *his friend* took the steamer through the lake at Whitehall. Wilson landed at Burlington, while his friend went on to St. Johns, where Wilson met him the next evening, told him how he had "chiselled" the teller, and gave him half the profits of the swindle.

"What do you think of that story, Wilson?" I asked.

"If I had any fear that the jury would believe those scoundrels I would pitch them out of this third-story window!" he answered. "Stanley ought to be in the State prison, I know; and from his appearance I think that other fellow has been there. I have not a hundred dollars, as you know. If I had a million I would not give them one copper to save their worthless lives. Pay them to go away after they have got all the money they can out of the bank? No! I prefer to trust a fair jury!"

"You make a mistake, Tom. You had better——"

"Stanley! don't you call me Tom! and you had best not tempt me farther. I have been robbed of everything, imprisoned, disgraced by and through you. You are a coward, I know. If I did not hope to be a reputable man and to keep out of trouble, I would brain you where you stand! Heaven knows that it is difficult for me to keep from choking the life out of your body!"

Wilson rushed from the room. I knew he went because he feared to trust himself, and I could not but respect him. Stanley tried to continue the interview, but I pointed to the door and told them that they had their answer. "Then we will have to swear," he said, and they departed.

The trial came on. We had what I have often declared to be the safe shelter and protection of an innocent man, a jury of twelve hard-headed, sensible Vermont farmers. The teller told his story as before. He was prepared for my cross-examination now, and I dropped him with a few indispensable questions. Stanley's companion then took the stand and testified to the story told in my room. His hang-dog look grew more villanous when I sharply asked, "When were you last in State prison?" The counsel for the bank objected that I must show the record of his conviction. The court sustained the objection. As a lawyer, I was bound to submit, but for a half-hour I put proper questions to him under which he broke down, and finally blurted out the statement that he had been pardoned out of Sing Sing that he might give his testimony on this trial.

Then Stanley was called. As he passed me to take the stand, he secretly placed in my hand a scrap of paper on which was written, " Ask me about Wilson's *whiskers and mustaches.*" On his direct examination he *almost* made a splendid witness for the bank. He knew a young man in a policy-office who was connected with a gang of counterfeiters. He was quite certain it was Wilson. The gang brought out some bills altered from one dollar to one hundred dollars on a bank in Boston. They were a skilful alteration. The gang scattered to "shove them." Wilson left the city for some weeks, and it was said that he had gone north to Canada to pass these bills. When he returned he had a lot of money. He knew it, for Wilson paid him fifty dollars, which he owed him, and showed him a large bundle of bills besides. He produced a memorandum-book showing the date of this payment. It coincided with the date of the crime.

As the testimony stood, it was unanswerable. My case depended on breaking down the statement of an utter wretch who was also an experienced witness. His direct evidence was completed, and the court adjourned for the day.

I was very cautious on his cross-examination the next morning. "Are you willing to swear," I asked, "that Wilson here is the person you knew in a policy-office in the Bowery?" He *thought* he was. He was *almost* certain of it, and yet he declined to say that he might not be mistaken. "Could he describe the person he knew there?" "Certainly. He was a young man, always well dressed, with dark hair and very black whiskers and mustache." "Might not his whiskers have been false?" *"Certainly not!* He had once pulled them playfully, to Wilson's great indignation. They were very black and very genuine." So much he *knew.*

Again Wilson was asked to stand in presence of the jury. His chin and upper lip were as innocent of any growth of hair as the face of a girl. The witness was required to examine and to say whether that face had ever borne whiskers or mustaches.

He made the examination, hesitated for a moment, and then exclaimed: "My God! gentlemen, here has been a fearful mistake! This man is not the person I once knew. He is not the man who was in the policy-shop—who was connected with the counterfeiters. I have been mistaken, and the least I can do is to apologize!"

This was the end of the plaintiff's case. I was satisfied that Stanley, having got from the bank all the money it would pay, deliberately deserted it, and decided that it was better not to persist in his perjury. A verdict in Wilson's favor was promptly returned by the jury.

A day or two after his acquittal, Wilson came to my office with two citizens of the town. He wished me to prepare a conveyance of a vacant lot of land adjoining the bank which had pursued him with such energy, and a contract for the erection upon it of a building. He then explained to me that he should never leave the town until every citizen who was unprejudiced had become satisfied that he was neither a counterfeiter nor a criminal; that he therefore intended to go into business and establish a family grocery-store *adjoining the bank* which had accused him and made him so much trouble.

I prepared the contracts, and in a few months he was established in business. He was industrious, he very soon had a large circle of good patrons, and was successful. He called for my bill of charges, and paid me liberally within a few months after his store was opened.

Within a year after his acquittal, one of our reputable citizens consulted me confidentially upon a subject of great interest to him. Wilson had asked him for the hand of his daughter. His conduct had been very honorable; he could not expect at present that he would not by many be looked upon with suspicion and not as a reputable man, but he hoped to live down all prejudices and establish himself in the good opinion of the public in the end. He had referred the father of the young lady to me, for I knew more about him than any one else and would no doubt give him advice upon which he could rely.

I assured the citizen that I supposed Wilson had an unknown origin and was almost literally a child of the streets; but I thought he deserved great credit for his efforts to overcome the disadvantages of his birth and the charges made against him by the bank, and to establish his innocence and become a reputable man; that his daughter would undoubtedly run some risk and sometimes be subjected to mortification, but I thought the chances were in Wilson's favor; that he would be a successful business man and a kind husband.

They were married and children were born to them. Mrs. Wilson was a plain woman, but the town contained no wife more contented, no more prudent, discreet, or devoted mother. The business of her husband prospered; he took his wife's parents into his family, where their remaining years were passed in ease and comfort. When they passed away Wilson closed his business, sold his property, and removed his family to New York City. He had a strong desire to conquer a position in the city from which he had been removed as a criminal. When I next had news of him he had become the purchaser of a church, left behind by the up-town movement of its congregation, and established in it the then new business of manufacturing and distributing mineral waters. His neat wagons, with fine Green Mountain horses and well-dressed, civil drivers, became as common in the streets as the milk-wagons of country dairies.

My recreation at that time was the study of the natural sciences, and I was engaged in making a collection of all the birds of Vermont. One Christmas Eve there came to my house a large box, upon which the express charges were paid. It contained an early copy of the author's editions of Audubon's Birds and Audubon and Bachman's Quadrupeds of America in ten elegantly bound octavo volumes. They were my Christmas present from Wilson. Their money value was several hundred dollars, but they had a greater value to me. They have stood on my library shelves for nearly forty years—they stand there still, their gloss worn off by many consultations.

This story has a moral. The bank no longer exists. Of its officers, directors, and principal owners, not one survives. Their descendants are not numerous; I do not know one who has been conspicuous in any department of human industry; some have been no credit to their ancestors or their advantages.

Wilson's children have grown up and each has gone out into the world to fight his or her own battle of life. At home they were trained by a careful mother, with the good example of the father as an object-lesson. The university, the mercantile college, the seminary were all laid under contribution to give them the advantages of a good, practical education. The daughters without exception are good wives, the sons are successful men—one of them may be called an eminent mechanical engineer. All are useful members of society.

At the time there were many who believed that my intervention had enabled a reprobate to defeat justice and evade the State prison. Most of them have since revised their conclusions. I, at least, have never regretted that I had faith in a young man when appearances were against him, that I defended him on credit, and so secured to myself at least one grateful client.

CHAPTER IX.

Hypnotism—Spiritual and Other Isms.

"The thing that hath been, it is that which shall be; and that which is done, it is that which shall be done; and there is no new thing under the sun."

It is a common expression when any novel and extraordinary thing is seen by us for the first time to say that nothing like this was ever seen before. This is almost universally asserted of what are called novel spiritual manifestations. A year seldom passes without producing them. I profess no ability to explain or account for them. I shall describe a spiritual exhibition which I once witnessed, just as well as I am able to, exactly as we supposed we saw it, and leave my readers to make their own explanations. I think the story will at least tend to confirm the words of the "preacher."

It is useless to assert that all believers in modern spiritualism have some defect in their intellectual organization. I have met with close thinkers, men who possessed the *mens sana in corpore sano*, who believed that they received frequent visits from the spirits of their deceased friends, as thoroughly as they believed in the existence of any object which was affirmed by all their senses.

A very pleasant writer and sound thinker was S. C. Hall, for so many years editor of the London *Art Journal*. And a very entertaining writer was Anna Maria, as he called her—his wife. They were charming in their own beautiful home, and none who were admitted to their society ever failed of delightful memories. Before he was an author Mr. Hall was a barrister, trained to intellectual controversy, and those who discussed moral subjects with him soon learned not to despise their adversary. I was once present in his home by invitation, where he was to show me a collection of Wedgewood pottery, which, on my recommendation, an American friend purchased. He was thoroughly familiar with the history of all the Wedgewood pottery, and was in the middle of a most interesting story of some of Wedgewood's disappointing experiments, when he very abruptly said:

"Excuse me! It had entirely escaped my memory, but I have a positive engagement at this hour. It will occupy but a short time. Pray amuse yourself with a book while I keep it."

I said, "Certainly," and went to an open bookcase, expecting to see him go out, or at least leave the room. To my surprise he remained sitting silent in his chair. I was embarrassed. I did not know but he wanted to be rid of me before attending to his appointment, but the cordiality of his manner and his suggestion of the book made that conclusion impossible. I waited; it was for him to resume the conversation when he thought proper.

It was fifteen minutes by the watch before he spoke. "I have a very dear sister," he said. "We have long been accustomed to meet in this room every Tuesday at this hour. She is very sensitive and I could not endure the thought of disappointing her. But I do deeply regret my apparent neglect of an American visitor."

"I beg you will not think any apology is necessary. My apartments are only a few blocks away. It will put me to no inconvenience to come again. Does your sister reside near you?"

"Very, very near," he replied. "She is in the spirit-world. She went there twenty years ago. But you need not go," he continued, as I rose to take my leave. "We have had our meeting and she has gone!"

He resumed the subject of our conversation and completed his relation. I referred to the subject of spiritualism. He told me that much the larger portion of his intercourse now was with persons in the spirit-world, that Mrs. Hall was in full sympathy with his belief, and that some of their most delightful companions were no longer in the body. It was as impossible to doubt his sincerity as his personal presence. Nor was his belief at all unusual. It is entertained by many who will not and a few who are quite willing to confess their faith.

Forty years and more gone by; a showman gave exhibitions in New England. He was a bullet-headed, loud-voiced fellow of the regular circus type. He usually selected from his audience a dozen or more persons whom he seated in the front row. In the right hand of each man he placed a small disk of copper, with a round piece of brass in its centre. Each person was directed to fix his mind intently on this disk, while the "Professor," as he called himself, gyrated with his hands and looked fierce with his eyes. After a few minutes of this senseless performance he assorted his subjects. Some he returned to their seats, the majority of the others he seated together in view of the audience.

Without any explanation he began his exhibition. "It is very cold! I am almost freezing!" Each of his subjects began to shiver and tremble with apparent cold. "How hot it is!" and while some threw off their coats, others fanned themselves, still others rushed to and opened the windows, and all appeared to be suffering from the heat.

"Look," said he, "at that lovely picture. See that mother with the child—could anything be more lovely?" They clasped their hands and gazed with adoration. "This is my garden. Here are roses and flowers, peaches and plums of exquisite taste! Gather as many as you like!" Some picked flowers and pinned them on their breasts; others ate the peaches as if they were luscious. "Be careful. Those are not peaches, they are wild turnips." Wild turnips sting the mouth as severely as red peppers. Forthwith they expelled the turnips from their mouths and called for water, ice, and snow. "Look," he said, "at all those gold eagles," pointing to a corner. "Every one may have as many as he can pick up." They rushed against and over each other, tore one another out of the way, and sprawled upon the floor in their efforts to get them. When the scramble was the worst, he made a single pass with his hand which restored each to his senses. They went to their seats, looking as sheepish as possible.

Then he prepared for the exhibition of tying a man in a closet, who played on the banjo and went through other performances too common to require description. This was followed by mind-reading and finally by professed communications with the spirits. To all which the more intelligent of the audience paid little attention.

But on the following evening one of his subjects, an intelligent young mechanic, described to a party of half a dozen gentlemen the vivid reality of his sensations. So far as he was concerned, there was no deception. Another gentleman declared that the spirit of his wife had answered his mental inquiry by a fact unknown to him, but which he had since learned was true. Then one proposed that we should all go and have a private exhibition, which the showman advertised to give. We went, we saw the exhibition, and the following is an accurate description of the audience, the *dramatis personæ*, and the display.

We were six in number: two doctors—one very learned in the Hebrew, Arabic, Greek, and Latin, as well as the modern languages—two lawyers, a clergyman, and the collector of the port. All were educated, intelligent gentlemen.

We went to a small but very respectable boarding-house, rang, and asked for the showman by name. We were shown into the small, plainly furnished "square" room. Soon entered a girl of some eighteen years, having every mark of an ignorant, gawky, impudent country wench.

"Do you fellers want a see-ants?" she demanded.

We had agreed that Dr. H. should be our speaker. "We would like to see whatever there is to be seen," he civilly replied.

"Wall, the Perfessor charges a half a dollar a head for a private see-ants," she said. "I'm his meejum."

She was assured that the entrance-fee of four shillings each should be forthcoming. She passed into the hall, and as the servant expressed her reply to her mistress' call in "A New Home," "we thought we heard a yell." "Perfessor," she screamed, "here's six gents as wants a see-ants, right off!"

There was as little that was spiritual in the appearance of the *Perfessor* as in his "meejum." He was an uneducated man who had acquired some polish by contact with others. He entered, collected his half-dollar from each, and proceeded to business. A circular table stood in the centre. From this he removed the cover and placed seven chairs around the table. Except a piano with no cover, the room contained no other furniture. We were directed to be seated and "jine hands" with the meejum.

We were all disgusted with the absurdity of the performance, when the medium said to the clergyman, who sat nearest to her: "Naow don't you tickle my hand. If you do I shall giggle right out." We were indisposed to speech. In a few minutes the girl was apparently asleep. The showman declared that he could understand anything said through her by the spirits, but she could only communicate with a stranger by raps and by spelling out the word. Thus one rap meant yes, two raps no, other letters being indicated by numbers on cards which were distributed to each of us. This apparently slow method was used by the medium with great rapidity. The raps were very distinct and apparently made all over the room—on and under the table, in the lamp-shade, on the back of a chair, and in other localities.

"I will now put the medium in communication with any one of you," said the showman. "She will summon any spirit called for. The spirit will not always come, and some that come will not answer."

I was first put into correspondence with her by taking both her hands, and the showman made some passes over us. This done, I mentally invited the spirit of a deceased doctor in my father's family. His presence was announced by a rap. The serious part of the business now began. I asked my questions in an audible voice.

"Are you a spirit?" Answer—"Yes."

"Whose?" Ans.—"I am Dr. Matthew Cole."

"Are there any scars upon my person?" Ans.—"Yes. Two."

"Where?" Ans.—"On your right ankle and under your left arm."

"What caused them?" Ans.—"A cut with an axe that on your ankle; an explosion of powder that under your arm."

There was not a person in the room but myself who could have known these facts. The answers were perfectly accurate. Dr. Cole attended me when I came near losing my life in my boyhood by the explosion of a half-pound paper of powder ignited in my pocket by the discharge of a musket. There was no fact stated, however, which I did not know.

The clergyman then took his turn and was put into communication with the spirit of his deceased wife. As in my own case, questions relating to his former settlement, residence, marriage, and other events were correctly answered. The clergyman then asked whether he had had any differences with a member of his former congregation. He was answered yes, and the full name of the person was given. "What was the origin of it?" "An unsigned letter which he believed was written by you."

The clergyman declared that he never knew the origin of what came to be a very serious trouble to him. Now, in the light of well-known facts, he believed the answer to be accurate.

Our learned physician now called for the spirit of his brother and he came. He was, when he died, professor of the Hebrew and allied languages in a German university. After several questions had been correctly answered, the doctor said: "Brother, it would give me great joy to be convinced that you are my brother. Can you make me certain of your identity?"

"I will try," was the response. "I will translate for you from the German into the Hebrew tongue what is known in our mother tongue as the first verse of the 34th chapter of the Second Book of Moses. It commences, as you know, 'Und der Herr, sprach zu Mou——'" "Mein Gott!" interrupted the doctor. "This is most wonderful. You are my brother or you are Satan. Nothing ever happened to me so extraordinary as this!"

He then explained that his brother differed from the authorities in the orthography of the name Moses. The Germans wrote it Mose; the French, Moise or Moyse. His brother always wrote it Mousse. That thought was not in his mind when he asked for the proof. It was natural that his brother should have selected it to prove his identity.

We asked that the proposed translation be made. The doctor assented and wrote from the raps the verse. In English it read thus: "And the Lord said unto Moses, Hew thee two tables of stone like unto the first: and I will write upon these tables the words that were in the first tables, which thou brakest." He took from his pocket the Hebrew Pentateuch and compared what he had written from his brother's dictation, and said that the words and characters agreed. None of us were Hebrew scholars, but we were none the less certain of the accuracy of the doctor's statement.

Striking as was the illustration, it only served to confirm an opinion which I have ever since entertained. In attempting to carry the translations farther, we found that the spirits would only translate for those who knew both tongues. They would translate a couplet of Virgil into French or English for me, but failed when they tried the Greek, which I did not understand. The trials of others met with the same fate. No one but the doctor could extract from the spirits a translation of one Hebrew character.

It may be the prevailing opinion that this incident is scarcely worth the space given to it. But pray consider the spectacle: A coarse, uneducated, and very common country girl, under the direction of a common showman, translating accurately a portion of the Hebrew Bible for a German scholar. It was an impressive experience to me, and set my mind at rest on some subjects which have much disturbed others. That there is a mysterious process by which one mind operates upon, influences, and in some cases controls another, seems to be incontrovertible. That there is any communication between the spirits of the dead and the living there is not the first particle of satisfactory evidence.

CHAPTER X.

"The Beautiful American Nun."

AT the close of the first half of the nineteenth century Vermont was an isolated province on the northern border of the spiritual kingdom of the Catholic bishop of Boston. Too remote for the personal supervision of that prelate, he had permitted the Rev. Jeremiah O'Callaghan to control it for so long a time that he had come to regard his authority as equal to that of the head of the church. The Reverend Jeremiah was an Irish priest of peculiar opinions never entirely in harmony with Catholic principles. On account of these he had been compelled to leave Ireland and had come to this frontier, where he could enforce his uncanonical views of usury, banking, pew-rent, and monopoly without interference from any superior authority. Catholicism had flourished under, or rather in defiance of, his rule; many new churches had been built, much valuable real property acquired, the deeds to which were taken to "the Reverend Jeremiah O'Callaghan and his assigns."

The new congregations were formed of Canadian-French and Irish Catholics in nearly equal numbers. All were good Catholics, but in temporal matters they were as discordant as the poles of an electric battery. Their united action in a congregation would have been impracticable under the most judicious management.

The combative disposition of the Reverend Jeremiah, who usually sided with his countrymen, always intensified, never reconciled these differences, until they produced numerous actions of ejectment, for assaults, batteries, and other proceedings disreputable to the church and profitable only to members of the legal profession.

These controversies increased in number and intensity until a very quiet and unassuming priest appeared upon the scene. This was the Rev. Louis de Goesbriand, who brought with him his commission as bishop of Vermont, which had been made a new Catholic diocese. He was a French Jesuit who came to us from some Western city. He frequently consulted Hon. E. J. Phelps and myself upon the law of conveyances and the methods of compromising suits, and impressed us both by his discretion and his skill in controlling the passions of angry men. He at once transferred the Reverend Jeremiah O'Callaghan, whose combativeness increased with age, to a church in the beautiful town of Northampton, Massachusetts, and in that way removed the principal cause of controversy. He separated the Canadian-French from the Irish, and impartially provided each with churches, schools, and pastors of their own nationality. In a few months every Catholic lawsuit had been settled, the titles to every parcel of church property had been brought into conformity with the church regulations, and peace was restored to every Catholic congregation in the new diocese.

The discretion and energy of the bishop commended him to the respect of all good citizens. He co-operated with the local authorities in good works, established excellent schools and gathered into them the children of the streets, where they were clothed, fed, and trained to respectability. From a sandstone which up to that time had been unappreciated, he built a cathedral in the city of Burlington which was a poem in stone, and which has come to be known as one of the most beautiful structures in New England. Notwithstanding their inherited aversion to the Jesuits, the people entertained a sincere respect for the Catholic bishop of Vermont, and his diocese was one of the most orderly and prosperous under the jurisdiction of Rome.

On a visit to Burlington after an absence of some years I called upon Bishop de Goesbriand and asked to see the interior of his cathedral. He assented cordially to my request and accompanied me to the structure. In his modest way he was pointing out some of its novelties, when I noticed a group of statuary in wood, which apparently represented some mythological subject. To my inquiry what it was intended to represent, he answered that he would tell me after we had completed our inspection. We visited all parts of the cathedral and its grounds, finally came to his residence, and entered his library. There I claimed the fulfilment of his promise, and there he told me the story of the "Beautiful American Nun." All its details connected with the sisterhood he gave me. Some facts of the early life of the principal character were derived from descendants in the family to which she belonged.

"The group of statuary which you saw in the cathedral is an attempt to commemorate the only accepted and well-authenticated miracle ever wrought within the limits of Vermont. After the war of the

Revolution, as you know, General Ethan Allen came to reside on the Winooski intervale in this town, where he lived at the time of his death. His dwelling was a farm-house on an unfrequented road, and he had no near neighbors. One spring morning when his daughter Fanny, aged nine years, was gathering wild-flowers on the river's bank, she was startled by the sight of a monster which was rushing through the water, apparently to devour her. Stricken with fear, she was unable to move and utterly helpless. Just as the savage beast was about to tear her with his ferocious claws, she heard a kind and gentle voice saying, 'Have no fear, my daughter, the monster has no power over you.' Trustfully raising her eyes, she saw standing by her side an aged man of venerable aspect, white hair and beard, wearing a long cloak and carrying a long staff in his hand. His words reassured the frightened maid; her fears departed and she started for her home. There she related her fearful adventure and described the appearance of her deliverer. Her father and mother immediately went in search of him, but he was neither to be found nor heard of. No one had seen him along the road where he must have passed; her parents gave up the search, believing that their daughter was the victim of her own imagination and that no such person existed as she believed she had seen. The incident passed from their minds and was for the time forgotten.

All accounts agree upon the piety and loveliness of the daughters of Ethan Allen. It was of Fanny Allen's elder half-sister that the touching story is told of her last interview with her unbelieving father. The rough warrior stood by her bedside

"THE BEAUTIFUL AMERICAN NUN."

holding her emaciated hand. 'My dear father,' she said, 'I am about to die; shall I die believing with you that there is no heaven, no Jesus, no future life, or shall I believe what my mother and her Bible have taught me?' The strong man wept bitter tears as he replied, 'My child, believe what your mother has taught you.'

"The years sped on. The hero of Ticonderoga was gathered to his fathers, and his lonely wife, after a season of mourning, sought protection and comfort in the home of her third husband, an eminent physician of an adjoining town. Fanny Allen was a beautiful girl of seventeen when she left her father's home to enter upon a new and very beautiful life which you will find recorded in this history."

The bishop handed me two royal octavo volumes in French, which comprised the History of the Hotel Dieu convent in Montreal, in which he said I could read the subsequent life of Fanny Allen. But I had been so charmed with his simple relation that I insisted upon hearing the account from his own lips. His narrative comprised all the facts described in the book. From that relation and facts derived from other authentic sources I have condensed the sequel of the story.

The remarkable beauty and rare intelligence of Fanny Allen appear in every account of her which has fallen under my notice. Her mother, whose name she bore, a widow at the time of her marriage with Colonel Allen, is described as a lady of commanding presence, graceful figure, and a queenly style of beauty. The daughter inherited all her mother's gifts, united with a sweetness of disposition and a confiding manner which charmed every one who knew her. Before her sixteenth birthday she had met a student in the then young University of Vermont. H—— D—— was the son of a wealthy Boston merchant; he lived in the family of President Sanders, a friend and neighbor of Dr. Penniman, the step-father of Miss Allen. He possessed an irreproachable character and was a thorough gentleman by birth and education. He loved Fanny Allen with all the devotion of a brilliant mind and a pure heart. She gave him in return the treasure of her first love. They were made for each other. The parents of both approved their union. For nearly a year they had lived for and loved each other. D—— was a welcome guest in the home of his beloved, and both looked somewhat impatiently forward to his graduation, when they were to be married and he was to enter his father's firm in Boston, where the young couple were to reside. The voluntary withdrawal of either from the promise of such a future seemed impossible. The love and society of her promised husband were completely satisfying to Fanny Allen. She envied no one, wanted nothing more. The year which closed on her eighteenth birthday was a year of contentment and unalloyed happiness.

Miss Allen had received an excellent English education, and at this time she conceived an irresistible desire to acquire the French language. She had never experienced it before; now it was more powerful than her love. Her mother resisted it at first. The French was a useless accomplishment which, before the days of railways, ocean steamers, and European travel, formed no necessary part of the education of a young American lady. The longing of Miss Allen increased when it was resisted.

She became despondent and melancholy; her face lost its fresh color. Her friends feared she was going into a decline.

As farther resistance promised to imperil the health and possibly the life of his adopted daughter, her step-father yielded and her mother accompanied her to the city of Montreal in search of a school in which the daughter might be taught the French language. Then, as now, the schools in the convents bore a deservedly high reputation, and were successively visited by the American strangers. Their final visit to the convents was to the celebrated sisterhood known as the Convent "Hotel Dieu." They entered its chapel, walked up one of the aisles until they stood before a large painting near the altar. To the mother's amazement, the daughter suddenly fell upon her knees, bowed her head in prayerful adoration, and pointing to a figure in the painting, exclaimed: "There is the man who saved me from the monster." It was the figure of the venerable Joseph, the husband of the Virgin, in a large painting of the Holy Family.

Believing that she had been directed hither by a divine influence, Miss Allen would listen to no suggestion of farther inquiry. Her mother left her as a scholar in charge of the sisterhood and returned to her Vermont home.

A new life now began for Fanny Allen. Her conduct was irreproachable. She made rapid progress in her studies, but they assumed a minor importance. She was powerfully impressed by the unselfish piety of the sisters who had withdrawn from the world and given themselves to the service of the church in the conversion of the unbelieving and incidentally to works of mercy and charity. She determined to enter the sisterhood as soon as her season of probation was ended. The grief of her mother over this decision could scarcely have been more poignant over her death.

Her mother, her friends, and her lover united their efforts to dissuade her from her purpose. In the hope of diverting her mind and of awakening her interest in worldly things, she was taken from the convent into the most fashionable circles of city life, where she was qualified to shine and where she attracted universal admiration. Her affianced lover, overwhelmed with grief, made to her the most tender and pathetic appeals. He painted the attractions of the social life which opened its doors to welcome them. He would give her comfort, luxury, position, everything that wealth could purchase or her heart desire. They would travel, they would store their minds with precious memories of old civilizations. Together they would float upon Italian lakes, read great poems among the mountains that inspired them. They would ascend the Nile, study the beauties of the Alhambra, and read the story of the cross on the shores of Galilee. Would she become a minister of charity? His fortune was hers to bestow. All he asked was that he might work beside her, sustain her strength, and see generations rise up to call her blessed. They had been, they might be so happy in each other's love! He prayed, he implored her not to give up a future of so much promise for the restricted opportunities and prison life within the stony walls of a convent cell.

But Fanny Allen was inflexible. She had the energy, decision, and firmness of her father, controlled by the gentleness of a trustful nature. Nothing could have surpassed the sweetness of her cheerful acquiescence in the wish of her mother that she should enter society. There she seemed to exert herself to add to its attractions. She was very beautiful; above the medium height, her complexion fair, her eyes dark blue with a singular calmness and depth of expression, united to a regal dignity and repose of manner which made her attractions irresistible while they indicated the refinement and loveliness of her character. Nor did her first love grow cold. Her lover was dearer to her than ever. It was because she loved him so well that she was constrained to obey the call of One through whom she hoped to secure his eternal welfare.

In due time Miss Allen, confident of the genuineness of her conversion to the Catholic faith, returned to the convent to prepare for her final withdrawal from the world. At a time when so little was known of Catholicism in Vermont, this announcement created an interest and excitement which the present generation cannot appreciate. In the popular ignorance of the time "taking the veil," as it was called, was regarded as the voluntary suicide of the novice, as the suppression, if not the destruction, of a human soul. The ceremony was described in the press. The gloomy half-light of the chapel filled with mourning friends; the funereal tones of the organ; the shaven priests; the angelic beauty of the novice in her dress of unstained white; the saddened, sweet resignation of her face; the grief of her last glance toward those from whom she was about to part forever; the final scene when, in the dark robe of her order, she fell into keeping with the awful ceremony;

the fall of the curtain which was supposed to separate her forever from all she held dear, was thought to represent a truthful exhibition, as dreadful and almost as cruel as the nameless ceremonies of the inquisition.

But if the information of Bishop de Goesbriand was reliable, the blessings which followed the consecration of the beautiful novice more than compensated every one for their sorrow for her temporal loss. She immediately became one of the celebrities of the city of Montreal. Her convent was no longer a place of seclusion. It was besieged by throngs of visitors who would not leave the city until they had seen "the beautiful American nun." Although she brought benefactions to the convent, these numerous visitors became not only annoying to her, but she was not strong enough to endure the fatigue of receiving them. Her Mother Superior at length decided to refuse to put her upon exhibition, and she was permitted to enjoy a season of seclusion.

After assuming the religious habit she lived only eleven years, and came to the end of her beautiful life at the age of thirty-five years. Those eleven years witnessed so many conversions of her relatives and acquaintances to the Catholic faith as to establish the miraculous character of her own experience. The physician who attended her last hours, a Protestant, was so touched by her faith that when at the last moment her confessor exclaimed, "Come to her assistance, all ye saints of God," he fell upon his knees and registered a solemn purpose, which was executed by leaving his profession, joining the church, and entering a religious community. Her intended husband sold what he had and gave it to the poor and himself to the service of the church. The Rev. Mr. Barber, who gave Miss Allen the rite of baptism into the Episcopal church, at the age of sixty-two years became a Catholic—his son and his grandson became priests of the Jesuit order and missionaries to the Indians. Her relatives and those who knew her well, almost without exception, followed her example; one of them, a clergyman, with his wife were separated by a papal decree, in order that the husband might become a priest and his wife the lady superior of a convent in a Southern city. The incidents of her life and the results of her noble influence would fill a volume. Indeed, her example has not yet lost its power, for many conversions from Protestantism of her posterity continue to occur, some of the most conspicuous under the ministry of the present bishop of Vermont.

"You do not believe in the Vermont miracle or in its marvellous consequences and conversions, but we do—we believe them thoroughly," were the sincere and artless words with which the good bishop terminated our interview and the story of "the beautiful American nun."

CHAPTER XI.

SECRETARY CHASE AND HIS FINANCIAL POLICY.

IN the judgment of thoughtful men, the Treasury was the weakest portion of the national defences during the civil war. Of the courage and patriotism of the loyal North and West there was never any doubt. But the soldier cannot fight upon courage and patriotism alone. He must be clothed and fed, as well as provided with arms and ammunition, and these cannot be furnished when the money and credit of the Government are exhausted. The rebel armies were never destitute of guns, powder, or ball. England and some of the Continental powers took good care of them in this respect. But toward the close of the war, when other supplies were exhausted, the military strength of the South rapidly weakened. Exposure and want of tents, clothing, and proper food were as damaging to the South as any powerful reinforcement of the Northern armies.

The management of Secretary Cobb had thoroughly depleted the Treasury: he had spared no efforts to accomplish this result. On the 4th of March, 1861, there was not money enough left in its vaults to pay for the daily consumption of stationery; no city dealer would furnish it on credit. When Secretary Chase entered upon his duties, the most thorough search was made to find something that could be turned into money. It was suggested that the surplus revenue which had been loaned to the States might be collected. But of the obligations for its return executed by the slaveholding States, every one had mysteriously disappeared, and that subject was laid aside. No authority for the issue of Treasury notes existed; the prospect of raising money was as remote as could be imagined.

The last Congress had authorized a small loan, at six per cent interest, payable in gold coin. Secretary Cobb had offered it; the whole amount had been taken, the subscribers depositing the customary one per cent as a guarantee that the remaining payments would be made. The Secretary had so frequently and so confidently predicted the dissolution of the Union, and that the loan would never be paid, that some of the subscribers in Washington and the South declined to make good their subscriptions and forfeited their guarantee. The amount not taken was about $9,000,000. This amount was available if subscribers for it could be obtained.

This balance was accordingly advertised in the usual manner. It was announced that on an appointed day proposals for it would be received, opened, and considered by the Secretary.

When the day arrived there were so few offers for it that the Secretary decided to postpone opening the bids and to advertise for proposals a second time. It was in this connection that I first heard the word "syndicate" in relation to a financial transaction. Mr. Jay Cooke, a personal friend of the Secretary, came to Washington from Ohio, and proposed that all loyal Republicans should form "syndicates" to subscribe for this loan. Such syndicates were formed and the subscription was considerably increased thereby.

That was a memorable day on which the bids were opened. Three persons were present: the Secretary, one of his assistants, and the Register. The Assistant Secretary opened and read the bids— the Register recorded them. There were a few offers for small amounts, as high as ninety-five; the offers of the syndicates were about ninety. Then the bids fell off—some of them were as low as forty. Think of it! Four hundred dollars offered for a bond of the United States, at six per cent interest, payable in gold coin, for one thousand dollars! The defeats at Bull Run were not so disheartening to the Treasury officers who comprehended the situation as the summing up of these unpatriotic offers.

No word broke the silence while the Register was adding up and averaging the offers. When this was done he inquired:

"Well, what is to be done?"

"Have you any suggestion?" asked the Secretary.

"I have," said the Register. "A little money we must have. There are between three and four millions bid for at eighty-five and above. I suggest that these offers be accepted."

"Very well," responded the Secretary. "Let the notices be given."

"But what then?" pursued the Register. "Our liabilities are accruing at the rate of $2,000,000 daily. The proceeds of this loan will not pay them for more than forty-eight hours. Is the Treasury to suspend payment?"

The Secretary was seated at the table, upon which his elbow rested; his massive head was supported upon his opened palm. His countenance wore a look of weary depression. Suddenly he started, raised his head, and the look of depression was followed by one of determination, almost fierce in its intensity.

"What then?" he exclaimed, "is a serious question. It is less difficult to say what we will *not* than what we will do. We will *not* try this method of raising money farther! Let this loan and these books be closed!"

At this point he rose and stood upon his feet. Erect, he was a model of strength and dignity—the finest man in carriage and appearance in the nation. Scarcely raising his voice, the words fell from his lips like a decree from the throne of an omnipotent monarch:

"There is money enough in the loyal North and West to pay for suppressing this wicked rebellion. The people are willing to loan it to their Government. If we cannot find the way to their hearts, we should resign and give place to those who can. I am going to the people! If there is a farmer at the country cross-roads who has ten dollars which he is willing to loan to the Government, he shall be furnished with a Treasury obligation for it, without commission or other expense. When we have opened the way directly to the people and they fail to respond to the calls of their Government in the stress of civil war, we may begin to despair of the republic!" With these words ringing in our ears, the conference ended.

This expression disclosed the source of the financial strength of Secretary Chase. His confidence in the people was absolutely supreme; it never for a moment wavered. He saw himself, and he could make others, even an assembly of bank presidents, see that their possessions were worthless unless the Treasury, a synonym in his mind for the Government, was sustained. But he addressed no such selfish arguments to the masses. They knew that it was their duty to support the Government with their lives— much more with their money. The plan of dealing with them directly was the strongest that could possibly have been devised.

Able as the Secretary was, it would be erroneous to assume that his financial policy, which culminated in "An Act to Establish a National Currency," was struck out at a sitting, and came from him perfect, like Minerva from the front of Jove. It was the subject of growth and development, enlarging with the necessities of the country and always adequate to its relief. A rapid sketch of this growth, as shown by the successive acts of Congress, may not here be out of place.

The extra session of July 4th, 1861, was called when there was in the Cabinet more than one believer in the suppression of the rebellion within sixty days. The Secretary was confident that its suppression would not involve any permanent disturbance of the financial institutions or systems then in existence. Accordingly, the first loan act of July 17th, 1861, comprised important provisions, which were never used and were soon abandoned.

This act authorized the Secretary to borrow not more than $250,000,000, and to issue bonds bearing seven per cent and Treasury notes bearing interest at the rate of seven and three-tenths per cent, the latter popularly known as the "seven-thirty notes." He was authorized to issue not more than fifty millions of dollars in Treasury notes, bearing no interest and payable on demand. These "demand notes" were made receivable for all public dues, including duties

SECRETARY CHASE AND HIS POLICY. 95

on imports, and were convertible into other notes bearing interest at the rate of 3.65 per cent per annum. The defeat at Bull Run on the 21st of July led to the passage of the act of August 5th, which authorized the conversion of the "seven-thirties" into bonds bearing six per cent interest; another act of the same date increasing the duties on imports, and another imposing a tax upon real estate and incomes, constituted the financial legislation of the extra session.

The "demand notes" were immediately issued, and there were small issues of the other Treasury notes authorized. But there were no conversions into bonds under these acts. The second or December session of the Thirty-seventh Congress was approaching; the necessity for an increased issue of notes for general circulation became apparent, and the Secretary turned his attention to the new measures demanded by these necessities.

The first loan act of the December session provided for the issue of one hundred and fifty millions in non-interest-bearing Treasury notes, constituting the first issue of those popularly known as "greenbacks." Fifty millions of these were to take the place of the "demand notes," which it was determined should be withdrawn from circulation. They were receivable for customs duties and took the place of so much gold. They commanded a premium nearly equal to that of gold. The new issue of $150,000,000 were receivable for all public dues except duties on imports. This act authorized the funding of all outstanding Treasury notes, together with any part of the floating debt, into six per cent bonds, to the amount of $500,000,000, bearing six per cent interest, redeemable at the pleasure of the

United States at any time after five and payable in twenty years. These were the well-known "five-twenties" of 1881. The act of March 1st, 1862, authorized the issue of certificates of indebtedness, payable in one year, with six per cent interest, to any public creditor. An act of July 11th, 1862, increased the issue of greenbacks $150,000,000, making the whole issue $300,000,000. The duties on imports were again increased. The internal revenue system was created, and these acts comprised the financial legislation of the Thirty-seventh Congress.

While these acts created a large additional revenue and increased the authorized funding of the debt by nearly eight hundred million dollars, they were obviously inadequate to the necessities of the situation. Secretary Chase foresaw, before the Thirty-seventh Congress closed, that the Government credit could not be sustained unless more thorough and permanent measures were adopted which should close the State banks and create a national currency secured by the bonds of the United States. He was aware that such a measure would encounter the powerful combined opposition of the existing banks; that its expediency would be questioned and its necessity denied. But he clearly anticipated its beneficial influence upon the country, and that it would eventually become the crowning glory of his financial administration. He therefore made no secret of its purposes and proposed operation, and addressed all the powers of his mind to its perfection and passage.

While the bill was before the House of Representatives, Hon. Brutus J. Clay, a loyal, conservative member of the House from Kentucky, himself a banker, called at the Treasury to show the Secretary that he ought to consent to a reduction of the proposed tax upon the circulation of the State banks. He argued that the tax was greater than the average profit on the circulation, and demonstrated that the circulation would inevitably be withdrawn. The Secretary admitted the force of his argument, but declined to consent to any reduction of the tax. Disappointed and somewhat irritated, Mr. Clay exclaimed, " Why, Mr. Secretary, you act as if it were your purpose to destroy the State banks!" " My own purpose is unimportant, but I am of opinion that the act justifies your criticism, and that such a purpose may be inferred from some of its provisions," observed the Secretary. Mr. Clay was almost speechless with astonishment. He rose from his seat, clasped his hands above his head, and left the office, exclaiming," My God! My God!" It was clear to the Secretary that the two systems could not co-exist—that one or the other must give way. Justice to Mr. Clay requires me to say that he became a firm supporter of the bill.

No fewer than a score of men have claimed to be the originators of the " Act to Provide for a National Currency." The list comprises bankers, lawyers, gentlemen of leisure, and at least one clergyman. Far be it from me to intimate that all these gentlemen are not entitled to all the laurels they claim. I would sooner take the part of one of the cities claiming to be the birthplace of Homer. But we who were in the Treasury and who had discussed all the important clauses with the Secretary and each other must be excused if we adhere rather firmly to the opinion that the real author of the bill was Secretary Chase.

The manner in which the important sections of this bill were perfected shows the great ability of the man and his superiority to any feeling of personal jealousy. There is no doubt whatever that he submitted the bill to every person he knew or heard of who could improve it by his criticisms or suggestions. Himself one of the best lawyers in the nation, whose facility of expression rendered his business letters models of English composition, he would not trust himself to perfect this bill. After it had been improved as much as possible in his own department, he one day asked the head of one of his bureaus who was the best lawyer to remove from the bill all the clauses of doubtful interpretation. The name of an eminent Senator was suggested, but it was mentioned as an objection to him that his great experience was associated with an unyielding obstinacy of opinion, that his views of "legal tender" differed from those of the Secretary, that he would insist upon their application to an act intended to survive all military necessities, and that instead of perfecting the bill he would eliminate from it everything which did not conform to his views. Judge Collamer was well known to the Secretary. He recognized his fitness for the work, declined to listen to the objections, but invited him to the Treasury, where he spent several weeks in close, intelligent, and most judicious labor upon the bank act. Judge Collamer might well claim the authorship of many of its provisions. But it never occurred to him nor to any officer of the Treasury to attribute the origin of this bill to any other than Secretary Chase. The removal of the prejudices of the bankers, their acceptance of and their organization under it, was largely the work of Hon. Hugh McCulloch, the first Comptroller of the Currency.

SECRETARY CHASE AND HIS POLICY. 99

Considerable time elapsed after the passage of the "Act to Provide a National Currency" before the first national bank under its provisions was organized. The officers of the State banks, who had generally managed them with safety to the public and credit to themselves, were naturally averse to any change and unwilling to concede that any better system could be devised, especially by a Secretary who, although he had established his reputation as a great financier, had no experience in the practical business of banking. The bank presidents of the principal cities, in making previous loans to the Government, had become accustomed to act together, and there was some evidence of an organized resistance on their part to the national-bank act. They did not believe it could be set in motion without their co-operation.

In this opinion they were mistaken. The first impulse was given to the new system by a New Yorker who was quite outside their powerful financial circle. The "First National Bank" was organized by Mr. John Thompson. It had a moderate capital and no business except such as itself created. It was by the act entitled to become one of the depositories of the Treasury moneys, and to other privileges having a pecuniary value, from which the State banks were excluded. These advantages immediately demonstrated that banking under the national act might be made very profitable, and resistance to it on the ground of prejudice could not long be maintained when it involved a pecuniary loss. The alternative was presented to the bank officers of banking under the old system at a loss or under the new at a profit. Their prejudices began to give way, and as soon as one or two of the State banks had decided to make the change, all the others were so ready to follow that it was simply a question which could get into the national system first. In a few weeks opposition to it from the old banks had disappeared.

The wise and conservative administration of the act by Mr. McCulloch, the first Comptroller of the Currency, was most efficient in removing all objections of the State-bank officers; and the readiness with which Secretary Chase accepted suggestions for amendments made friends of many who would otherwise have been its enemies. It was at first intended that the national banks should be numbered consecutively in order of their organization, and that the former names of the State banks should be wholly suppressed. The suggestion that these banks should be permitted to retain the old and honorable titles was made by Mr. Patterson, one of the oldest and most experienced bank presidents of Philadelphia. The value of this suggestion was immediately recognized by the Secretary and the Comptroller, and it was adopted. Its effect was equivalent to a retention by the old banks of the "trade-marks" of their business. Thus, for example, the "Chemical Bank," which would have become possibly the "Nine hundred and seventh National Bank," under Mr. Patterson's suggestion became the "Chemical National Bank." The change was so slight that it preserved whatever of advantage was associated with an old and honorable name. The influence of this change was very great; in fact, it seemed to remove the last prejudice against the national system, which, tested by an experience of twenty-five years, has proved to be the best, safest, and most satisfactory known to the history of banking.

CHAPTER XII.

Some Notes about Birds—A Lesson in Engineering.

I HOPE no reader will turn away contemptuously from this chapter because he assumes that the subject is unworthy of men who have to deal with the serious concerns of life. I have never had much time to throw away, but I have spent a good many days with our common birds, and a much larger number with men, infinitely less to my profit and pleasure.

If he hopes to gain the confidence of the public, no writer of political literature should fail to acquaint himself with the elements of natural history. I have in mind a very delightful author, eminent as a poet, a statesman, a diplomatist, and a historian, yet because of his gross perversion of ornithological facts I cannot read anything that he has written with any pleasure or give credit to facts upon his unconfirmed evidence. One who describes humming-birds perishing in a snow-storm, the robins pairing in midwinter, the crows nesting in the evergreens around his garden, will never gain the confidence of the naturalist. When he affirms that the blue-jays unravelled an old carpet for the materials for their nest built in his fruit-trees, and that the parent birds looked on with silent admiration while he amputated the limb of one of their young, broken by being entangled in one of the strings woven into their nest, he taxes our credulity quite as heavily as old Sir John Maundeville when he declares that "the Ravenes and Crowes, everyche of hem bringethe in here bekes a braunche of olive, of the whiche the monkes maken gret plentee of Oyle to feed the lampes in the Chirche of Seynte Kateryne," a fact which he solemnly declares is "the myracle of God and a gret marvaylle." The humming-bird never comes to us until the honeysuckle is in flower, the male robin precedes the female by some weeks in its spring migration, and every tyro knows that in New England the *corvidæ* are the most secretive of birds in their nesting and incubation. The nest of the common crow, always in the thick boughs of the lofty pine or hemlock, is seldom found until it is betrayed by the hoarse cawing of the young; the egg of that very common bird, the Canada jay, was unknown to science until 1859, and no nest of a New England bird is more difficult of discovery than that of the blue-jay. It is to be found only in some ravine in the depths of the forest where the thick tops of the evergreens effectually screen it from human observation. When found, like all the nests of the *genus*, it is formed exclusively of dried twigs, with no spear of grass or anything but woody roots and twigs in its construction. No improbability could surpass the story of the young jay losing its leg by becoming entangled in a string, except that of the nest being made from the ravellings of an old carpet hanging in a flower-garden!

The blue-jay is one of those birds that change their habits with their locality. In New England they are never seen in flocks and seldom more than a pair are seen together. In the Southern States, where they winter, they collect in flocks, and their watchfulness for every grain of rice or corn makes them the pest of the plantation. Those which remain there do not lose their attachment for human society, and are said to nest and rear their young near the houses of the planters.

Do the birds reason? Do they know when it is necessary to protect themselves and their young against man and the lower animals and when it is not? I will not attempt a comprehensive answer to these questions. I will state some facts which will be interesting, and I know that they are credible.

The crows are a knowing family. They comprise the ravens, the magpies, the common crows, and the jays. The raven lives in the depths of the forest or on the shores of our solitary lakes in the silent wilderness. Why men pursue him to death it is bootless to inquire. Under no circumstances does he ever cultivate or injure human society. The crow is a very common bird and is, as his wants demand, a pest and a blessing. In the winter of 1862, when in the vicinity of Washington the unacclimated horses and cattle died by thousands, I used to welcome the mighty army of black-winged scavengers that devoured the carrion and protected us against epidemics. But every New England farmer's boy knows what a pest they are to the newly planted corn-fields and has had some opportunity to study their predatory habits. They never raid the sprouting grains without first placing on the lookout an experienced veteran, who never fails to give loud warning of the approach of any danger. If the farmer is unarmed and the crows are hungry, he may approach within a very few yards before they take flight. But let him bear upon his shoulder an old

Springfield musket or other fire-arm not dangerous to be handled, and the alert sentinel will not suffer him to come within a fourth of a mile of one of his family. Their affection for their young alone renders them insensible to danger. Capture a young crow and make him cry out, and every other one within hearing will come to his assistance. The sport of shooting them under these circumstances was always too cruel for me to engage in, even against such a notorious marauder.

The blue-jay is as knowing a bird as his congeners, the magpie and the crow. In the Southern States, as I have said, he lives in flocks near human dwellings. In the Middle States he is more retiring and not inclined to human society. In New England he is a solitary bird, and in pairs seeks the depths of the forest, where he is as difficult of approach as the common crow. He is omnivorous and savage enough to attack and destroy a wounded bird or animal much larger than himself; he can make his neighborhood very uncomfortable for the smaller predaceous animals.

Wilson, one of the most delightful of writers, commences his ornithology with a sketch of the habits of the blue-jay. I will add to his most entertaining account a few observations of my own. There was upon our homestead farm an extensive wood of the first growth. There were hills covered with pines, hemlocks, and other evergreens, plains of sugar-maples and beeches, and on its three hundred or more acres grew almost every New England tree and shrub. The crows and jays nested in the evergreens, the myrtle-bird and thrushes in the groves of deciduous trees, and many species of natural enemies seemed to live together as a happy family. On one occasion I noticed a pair of jays screaming in imitation of a sparrow-hawk, with butcher-birds and several other species, all pursuing some animal running on the ground in the edge of a cleared field. A hawk made a descent, as I supposed, to strike one of the birds, but when he rose in a graceful curve I saw writhing in his talons the weasel which the birds had been pursuing. Later I saw an owl and finally a mother fox pursued by the same winged hunters. I could not avoid the conclusion that these birds of different species, so unlike each other, had banded together for their mutual defence, which they were successfully maintaining. Although I was unable to discover the nest, the young family of jays in due time appeared and grew to maturity.

The ruffed grouse, or, as it is commonly known in New England, the partridge, sometimes exhibited an intelligence almost and a pride more than human. In the wood I have mentioned there was a fallen tree, and I had discovered an opening through the branches where its whole length was visible. This fallen tree was the throne of one of the proudest birds that ever existed—the drumming-log of Mr. *Tetrao Umbellus*. With his tail, marked with transverse bars of black, expanded, his wings drooping, the tufts on his neck elevated, he marched along his log as stately as a male turkey, a peacock, or a drum-major. At the end he turned about and struck his stiffened wings together over his back, slowly at first, the strokes increasing in rapidity until they ran together, producing that drumming sound which so frequently attracts the pot-hunter and costs the musician its life. I watched this exhibition for hours, his performance being varied at times by affectionate endearments to the female under the log, where, with wings greatly expanded so as to cover a score of eggs, Mrs. *Tetrao* patiently incubated. Without disturbing, I watched her closely until she left the nest and, with soft cluckings, kept her peeping, fuzzy young ones within the shadow of her maternal wings. Then I thought it would be interesting to capture two or three of the young. I may tax the reader's credulity, but I must ask him to believe this story. There was an open wood-road leading away from the log. All else was a thicket. The moment I appeared near the log the mother limped a few yards down this open road, and then, with drooping wings, fell apparently helpless on the ground. I ran to pick her up; she rolled over and over several times, always just beyond my reach. I continued the pursuit a dozen yards or more, when she deliberately rose from her helpless condition on the ground and gracefully sailed away into the forest. I hurried back to the abandoned nest, but no young one was to be found. They too had betaken themselves to the covert, with sense enough not to betray themselves by a sound. If this was not the act of a *reasoning* mother to protect her young by drawing me away from them, it was certainly an excellent imitation of the reasoning faculty.

The blooded setter readily follows the game-bird by its scent, as every true sportsman knows. Has the bird the power of withholding or suppressing its scent? I will answer by an experience of my own, to which, if required, I could call a living witness.

We were shooting over "Bang," an Irish setter with as fine a nose as was ever carried by any animal with four or a less number of feet. It was a morning for English snipe. We had picked up a few individuals, one at a time, when we reached a narrow marsh near the mouth of the Winooski River, where, if anywhere, *scolopax gallinago* was to be found. At the lower end we sent in the dog and followed within shot. I firmly believe the dog quartered every square yard of that ground without finding a trace of a bird. We were about leaving it, when at the extreme upper end the dog turned in the opposite direction and immediately flushed three birds. Two of them fell, but the third was missed. Instead of moving off in his usual zig-zag flight and alighting, he ascended in a circular movement, uttering his feeble *squeak*. Before we had charged our muzzle-loaders the snipe began to spring up from the very ground over which we had walked, moving in similar circles until there were as many as a dozen in the air. We brought down two, when the others at a lofty elevation started southward, and gathering in a flock disappeared from our sight. Not a bird was left on the marsh. If these birds did not suppress their scent, how did it happen that the dog passed them until he turned to hunt in the opposite direction?

Where, tell me where, has *columba migratoria* gone? I have no need to describe the immense flights of passenger-pigeons which darkened the sky and made a sound of thunder in Kentucky and Ohio, one of them estimated by Mr. Audubon to comprise one billion one hundred and fifteen million individuals. In my boyhood they nested in the second growth of pines near our homestead, where I have picked up of a morning as many fat squabs as I could carry. We had to watch closely to protect the ripening fields of wheat and rye from their depredations. There was no other species of bird half so numerous.

I speak of them here to record an incident. In 1890 I was driving with a friend near Burlington, Vt. Our conversation was of the passenger-pigeon, and he had just informed me that he had not met with an individual in several years. We were then passing a field from which the crop of buckwheat had just been harvested. I observed to him that thirty years before I had killed pigeons on that field—many of them; that they were numerous there after the crops were harvested and were careful gleaners. My friend was telling me how complete their disappearance was over all our hunting-grounds of thirty years before, when six birds of the species alighted on a dead tree in the middle of the field! Three were males with the lively red color on their breasts and the long pointed tail and upper parts of cerulean hue which always made them so graceful and attractive. They were almost the last of their race in New England.

It was the opinion of that veteran observer, Mr. Audubon, that the passenger-pigeon was capable of a sustained flight of several hours at the rate of a mile per minute. Of our American birds, only the swallow family have been endowed with greater activity and rapidity. I know of no living creature which either of our genuine swallows cannot give time to and defeat in a race. For two or three spring days in each year there is an exhibition of the poetry of flight over the surface of either of the lakes in the New York Central Park. It is given by one of the most beautiful members of the family—the green-blue or white-bellied swallow. They have been mated and are on their bridal journey. The insect life on these lakes is attractive to them, but they rest and recruit here for two or three days only. In the early morning there will be some thousands where there were none the preceding sunset. Always apparently on the wing, describing all manner of circles, curves, straight and irregular lines, yet never colliding with each other or with any stationary object, when or where they sleep I cannot tell, for I have never seen one at rest. The males are quarrelsome and fight battles in the air. Suddenly a common impulse seizes them—they disappear, not to be seen again until another spring.

The habits of the barn swallow have given to that common summer visitant a singular reputation among the unlearned. They come and go so suddenly, with no advance agent or stragglers, that they are by many supposed to betake themselves to the soft mud in the bottom of the ponds, where they hibernate until their reappearance in new and glossy plumage in the spring. Like some half-human animals, they prefer to sleep closely packed together in a lodging-house. All the swallows in the locality hang themselves up in the inside of a hollow tree for their night's repose. After serving as the lodging of many generations the tree is cut down or falls, disclosing a mass of feathers and exuviæ, with a few skeletons of birds that lost their lives there. Straightway it is announced that the place where the swallows winter has been discovered and destroyed.

An incident in my own experience illustrates the very social habits of this graceful bird. I had had excellent sport with that noble game fighter, the black bass, around a small island of a few acres in Lake Champlain, east of Grand Isle, and determined to put up my tent and pass the night there. Except a few open spaces covered by a soft moss more than twelve inches thick, the surface was covered with red cedars, none more than a dozen feet in height, with lateral branches so interlaced that it was difficult to move among them. There was not apparently any animal or bird to be seen.

As the sun approached the horizon a few swallows came and alighted in the cedar branches, then more swallows, and still more until flocks of many hundred, coming from every point of the compass, were converging upon the island. They kept coming while the daylight faded into darkness. Their noisy chattering increased with every fresh arrival. I fancied that those who retired early and were comfortably settled for the night objected to being crowded upon their branches by the late arrivals. My supper was prepared and served to the accompaniment of innumerable angry but musical voices.

After some time the disputes appeared to be adjusted and there was a profound quiet, only broken here and there by some individual apparently talking in his sleep or disturbed by the nightmare. Then, making as little disturbance as possible, I forced myself under the branches, well into the grove, disturbing many sleepers in my progress. I *felt* that I was surrounded by life. Raising my hand to a branch, I discovered that the swallows were literally packed along it side by side. By striking successive matches I saw that every branch in view was laden in the same manner. The light seemed to awaken them for a moment, but they fell asleep again as soon as it was extinguished. I could have captured scores within reach of my hand, but I would not disturb these innocent creatures which had selected for their nightly repose what they supposed to be the security of an uninhabited island.

As the gray dawn was creeping over the eastern mountains there was a clear-ringing, silvery note from one of the tallest cedars in the grove. It was the *reveillé*. There was an answering note, then another, then many, and in a minute the grove was alive with voices. They were not the weary, complaining notes of the evening, but they were full of life and animation. There had been disputes, now there were voices in council. They were not protracted. As the first rays of the morning leaped skyward, touching the rock face of Mansfield with their golden splendor, a single swallow shot out from the grove and made one circuit sounding its call. Others followed until a small flock was collected, which moved westward over ten miles of water to the shore. Others followed, collecting in separate flocks and taking flight in different directions. Within five minutes the last swallow had departed and solitude reigned in the island.

There are mechanical engineers among the birds, and one of the most practical is a member of the swallow family, as the following incident will prove. Between the Winooski Valley and Lake Champlain, north of the city of Burlington, lies a broad sand plain high above the lake level, through which the Central Railroad was to be carried in a tunnel. But the sand was destitute of moisture or cohesiveness, and the engineers, after expending a large sum of money, decided that the tunnel could not be constructed because there were no means of sustaining the material during the building of the masonry. The removal of so large a quantity of material from a cut of such dimensions also involved an expense that was prohibitory. The route was consequently given up and the road built in a crooked ravine through the centre of the city, involving ascending and descending grades of more than one hundred and thirty feet to the mile. When the railroad was opened these grades were found to involve a cost which practically drove the through freights to a competing railroad.

There was at the time a young man in the engineers' office of the railroad who said that he could tunnel the sand-bank at a very small cost. He was summoned before the managers and questioned. "Yes," he said, modestly, "I can build the tunnel for so many dollars per running foot, but I cannot expect you to act upon my opinion when so many American and European engineers have declared the project impracticable." The managers knew that the first fifty feet of the tunnel involved all the difficulties. They offered him and he accepted a contract to build fifty feet of the structure.

His plan was simplicity itself. On a vertical face of the bank he marked the line of an arch larger than the tunnel. On this line he drove into the bank sharpened timbers, twelve feet long, three by four inches square. Then he removed six feet of the material and drove in another arch of twelve-foot timbers, removing six feet more of sand, repeating this process until he had space enough to commence the masonry. As fast as this was completed the space above it was filled, leaving the timbers in place.

Thus he progressed, keeping the masonry well up to the excavation, until he had pierced the bank with the cheapest tunnel ever constructed, which has carried the traffic of a great railroad for thirty years, and now stands as firm as on the day of its completion.

The engineer was asked if there was any suggestion of the structure adopted by him in the books on engineering. "No," he said; "it came to me in this way. I was driving by the place where the first attempts were made, of which a colony of bank-swallows had taken possession. It occurred to me that these little engineers had disproved the assertion that this material had no cohesion. They have their homes in it, where they raise two families every summer. Every home is a tunnel, self-sustaining without masonry. A larger tunnel can be constructed by simply extending the principle. This is the whole story. The bank-swallow is the inventor of this form of tunnel construction. I am simply a copyist—his imitator."

There are fine points in animal engineering. Like those of the ants and the timber-eating beetles of the tropics, or the *calamitas navium* or ship-worm of Linnæus, the excavations of the bank-swallow never trespass upon each other, however numerous or proximate they may be. They are separate, though sometimes the partitions are little thicker than paper. This swallow is a cosmopolitan. He lives upon all the continents, in all the hemispheres, from the equator to the ice-bound shores crossed by the 68th degree of latitude.

CHAPTER XIII.

Judge Lynch—An Incident of Early Pacific Railroad Travel.

The train for San Francisco was standing in the Omaha station awaiting the transfer of the passengers, luggage, and the mails from the East. I stood before the window of a telegraph office writing a dispatch, when a rather roughly clad person of unprepossessing appearance said to me:

"Neighbor, would you mind writin' one of them telegrafts for me?"

"Not at all," I said, "if you will dictate it."

"Oh, yes!" he exclaimed, "I'll pay the shot; I ain't no sponge!"

"I mean," I said, "that I will write it if you will tell me what you wish to have written."

"Sartain!" he replied, scratching his head as if reflecting. Then after a moment he said: "Write—'On the train, four o'clock, in Omaha. We've got him!'"

"But no one can understand such a dispatch. To whom is it to be sent? Whom have you got? What name shall be signed to it?"

"Send it to *the boys*. They will know who it comes from. Oh, they will understand it."

"The message cannot be sent unless you name some place."

"Yes, thet's so! Well, tell the ticker sharp to

send it to Evanston, Echo, Green River, any of them places along there, just as he likes."

Finding that I had an original to deal with, and in order to make him solely responsible, I said: "I will write whatever you say. Now begin!"

"All right!" he exclaimed. "Now I will give it to you straight. Write!" And I wrote as follows:

"To the Boys. We're on the train in Omaha. It's four o'clock. We've got him."

"Tell the ticker chap to send it to Evanston."

He handed the message to the operator, offering him two prices if he would "crack her right along," thanked me, entered the smoking-car, and the train rolled away.

I arranged my section for the long ride and went forward. In the small room in the smoker were four men. One of them, who sat in a corner, was a man of gigantic stature, with the most repulsive face I ever saw on a human being save one—that of Judge Terry, of California. It was deeply pitted by the small-pox and crossed by scars which distorted his mouth and gave a savage leer to his right eye. His mat of coarse black hair was partly covered by a broad sombrero, once white, but now the color of alkali-dust. His huge hands were locked in handcuffs—each of his splay feet was shackled to an iron bar which was fastened to the iron support of the seat by a heavy chain and padlock. He wore a coat and breeches of smoke-tanned leather, ornamented with long fringes of the same material. Altogether he was a person I would have avoided as carefully in the open day as in the darkness of midnight. His fellow-travellers evidently had the monster in charge. They were men of the same type as my friend of the telegram, and each openly carried, with the handle projecting from his hip-pocket, a Colt's revolver of the largest calibre. My new acquaintance shook me cordially by the hand, motioned me to a seat opposite him and near the door of the small room. After some indifferent talk, he said he supposed I would like to know *what the game was*, and proceeded to give me the following explanation:

"Me and my mates there watching the Greaser work in the coal-yards at Evanston, near Green River, where we buy our truck and are well known. Last winter a young Englishman came to Green River to hunt elk and b'ar. He didn't freeze to his money, neither did he throw it away. He was a tender-foot, but a white one. No man went cold nor hungry around his camp, and when the black fever come he never run a rod. He stayed by the boys, for he was a young doctor, and them that did as he told 'em got well. There was nothing he wouldn't do for the boys, and you may just bet your pile the boys swore by him. He took an old mate of mine for his pard; they made long trips, and sometimes were gone for a month. Each of them carried a Winchester besides his knife and revolver. He had two good saddle-horses and fixings, with burros to carry the camp traps and provisions.

"One day they started for a trip down to the big canyon. Two days later one of the horses came into Green River with a broken bridle. It was suspicioned that they was in trouble. The sheriff, a square man, who didn't scare for a tribe of Injuns, said he was bound he'd find out what was the matter. He started alone on the trail—which was keerless.

"After three or four days, when nothing had been

heard of the sheriff, that Greaser that you see and a half-breed Comanche rode into Green River, one of them on the sheriff's horse and one on that of the Englishman. They flourished the guns and other arms of the hunting party, hazed the whiskey-shops, drank and took what they pleased without pay, got whoopin' drunk, fired off their guns, and rode off toward Evanston. The Green River fellers ain't no sneaks; but it was done so sudden that they were s'prised-like, and the rascals got off without a shot.

"That Greaser's name is *Jesus* Ramon. Any Greaser is a bad egg, but he is the worst of the lot. He is as strong as a bull, as quick as a cat, as mean as a thief, and as murderous as an Arrapahoe. He has lived by murder and robbery and horse-stealing, and most of the ranchmen are afraid of him, though at the bottom he is a coward. The Injun was afraid of him, though he too was quick on the shot. Well, this Ramon and the Comanche came over to Evanston to try the Green River game over again. But some of our boys got the drop on them in the first pulque-shop they struck in our pueblo. They had to come down and go to the corral, where watchers were put over them for the night.

"Four of us then started out on the southern trail. We only had to ride about sixty miles. The buzzards were sailing in the air over an arroyo where a pack of coyotes were snarling and snapping over what was left of the sheriff, the Englishman, and his pard. Their heads and enough of their bodies were left to show that the hunters had been brained with hatchets, probably while they were asleep; and the sheriff had been shot in the back just as he had reached the bodies of the others. We didn't waste any words. We buried what the wolves had left under a big mound of heavy stones. Not a word was spoke, but each of us knew that the three others had decided to attend personally to the case of Jesus Ramon.

"When we got home we found that he had bolted. The night had been cold, a fire had been built, and in some way the Mexican, who was bound with cords, had contrived to burn them off. I have told you how strong and cute he was. He waited till midnight, when he made a dash, struck down his two guards with a stick of wood, and got away in the darkness. At the nearest ranch he stole a horse and made off.

"Then we had a caucus. The Comanche, who had slept off his drunk, found he was to leave for the happy hunting-grounds, and told us the story. The Greaser had murdered the first two in their sleep and shot the sheriff in the back while he was examining the bodies of the others. We talked the matter over, and made up our minds that our camp would be disgraced if the Greaser was not brought back and punished. We four volunteered to bring him."

"What became of the Indian?" I asked.

"We hung him to start with. He wasn't no account, anyway. He was best out of the way. We've got a rule in our camp that when a man is sent for he's bound to come back or be accounted for. The men who go for him have got no call to come back until they bring their man. Sometimes they bring him on a horse, sometimes in a box. I don't remember no case where the man didn't come.

"The chase this Greaser led us would have thrown

off a tenderfoot at the start. He stole a horse at a ranch east of the camp, where he left his own big tracks in the corral, and the horse appeared to have started over some soft ground on the gallop. We knew he left that plain trail to mislead us, and we lit out in the opposite direction for the Laramie Plains, and struck his true trail in twelve hours. I needn't tell you what a run he gave us. He struck the Northern Pacific, got on the train, and went to Seattle. We tried the telegraft, but he had been smart enough to cut the line. There he shipped on a brig bound for a port near Los Angeles with lumber. We guessed he would get on the Southern Pacific and try for the mountains of El Paso, for we knew he would not go to Mexico, where he was wanted. We put for 'Frisco by stage and train, then on the Southern Pacific to Fort Yuma, where we found he was still ahead of us. Some one must have let him know that we were after him and that the scent was hot, for he kept on east. We followed him to 'Orleans,' where we lost the trail. We wired his description and what he was wanted for north and northeast. He was so marked that you could describe him easy. One day while we was halted in 'Orleans' came a telegraft that our man had killed another in a drunken scrap in St. Louis and skipped north. We again took up the trail and followed it up the Mississippi, over into the Dominion to the Canada Pacific Railroad. He had struck it, started west, but left it at Saskatchewan. There we lost him again, and if it hadn't been for that ugly *cabeza* of his he might have got away for the time. Here we had to stay six weeks, until the boys could send us money, for we had spent the last nickel. One day, in the tepee of an Injun on the west shore of Lake Winnipeg, two of my pards there got the drop on him. He had to hold up his hands and give up, peaceful-like, for he was looking into the barrels of two Winchesters, and he knew the boys was quick on the pull.

"We cleaned him out of knives and guns, down to a toothpick, took him to a blacksmith, and had the bracelets just riveted on his arms and ankles. We brought him to Omaha without much trouble. But now, when we're only a day or two from home, he's got some scheme in his head which may break out any minute. Since they sent us the last money, nearly four weeks ago, the boys hadn't heard from us until I sent that telegraft. I got you to write it," he said with a roguish expression, "because I write a back hand, and I wasn't sure they would be able to read it. They will be on hand at Evanston."

"How could they make anything out of that dispatch?" I asked. "It was unsigned and not directed to anybody. It didn't say whom you had got, and what was that nonsense about the time of day?"

"You couldn't make it plainer," he replied. "All the boys are in the game, so it wasn't no account who got the dispatch. Nobody but us was on the trail, and we warn't hunting anybody but the Greaser. When it said it was four o'clock on the train, they could figger when we'd get to camp. It was as plain as a badger's trail in the alkali-dust. The boys will be on hand, sure!"

"I suppose you will turn your prisoner over to the sheriff," I said. "Where is the jail in which he will be kept until he is tried?"

"Sheriff! Jail!" he exclaimed, as if he did not

understand me. "Not much! We've got no sheriff! He murdered him. The corral is all the jail he will want. Maybe he will have a trial, maybe he won't. What's the good of a trial? Didn't he shoot the sheriff in the back and murder the Englishman and my old pard in their sleep? He didn't give them no trial, why should he have one? But likely the boys will have settled that."

"I hope you don't intend to have Judge Lynch try this man? That would be a crime in this country of law and order."

"I don't know that Judge Lynch," he said. "Our judge's name is Bascom. He's a very strong law-and-order man. Suppose you stop over one train and see. If there is a trial you shall be on the jury. Then you will see how regular our trials are. I wouldn't wonder if the boys held the train so that everybody may see what a fair show he'll get."

It was in the afternoon when we approached Evanston. I again went forward to the smoking-car. The train slowed and ran up to the station between two lines of stalwart men. The boys had understood the dispatch, for as soon as the train came to a stop six of them entered the car.

"Come, Jesus Ramon!" said their leader. The Greaser began to jabber something in Spanish, when he was seized and torn out of the car so quickly that he carried the seat to which he had been chained with him. Some one released him from the seat, a lasso was deftly cast over his head and tightened around his chest and arms. A single order was given, "To the corral!" and the procession moved. A guard had in the mean time taken control of the locomotive, and it was announced that the train would not leave until notice should be given that the exercises had closed.

The passengers followed the crowd to the corral, an inclosure where horses and cattle were kept, surrounded by a strong close and high fence. Near its centre stood a lofty pine tree, which threw out its first branch forty feet above the ground. The ends of two lassos were knotted together and the double length cast over the branch. The end which carried the noose was lowered to within a couple of yards of a wooden stool, the other end was carried outward and attached to two additional lassos. The prisoner was brought forward, forcibly seated upon the stool, and the noose was adjusted to his neck.

There were about two hundred men present in their working clothes; the passengers and men from the train counted another hundred. The silence was oppressive. At last one of the men stepped forward and addressed the Mexican substantially in these words, written down by me on my return to the train:

"Jesus Ramon, you have come to the last day of your life. You are no good. You have spent your life in drunkenness, fighting, horse-stealing, and murder. You have been a thief and a murderer for forty years. When a boy you shot Indians for fun. You always shot your victims in the back. You are a terror to women. Your last crimes have been the meanest. This Englishman had been kind to you. When you said you were poor he gave you a horse, a rifle, and money. While he was off on a hunt and you knew he had but little money with him, you stole upon him like a coward and killed him and his pard in their sleep. The sheriff had befriended you, and you shot him in the back for his reward. You insulted the people of Green River by riding through their town on the horse of one of your victims, and you dared to give us the same insult. We have considered your case and find that you don't want any trial. You were guilty of three fresh murders, and you ran. You have cost us some time and money. You are now standing very near to the end of your worthless life. Have you any words or message to send or leave before you die?"

The wretch muttered something in Spanish to the effect that he understood nothing. Many voices declared that he had often spoken English. His anger betrayed him. "One chance!" he yelled. "Give me one chance and I fight you all!"

"No, Ramon; your fights are ended. Do you want a priest?"

"*Caramba!* No!" he snarled, with the expression of a tiger. "I give you six, ten *mil pesos* for liberty! Ten thousand dollars!"

"You might as well promise to give the earth. You never had a peso of your own, and if you had ten million of them they would not help you now."

"I haf an *amigo*. He gif me *plata* and *oro*. I bring it here in tree day!"

"Jesus Ramon!" and there was no one present who was not impressed by the solemnity of the voice, "do you see that train?" He pointed to an in-coming train far out on the level plain, not less than six miles away. "If you have any request to make, any message to leave, any prayer to make to God, make it! For when that train whistles for the station you die!"

I felt some inclination to intervene for law and

order, but it was very slight. The scene was singularly impressive. The open country at the base of the foot-hills on one side, with the naked mountain two miles high overlooking it, and the rays of the setting sun projecting lengthening shadows toward the east. In the other direction the alkali plain, with the train crawling slowly over it, and in the corral the wretch gloomily awaiting his doom. It was an experience never to be forgotten.

Then the stern voice of the leader again broke the silence. "Men, form your lines!" A double line moved outward, the hand of each man grasping the free end of the lasso, for no one was to fail to take his share of the responsibility. "Men!" said the leader, "let it not be said that we did not give even this miserable Greaser one chance to live and become a better man. We know his past life. There is not within fifty miles a ranch that he has not robbed, a corral from which he has not stolen, a pulque-shop which he has not laid under contribution. We have never known him to earn a dollar or pay for anything. He never saw an Indian woman without insulting her, a man with money without trying to rob him. We know of twenty murders he has committed, every one, so far as we know, cowardly. But if there is in this crowd one man who ever knew Ramon to do any decent act which made any man or woman better, or who believes that if we let him go he would be any better in the future, let him speak, and the criminal shall have, at least, a delay! No one speaks! We have another rule—If one man in twenty of those present is in doubt or would advise a postponement of the execution, it must be postponed. You that would postpone it, hold up your right hands; and the passengers and train hands, on this question, have a right to vote."

But not a hand was raised. It seemed to be my duty to testify for law and order, but my right arm felt as if a hundred-pound weight were pulling it down. The train was very near now; the lines were dressed so that each man stood erect, his face turned away from the tree. We almost held our breaths. Now! There was a puff of white steam from the locomotive—with measured step the men moved outward—there was a horribly spasmodic struggle—and in a few minutes all was over.

"Friends," said the spokesman, addressing the passengers, "you have seen that we treated this Greaser justly and fairly. We who live here and have to protect our property and our lives ask one favor of you. We don't like this business, but it has to be done. Do not give us away to the newspapers. They will send a swarm of reporters here, who are worse than a band of Piute Indians. Some of them will make it out that Ramon, the murderer and horse-thief, was a Christian martyr. We ask you to keep your own counsel."

The whistle sounded, the conductor commanded all aboard, the bell rang, and our train moved westward. We had been delayed exactly one hour, which was made up before we reached the next station on the plains of Laramie.

CHAPTER XIV.

Judge Lynch, Continued—An Experience in a Western Mining-Camp.

I was on a visit to a mining-camp down the valley from Austin, Nevada. The camp was in a canyon wide enough for the road and a row of buildings on each side. The mines in the rocks on either hand were entered through drifts nearly on a level with the road.

I had breakfasted with the family of the superintendent, and, with several of the leading men of the camp, was smoking a cigar on a raised platform in front of the counting-room, when we heard from a whiskey-shop on the other side of the way, a short distance above, the crack of a revolver.

"The shooting begins early this morning at Pat's!" remarked the superintendent. "That is the worst gambling and fighting hole at the camp. We count on a shooting game there as often as once a week."

While he was speaking a man ran out of "Pat's" into a groggery on the opposite side, then came out and started up an arroyo or dry watercourse at right angles to the canyon.

"Stop thief!" What magic is there in those words to collect a crowd. Except the fugitive, there had been no human being visible—within a moment after this cry there were fifty. They were multiplied by

"Stop the murderer!" "Shoot the rascal!"—and a crowd of old men and young boys and Indians streamed up the arroyo after the flying man. A young active runner was in the advance, rapidly overtaking the fugitive. "Stop!" I heard him cry. "Halt and throw up your hands, or I will drop you as I would a coyote!" He was obeyed. The man halted, held up his hands, faced down the hill, and coolly asked of his captor, "Well, what do you want of me?"

"I want you to march down the hill to the road. Then I will tell you what to do farther." To the crowd he said: "This man is my meat. I am a sheriff, and no man shall touch my prisoner! Put up your guns! No man shall have him until I have finished with him."

The crowd rather sullenly acquiesced. They got the sheriff and his prisoner in their midst and forced them into the road in front of where we were sitting. There they halted, and I heard subdued expressions of "Let's take him to the corral!" "Who's got a rope?" "A lasso will answer!" Some one in the crowd shouted, "He has shot *Billy Osborne!*" and the murmurs were increased.

"What do they want to do with this man?" I asked of the superintendent.

"Hang him, I reckon," he replied. "If he has killed Osborne I am rather in favor of it myself."

This cool proposition to lynch the fellow shocked me. Meantime the sheriff was shouting and threatening, but I saw that he was in fear that the prisoner might be taken out of his hands. I rose impulsively and addressed the crowd. I urged them not to commit another murder, but to have the man tried. "He didn't give Billy no show!" said one. "He was worth a hundred like him."

"No matter about that," I said. "Anybody is entitled to a trial. Convict him, and then hang him as soon as you like."

It was evident that I was making but little impression. They seemed to listen to my earnestness with a kind of amused expression. The young sheriff's deputy, however, took the opportunity to work his man toward the edge of the crowd, near the mouth of a drift into the mine. Suddenly he shoved his prisoner inside, placed himself in front of the opening, revolver in hand, and said:

"I don't like to disappoint you, boys, but I am an officer, and I am bound to hold this man and commit him to jail. I know the inside of this mine. There is no place to get into or out of it but here. No man goes into it but to help me. The man inside don't come out until I have bound him so that he cannot get away. You had better give up the chase, boys, or turn in and help me tie him!"

There were murmurs of dissatisfaction, but the crowd gradually dispersed. I attended the inquest. The prisoner, it was proved, was an ill-tempered, reckless gambler and cheat, who had been driven out of a mining-town some thirty miles south and had only come into this camp the previous afternoon. At a *monte* game at "Pat's" he had been caught cheating and had a fight, but the quarrel was made up and the game went on until daybreak, when the party separated, the gambler and the man who detected him apparently friends. The gambler went into a whiskey-mill opposite, borrowed a revolver, and came back. As he entered "Pat's" he aimed at his opponent, fired, and his ball struck in the forehead of a miner who was asleep sitting on a bench, killing him instantly.

Some of the testimony was pathetic. Osborne, the murdered man, was a general favorite. "He was my pard," said one. "He had a wife and kids in the East and he was working to pay for his little farm. In another month or two his pile would be big enough, and he was going home. 'I can't drink with the boys,' he used to say, 'if I don't set up the p'ison, and every dollar I spend that way puts off the time when my babies will be climbing on my lap and hanging on to my neck.'" And honest tears rolled down the rough face of the narrator as he said with a trembling voice, "He was a white man, was my pard, and it's an infernal shame to have such a man wiped out by a d—d skulking, good-for-nothing long-fingered *monte* sharp."

The verdict was wilful murder. Before it was given a wagon with a pair of horses on the gallop dashed down the road. The wagon contained three men. Lying on his back in the straw, bound hand and foot, was the murderer, who was being taken to the jail at the county town.

The same afternoon, after a weary tramp through the mines, I was seated on the same platform, resting. I had met in these Western mines graduates of our universities, thoroughly intelligent men. I was not, therefore, much surprised when a miner with grizzled hair, clad in his working dress, came to me and said:

"I suppose, sir, that you are pleased by the success of your intervention for that murderer this morning?"

I answered that it was only natural that I should

be gratified if any effort of mine had prevented a breach of the law and tended to secure the man a fair trial, and that I looked upon murder by lynching as no better than murder with malice.

"You are mistaken," he said. "Your opinion would be more valuable if you had my experience. Here is a wretch who lives by cheating; probably he never earned an honest dollar. He lives upon the industry of others. He wanders from camp to camp, robbing or cheating every one who gives him the opportunity. Driven out of Belmont, he came here, and naturally gravitated to the nearest dog-hole in the camp. He had not been here twenty-four hours before he had killed an industrious, worthy man, who was working for his wife and children in the East. Had you not interfered, the boys would have laid him away and covered him where he would never again have done any harm to anybody. You stopped the boys in their good work. You have done nothing to be proud of, sir!"

"He will not escape punishment," I replied. "Upon the evidence he must be indicted and convicted, and he ought to be hung."

"Do you think so? How little you know about this sage-brush country! He is in no danger from the law, and he knows it. He will employ lawyers, hire gamblers to swear falsely, and probably be acquitted. If not, the worst that will happen will be that the jury will disagree and he will get out on straw bail. There is only one way to deal with such wretches. They are only good to stretch a lasso. I have had twenty-five years' experience, and I know."

"Would you be willing to relate any experience of yours which justifies hanging a man without a trial?"

AN EXPERIENCE IN A MINING-CAMP.

"I will tell you a little story; you may draw your own conclusions," he said. "I was a forty-niner in Grizzly Gulch, in Nevada County, California. We had all kinds of men from almost every country. Our camp was a mile away from the Gulch, where we were placer-mining. Some lived in tents, some in huts. Every day all the men left the camp and stayed all day in the diggings—not a man was left in a camp in which there was not a bolt nor a lock and very few doors. We had no stealing—no claim-jumping. If two men disagreed and they were anyway fairly matched, they fought with their fists and then shook hands and were friends. If they were not matched, some one volunteered or we made it even some other way. That was a camp worth living in. There was a great deal of travel there. We used to set our pans of gold out in the sun to dry. A man would take up a pan and examine the dust, but he always put it down just as he found it. Along at first there were some scraps. Some horses and burros were stolen. But the thieves were always sent for and we hung them every time. We have sent after men to Mexico, Alaska, and over the Sierra.

"After people got acquainted with us and things got settled, we had the peaceablest camp on the coast. I don't remember one case where the thief got away with another man's money or property. We made our judges and lawyers as we wanted them, and when the trial was over they went back to work in the diggings. It was a pleasure to live there. I tell you that in a new country what you call law and order may do for milksops; men want something stronger."

"How many men do you suppose you hung before the country got, as you call it, settled?"

"I don't remember. Maybe twenty."

"Do you not think that as population increases laws and judges are necessary, or at least useful?"

"They may be; but, like other evils, should be postponed as long as they can be. They are not yet necessary in this camp. When they are I shall migrate."

"Was the condition you have described in Nevada County permanent, or did it soon change?"

"It was temporary. When the diggings were washed out, hydraulic and quartz mining came in and the forty-niners scattered. I went there a few weeks ago on a visit. Well! there was a change! They have got churches and a big school-house and two newspapers! And how those newspapers do abuse each other! They have got a big stone court-house and judges, three or four kinds, and sheriffs, and all sorts of offices. You would think that one-half the people were living on the others. One day while I was there a stage came into the town, the horses on the run and the passengers very white under the gills. What was the matter? Only two miles outside the town two masked gentlemen had stopped that stage, ordered the passengers out (five of them were called *men*), made them hold up their hands, and one robber went through them while the other watched with a cocked gun. The whole party were cleaned out of their watches and money. They even searched two women and took their trinkets. One of the passengers, a merchant, made some effort to defend his bar of gold, and they shot him down and left him dying in the road! Have you heard that these murderers were punished? Oh, no! The newspapers published columns about the 'horrible outrage.' A public meeting was called, resolutions were passed, rewards offered, and the biggest kind of a fuss was made. But the murderers have been as safe as a thief in a mill. What would we have done in '50? I will tell you. We would not have had any meetings or resolutions. We would have picked out our two best men for that kind of work. They wouldn't have been troubled by any orders. But they would have taken that trail and run it down, with two dead highway robbers at the end of it, or they would have been following it to-day! You may not like that kind of practice for murderers; I do. It makes a more quiet camp."

I could not deny some of the premises of the grizzly miner. To test his prophecies, I made it in my way to visit the county town where the fellow who had just shot Osborne was to be tried. I arrived late in the evening and was shown to a room in the hotel, where, after a futile attempt to rid myself of a coating of alkali-dust, I took my supper and retired. I could not sleep; there was a murmur of voices and a clink of coin in the room below. After tossing on my bed for two hours, I dressed and went below to investigate. Adjoining the bar was an improvised gambling-room. At one end of it a clerical-looking gentleman was dealing faro; at the other was a roulette-wheel and a man profuse in his invitations to the boys to try their luck. The landlord could not give me another room unless I would occupy the same bed with a stranger, and he said the boys would want to keep up their game until daylight. I spent the rest of the night in reading a blood-and-thunder novel which I found in my room.

Among the visitors I found the next morning my old acquaintance, the advocate of lynch law. He said the game was set up and the fellow would be acquitted on the ground of *self-defence*. But the boys had come over from the camp; there might be some chance for them to take a hand.

The room was filled with a very miscellaneous crowd when the court was opened. Scarcely three of the regular panel of jurors answered, and the sheriff filled the panel with talesmen from the crowd. The whole bar appeared to be acting for the respondent, and the young prosecutor seemed to be completely outweighted. He proved the facts, however, and made full proof for a conviction.

A cloud of witnesses appeared for the respondent. His defence was contradictory and almost impossible. It was a case of accidental shooting; he intended to kill the other fellow, but it was proved that the dead man had had a difficulty with the respondent at Belmont, and two witnesses, who were most undoubtedly suborned, swore that he had threatened the respondent's life. The jury made short work of the case, and in ten minutes brought in a verdict of *not guilty*.

After the verdict I again met my lynch-law friend. He did not say "I told you so!" He was in a serious frame of mind; said he had told the gambler to get out of town as soon as he could and try to live a decent life; but he was cocky, would not take his advice, and now he might go to the devil in his own way. His road might be a short one, for Osborne had many friends, some of whom had wit-

AN EXPERIENCE IN A MINING-CAMP. 135

nessed the sham of a trial and might pull their guns upon the murderer on any reasonable provocation.

I was compelled for want of a conveyance to pass another night in the town, and at the same hotel, for there was no other. As I passed the door of the gambling-room I saw that the acquitted felon had taken the place of the clerical-looking party and was dealing faro. He had been hired by the proprietor as a drawing card. I was weary and fell asleep notwithstanding the sound of profanity and the jingle of coin which came up from below.

The sound of a single shot awakened me. I sprang from my bed, on which I had thrown myself without undressing, and went to the foot of the stairway. Through the door I saw a crowd around the prostrate form of a man near the dealer's chair, and I heard expressions of "He's a goner!" "He's passed in his checks," and the like. My friend of lynch-law sympathies approached me, pointed to the motionless body, and whispered the single word "*Habet!*" The prostrate man was the gambler, and he was dead.

A witness at the inquest next day gave substantially the following account of the "scrap," as he called it. The table was full, and two boys from the mining-camp were bucking the tiger. Every time there was a pile on any card the bank won. One of the mining boys asked if it was a skin game. The owner swore it was square. "He never played anything but a square game. He didn't believe it would be safe to put up a skin game on that crowd."

"Right you are," said the miner. "It wouldn't be safe. I'd as lief not play; but if I am in the game has got to be square, or maybe suthin'll happen. Your dealer there is quick on the shoot, I know, and I don't believe he's square. Oh, you needn't slide your hand down to your pocket that way. See?" and in a flash he had the pull on him.

"I was not going to draw on you," said the dealer as he took up the pack.

"All right," said the miner. "I was only saying don't you deal two cards, nor try, again. I don't know as you dealt two cards, but I know you tried," he continued as he lowered his revolver.

After that the game went on very quietly. The mining boys lost a good pile, then their luck turned and they played it man-fashion. There were only three cards in the box when one of the boys coppered the nine of clubs for ten twenty-dollar gold-pieces. I never saw anything done quicker. The next card was the bank's. He dealt it and turned it up. Before he could lay it on the pile the miner had plugged him. As he fell, *two* cards dropped from his fingers. The miner said, "That play was for Billy Osborne!"

The jury returned a verdict that the shooting was in self-defence. It seemed to satisfy everybody. As I was about entering the stage the next day, my lecturing friend, who was in a reflective mood, said, "Was it Cicero or Tacitus who wrote '*Ab alio spectes, alteri quod feceris*'? It is as sound doctrine in a Nevada poker-shop as in the Roman Senate. The gambler got what he had given to Osborne and no doubt to many others. It was the best disposition that could have been made of him, for himself and certainly for the community."

The advocate of what he would have called "natural justice" was a singular illustration of the tendency of our race to retrograde toward its original condition. This man was a university graduate, of good family, in comfortable circumstances. Moved by a pure spirit of adventure and the attractions of the gold discoveries, he had crossed the plains and become a gold-digger. His habits appeared to be fairly good, and now for years he had experienced the vicissitudes of a miner's life, and at that time was a common workman for day wages. There came later another change. Within a year I heard of him as a judge of the highest court in one of the most enterprising of our Territories whic his now a State. My chance acquaintance is its Chief Justice. He occasionally sends me a copy of one of his opinions, which shows that he is equal to his judicial position and that he fills it to the satisfaction of his fellow-citizens.

Very recently my attention was called to an article in a legal magazine on "The Increase of Crime." It was written by a Western lawyer of ability who had been cautious and industrious in the collection of his statistics. Some of them may surprise the reader as they did me. He states that murders are more numerous at the present time than they ever were before; that the record of murders in this country for the six years 1884 to 1889, inclusive, gives a total of almost fifteen thousand—the last year exceeding by several hundred either of the preceding years in the number of lives taken by violence. It is interesting to note that only about ten per cent of these murderers were legally executed, and that much the larger number of them who paid the penalty of their crimes met retributive justice at the hands of Judge Lynch. Of the persons charged with murder in these years only five hundred and fifty-eight were legally executed, while nine hundred and seventy-five were lynched.

When it is shown that in a period of six years murder was legally punished only in about one case in twenty-seven, it is impossible to avoid the conclusion that there is some defect in our legal system. I do not propose here to discuss the cause of this failure of justice; whether it is due to the maudlin sympathy for great criminals or to ineffective prosecution is unimportant. The fact remains that while in new and especially in mining communities justice at the hands of the people is swift and certain, it fails in the majority of cases in law-abiding communities.

CHAPTER XV.

ADIRONDACK DAYS — UNTRIED COMPANIONS IN THE WILDERNESS—THEIR PERILS AND EXPERIENCES.

I AM to write of the past—of days that will never return because the conditions that made them delightful can never be reproduced. I was inexperienced in the woods in 1846 when I made my first visit to the Adirondacks. I did not then know that in the forest the true inwardness of man was revealed and that one should never risk association there except with true sportsmen and very honest men. But I was an apt scholar—my first lesson was effective. I have made many later excursions there, but always with carefully selected associates.

You who visit the Adirondack region now, after vandal hands have obstructed the outlets, raised the waters and killed the trees, so that along the banks of every river and around the shores of every lake there is a row of whitened skeletons of what were once the verdant glories of arboreal life, know no more of the original beauty of that scenery of mountain, lake, tree, and river than he who looks upon the cold marble and broken arms knows of the warm glow of life and beauty which shone in the living model of the Venus of Milo.

In those days the shores of Long Lake and many others bore no marks of the hand of man. The trees and shrubs covered them to the very edge of the clear water, so that as we floated along the surface it was impossible to distinguish where substance ended and shadow began. From the summit of Tahawus, scores of these lakes shone like jewels of purest emerald. From my first camp on the high western bank just above the outlet of Long Lake, looking eastward, there were eight well-defined masses of color, from the silvery sheen of the lake through shades of green to the deep blue of the mountain summit. It was a vision of color.

In that camp I lived five weeks and saw no human face save those which belonged to my own party. Then a saddle of venison, a brace of young wood or black ducks, or a half-dozen of ruffed grouse were to be had in an hour's shooting, and near the mouth of Cold River, just below the outlet, a couple of brook trout of four pounds weight were to be had in a cloudy day in half the time. Now there is a route of summer travel through the lake and down the river, and the game of those days has only a legendary existence. Nowhere in landscape scenery have more deplorable changes been wrought by thirty years of vandalism.

I knew no better then than to permit the addition to my party of an artist with a masculine Scotch wife who ruled him with a heavy hand, and a minister with his two boys of fourteen and sixteen years of whom I knew nothing. A chill comes over me as I think what a narrow escape I had from committing a felony upon those boys. They were unmannerly cubs who would not obey their father, and passed their time when awake in howling like untamed hyenas. They were nuisances—"from night till morn, from morn till dewy eve." I got rid of them at Newcomb, near the head of the lake, by alarming their father with the well-founded apprehension that the Indian guide would certainly contrive to rid the camp of them by accident or design.

My guides were Mitchell Sabattis and Alonzo Wetherby. Sabattis was a St. Francis Indian, a skilful hunter, and became afterward one of the finest characters I ever knew. At that time he got howling drunk at every opportunity. It is a pleasure to remember that he always attributed his reformation to his connection with me, and that for the last thirty years of his life he was a kind husband, an excellent father to worthy children, and a most reputable citizen. He died only a few years ago, a class-leader in the Methodist Church, universally respected. "'Lon Wetherby" was an equally good hunter, a giant in strength and a Yankee by birth. To hear the rich, liquid sound with which he rolled out his only oath, "By Ga-u-u-ll!" was worth a journey to the outlet of Long Lake.

I did not exist five weeks in a camp with the minister or the artist and his Scotch wife, and I may as well here describe our separation.

I wanted to have a personal experience in floating for deer. The night after we reached camp, Sabattis made his "jack" to carry the light and fitted up his boat for the trial. The minister wanted to go with us. He "would not make a sound," he said. He would lie on his back in the bottom of the boat and silently watch the operation. Mitchell cautioned him that the slightest sound would destroy all our chances, and after repeated promises of absolute silence we took him along.

We placed him on his back in the bottom of the boat, where he was not to speak even in a whisper. The jack or light was in the bow and I was just in its rear. Mitchell sat in the stern and paddled. It was a weird and noiseless, a ghostly performance, as our boat crept along the shore without breaking the silence of the wilderness. The falling of a dead tree on the flank of a distant mountain woke the echoes along the shore like the report of a cannon. The note of the screech-owl in the branches overhead—the grating of a rush along the keel of the boat, alike started the blood to the extremities. Far out upon the lake was heard that desolating sound at midnight, the chattering of the loon. Overhead the stars shone through the pure atmosphere, so pure that Venus and Jupiter cast shadows.

We had been out but a few minutes when we heard the threshing of some large animal among the lily-pads, just opposite the camp. Silently the boat was turned in that direction, and I knew that we were approaching my first deer. My gun was in the hollow of my arm—I was peering into the darkness to catch the first reflection of the light upon the eyes of the noble game, which was to be my signal for a shot, when like a bellow from a bull of Bashan there broke from the bottom of the boat and rolled out upon the silence of the night the words:

"Great and wonderful are Thy works, O——"

The rush of a noble buck as he bounded across the patch of light into the forest and the exclamation of the furious Indian, "Why don't you shoot his fool head off?" met a strong impulse in my mind to do what Mitchell suggested. But I restrained myself to the inquiry, "How many kinds of a fool do you suppose you are, anyway?"

He was profuse in apologies. He had not heard any sound—he was so overcome by the glories of the starlit sky that he quite forgot himself—the words escaped from his mouth involuntarily. If we would now go on he was certain he could keep quiet.

"There is no deer within two miles of Long Lake now," said Mitchell. "That sound would scare the devil. We go home—no use for waste time tonight."

And home we went with no venison. On the way I told the parson that we would have to part company; that Mitchell, like all his race, was of an unforgiving nature; that he was angry and might be dangerous; that I would loan him "'Lon Wetherby" to row him through Catlin Lake to Newcomb, where he might perhaps make up a party and go off in another direction. He was much frightened and very grateful. I gave 'Lon his directions, and when I arose the next morning the minister had departed and I saw him no more.

I separated from the artist and his dreadful wife on this wise. Wishing to take some exercise, on the following afternoon I took one of the boats and determined to go down the Raquette River to the mouth of Moose Creek and ascend the creek, by way of exploration. Sabattis said I should probably see nothing, but it was always well on such an exploration to take with me a loaded gun. The artist wanted to go along and make sketches, and I took him on condition that he was not under any circumstances to utter a sound or interfere with me.

I rowed down to the mouth of the creek, shipped the oars, and seated myself in the stern to paddle. My double gun loaded with buckshot cartridges lay on the bottom of the boat within easy reach. The artist sat on the rowing seat in the middle of the boat. The water in the creek was very low. I paddled slowly up, both of us looking forward.

I had turned a sharp point about half-way up the creek and was opening another, projecting from the opposite side, when on its extreme end, and at least fifty yards from the cover, I saw extended on the sand a full-grown black bear. Forcing the paddle into the sand, I had stopped the boat and was about to reach for my gun, when in a flash bang! bang! went both its barrels, and one cartridge hurtled by within a few inches of my head.

If I was ever furious it was then! The bear was not thirty yards away—he had to cross the gravel forty yards before he reached the bushes. I should certainly have planted both cartridges in his vitals. He was in no haste. After the painter had sent the last charge whizzing past my head in the opposite direction, the bear stood upon his feet, shook himself, and deliberately trotted across the open space into the bushes. He even stopped and took a good look at us before he disappeared.

It would be a weak expression to say that I was discouraged. It was useless to get angry—I could not do the subject of that artist justice. I was irritated, provoked, exasperated. After my experience of last evening with the minister, why did I take any chances with the painter? He of course was arguing, explaining, apologizing, expounding. He had been excited—he had seized the gun and discharged it before he knew what he was doing. He was very sorry—he humbly begged my pardon. It should not occur again!

"Young man!" I said solemnly, "you are right. It will not occur again! If I thought there was any danger that it would I do not know what I might do. Do not tempt Providence farther. We are going back to the camp, and you must prepare to leave at once. If that bear should meet you I would not give a farthing for your life. I feel like making an end of you myself, but I will give you one more chance if you will go to-morrow." He went, and his wife with him. Mitchell left them in a lumber camp and returned the next day. Thank fortune, I never saw them again!

We were much in need of venison. We were expecting company and there was no fresh meat in the camp. One rainy, foggy night, Sabattis and myself went to the same Moose Creek to try for a deer. The water had suddenly risen and the adjacent marshes were overflowed. We had ascended the creek as far as it would carry our boat and had found nothing. On our return about half-way to the river, we heard a deer. He was standing in the shallow water on the marsh and outside the curtain of willows which grew upon the bank. Mitchell stopped the boat opposite where he stood, so near that we could hear him chewing the leaves. It was impossible to get a sight of any part of him. If we made any disturbance he was certain to disappear instantly in the darkness.

Five minutes we stood endeavoring to pierce that curtain with our eyes. Then I estimated as well as I could his height above the water, aimed where I thought his chest ought to be, and gave him one barrel. Away he went across the broad marsh, dashing through the water until he reached the solid ground, where his measured gallop grew fainter, until to my ear it was no longer to be heard on account of the distance.

"Well! we have lost him," I said, in a tone of disappointment. "I am sorry, for he was a noble buck. I got one glance at his antlers."

"How can we lose what we never had?" was Mitchell's pertinent inquiry. "But we will have him yet before daylight. He is hard hit and will not run very far."

"Why do you say that?" I asked. "He bounded away in a very lively manner as if he was uninjured."

"For two reasons," he answered. "He did not snort or whistle as an unwounded deer always does when suddenly startled. Then one of his fore-legs appeared, by the sound, to be crippled."

He pushed the boat rapidly across the marsh to the hard ground, and with the light in his hand soon found where the deer had passed through the thick weeds and grasses. "It is all right," he said. "Here is where he went out, and it's as bloody as a butcher's shop."

I came near where he stood. "Show me the blood," I said.

"Why there! and there! and there! all over! Don't you see it?" he exclaimed.

"I see nothing but wet leaves and bushes," I replied. "Now stop and show me what you call blood."

He plucked a leaf with incurved edges, on the wet surface of which there was a discoloration which he said was blood. "It is as plain as can be," he said;

"you would not expect a wounded buck in a hurry to stop and paint a United States flag for our benefit. I am going for him," he continued. "You stay in the boat until you hear a shot, which may mean that I have found him or that I have given him up. Then you fire a pistol, which will give me my bearings and save time."

With the lantern in one hand and my gun in the other, he disappeared in the foggy night. How long I lay stiffening in the boat or stamped along the shore in an effort to keep my blood in circulation, I do not know. But after what seemed hours of weary waiting, away up on the side of the mountain I heard the faint report of a gun. I fired the revolver in answer and waited again until I heard something threshing down the hill.

"Is that you, Mitchell?" I shouted.

"Yes," he answered. "I have got him. He is a splendid buck; not too old and in prime condition. He will provision the camp for a week."

He now appeared, dragging the deer after him.

"How did you find him?" I asked.

"I followed his track over the wet leaves," he answered. "Where he stopped the spot was marked by a pool of blood. These were nearer together as we went up the hill. Finally I overtook him. He was standing with his head down and I saw he had been hard hit. I held the jack in one hand and shot him with the gun held in the other."

Mark, now, what this Indian had done. His ear had detected an injury to one of the animal's forelegs. In the dark and rainy night, by the light of the "jack," he had found his path out of the marsh, had followed it over fallen trees, through the thick brushwood, a mile or more up the steep hillside, until he had overtaken the wounded deer, and holding the light in one hand and the gun in the other had given him the fatal shot. Such a story seems incredible. Had I not seen the results I think I would not myself believe it.

We reached our camp just as the sun was climbing over the tops of the eastern mountains. The yellow fog retreated before it—the green of the forest, the blue of the lake, and the gold of the sun united in a landscape of glorious beauty, which drove the chill from our bodies and the weariness from our limbs.

When the deer was dressed it was found that my cartridge had struck his shoulder-blade in an oblique direction. Every shot save one had glanced outward —that one had passed through his vitals and would have ultimately proved fatal.

No account of the Adirondacks would be complete without a fish-story. Mine runs after this wise. I had made preparations and had great expectations. I had fly-rods and bass-rods and reels, books of flies, bait in imitation of all the monstrous and 'impossible animals which the trout are reputed to fancy. But the display did not excite the enthusiasm of either of my guides—on the contrary, they appeared to view it with contempt. The bass-rod, which had no elasticity and which was strong enough to lift fifty pounds at the tip, and a gaudy scarlet ibis fly they thought might answer, but a tamarack pole and "worms for bait" were preferable. The remainder of the lay-out was trash except a six-ounce thirty-dollar fly-rod which "might answer as well as a hand-line to catch minnows!" Such was the lesson administered to my fisherman's pride when I handed over to them my costly outfit and asked them to select what was adapted to Adirondack fishing.

For several days they seemed disinclined to fish. One day the sun was too bright, the next was too dark; one day was too hot, the next too chilly, until I began to despair of finding a day suited for fishing in the Adirondack wilderness.

But a day came when Mitchell said with Peter, "I go a-fishing," and like one of the other disciples I said, "I go with you." It was a yellow afternoon, when the clouds seemed to intercept the rays but not the color of the sun. He selected the rod which had landed striped bass and bluefish on Pasque Island, a heavy line and the large hook with the scarlet fly, also a tamarack pole and a box of earth-worms for emergencies. "He didn't care to fish himself—I would get enough if the trout was anyways lively."

About three o'clock in the afternoon, as the sun was sinking in the west below the crest of Buck Mountain, he rowed me down to the mouth of Cold River, ascended the stream to a place where it widened into a broad pool with bold shores, tied his boat to an alder, and proceeded to fill and light his pipe. I had meantime taken the rod from its case, jointed it and arranged the line, and reel, with three or four buckshot on the line, without which a cast of twenty feet with that rod could not have been made. Mitchell attached the fly, and pointing to a dcaying stump on the bank said: "Under that stump ought to be a good place for a trout."

I made the cast. The moment the fly struck the water the surface in the vicinity was seething like a whirlpool. There was a vicious jerk on the line, and the reel hummed like a buzz-saw as thirty yards of the line ran out. As I checked the fish he rushed past the boat within reach of Mitchell's landing-net. He made one sweep and a five-pound brook trout lay panting in the boat, my first fish in the Adirondacks.

What followed was mere repetition. Every time the fly struck the water a half-dozen trout leaped to seize it. My tackle was strong, and Mitchell looked upon playing the fish as a waste of time. In a short half-hour five brook trout lay in our boat side by side, weighing a little more than twenty pounds. It was enough to supply our table. I would not commit the crime of killing such splendid game for which we had no use. That short half-hour was an era in my life. The uniformity of size and weight, I suppose, arose from the fact that all the trout were full-grown.

In those delightful five weeks I formed an attachment for these guides which lasted as long as they lived. From Wetherby, and later from others, I learned that Sabattis was a generous fellow whom every one liked, but he would get drunk upon every opportunity, and then he was a madman. His wife was a worthy white woman. They had five children. The sons were as skilled in woodcraft as their father and inherited the excellent qualities of their mother. One of them grew up with the figure of Apollo, and when I last saw him I thought that physically he was the most perfect man I had ever seen.

CHAPTER XVI.

THE STORY OF MITCHELL SABATTIS.

I SPENT my last night at Mitchell's home in Newcomb, where a conveyance from Elizabethtown was to meet me. Mitchell and his wife appeared depressed by some impending calamity. I made them tell me their trouble. There was a mortgage upon their home and little farm. It was due, the property was to be sold about four weeks later, and they saw no way of avoiding this, to them, ruinous result. If his home was sold, Mitchell's habits would be worse than ever.

Mitchell's wife assured me that he was proud of the fact that he had never broken his word; she said he was a kind husband, and if she could induce him to promise not to drink, she would even be reconciled to the loss of her home.

The next morning when the horses were at the door and I was about to leave, I called Mitchell and his wife into their little "square room," seated myself between them, and asked:

"Mitchell, what would you give to one who would buy your mortgage and give you time in which to pay it?"

"I would give my life," he exclaimed, "the day after I had paid the debt. I would give it now if I could leave this little place to my Bessie and her children."

"It will not cost you so much as that," I said. "I am going to Elizabethtown. I shall buy or pay your mortgage. Your home will not be sold. On the morning of the second day of August of next year, I want you and ''Lon' with your boats to meet me at Bartlett's, between the Upper and Lower Saranac Lakes. If you there tell me that you have not drunk a glass of strong liquor since I saw you last, your mortgage shall not trouble you so long as you will keep your promise not to drink. If you break your promise I do not know what I shall do, but I shall lose all my confidence in Mitchell Sabattis. Your wife and children will not be driven from their home until you get drunk again."

He promised instantly, solemnly. He rose from his chair. I thought he looked every inch the chief which by birth he claimed to be as he said: "You may think you cannot trust me, but you can! Sabattis when he was sober never told a lie. He will never lie to his friend."

For a few minutes there was in that humble room a very touching scene. The Indian silent, solemn, but for the speaking arm thrown lovingly around the neck of his wife, apparently emotionless—the wife trying to say through her tears—"I told you you could trust Mitchell! He will keep his promise—he will never get drunk again. I know him so well! I am certain that he will not drink, and we shall be so happy. Oh! I am the happiest woman alive!"

"Well! well!" I said, "let us hope for the best; we must wait and see. Mitchell, remember the 2d of next August—Bartlett's—and in the mean time no whiskey!" And so we parted.

I bought, took an assignment of the mortgage and

carried it to my home. Other duties occupied me, and Sabattis had long been out of my mind. One evening late in the following February, just at nightfall, I was watching the falling snow from my library window in Burlington, when a singular conveyance stopped almost in front of my door. It was a long, unpainted sled, the runners hewn from natural crooks, with stakes some five feet high inclosing an oblong box of rough boards, to which were harnessed two unmatched horses. The driver travelled by the side of the horses, carrying a long gad of unpainted wood having no lash. He wore a cap and coat of bear-skin, which concealed his features.

Taking him to be some stranger who had lost his way, I went to his assistance. As I made some observation, a voice deep down inside the bear-skin said: "Why! it's Mr. Chittenden. I was looking for you and your house."

"Mitchell Sabattis!" I exclaimed. "In the name of all that is astonishing, what are you doing here?"

For a moment he made no answer. As I came nearer his arms worked strangely, as if he would like to throw them around me. His voice was tremulous as he said: "I am so glad. I was afeared I should not find you—this town is so big and there are so many houses and men and roads. I was looking for a place where they would feed and take in the horses."

"But what has brought you here, a hundred and fifty miles from your home in Newcomb?"

"Yes! yes! We have been very lucky this fall and winter. My wife said I had better come. I have had good fortune. Sold all my furs and my saddles of venison for money. Just now the season is over and I had nothing to do. So we talked it over, my wife Bessie and me. You remember Bessie. Somehow I can't get the right words. I would like to tell you to-morrow. Do you know of some place where they would take in the horses?"

"But what is this sled loaded with?"

"Nothing—much. Only a little game for you. I will tell you all about it to-morrow."

I went with him to a stable where his horses were taken in and his load put under lock and key. I took him to my house, although he protested that he had his own supplies and could just as well stay in the stable. His personal neatness, his civility, and the oddity of his expressions delighted every member of my household. A warm supper and a like welcome soon opened his heart, and I gathered from him the following details:

Good fortune had attended him from the time when he was relieved from anxiety about the mortgage. He had employment as a guide until the season for trapping and shooting for market began. He had never killed so many deer nor got so good prices in money for venison. He had paid all his little debts and saved one hundred dollars, which his wife said he ought to bring to me. They thought I would like a little game. So he had built a sled, borrowed two horses, made up a little load, and he had travelled that long and hard road from the head of Long Lake to Crown Point and thence to Burlington, not less than one hundred and fifty miles.

A refusal of his gift was not to be thought of. The next morning I took my butcher to his little load of game. There were the saddles or hind quarters of twenty-five fat deer in their skins, two car-

THE STORY OF MITCHELL SABATTIS. 155

casses of black bear dressed and returned to their skins, the skin of a magnificent catamount, with the skull and claws attached, which he had heard me say I would like to have, a half-dozen skins of the beautiful fur of the pine marten or the American sable, more than one hundred pounds of brook trout, ten dozen of ruffed grouse all dressed and braided into bunches of a half-dozen, and some smaller game, with some specimen skins of the mink and fox. There was more game than my family could have consumed in a year.

I selected a liberal supply of the game and took the skins intended for myself and family. For the balance my butcher paid him liberally, and this money with his savings would have more than paid his mortgage. But I would not so soon lose my hold upon him. He had told me that if he could build an addition to his house his wife could keep four boarders while he was guiding in the summer. I induced him to save money enough for this addition, and to purchase the furniture then and there. He paid the interest and costs and a part of the principal of his mortgage, and went home loaded with presents for Bessie and the children—a very happy man.

On the 2d of August, this time with two *gentlemen* and their wives, all safe companions in roughing it, as we approached the landing at Bartlett's, Mitchell and Alonzo were waiting for us. There was no need to ask Mitchell if he had kept his promise. His eye was as clear and keen as that of a goshawk. The muscles visible in their action under his transparent dark skin, his voice, ringing with cheerfulness, all told of a healthy body and a sound mind. His wife, he said, had her house filled with boarders, his oldest son had been employed as a guide for the entire season, and prosperity shone upon the Sabattis household.

Where should we go? I consulted him about the location of our camp. He said that " 'Lon" and himself knew what kind of a place we wanted. We didn't want visitors or black flies—we wanted a beautiful location, with mountains, lakes, brooks, and springs, with abundance of game. Himself and " 'Lon" knew such a place—they had left home, built a camp for us there, and if we would make a long day of it they would row us there at once.

This chapter is already too long. I have no time to tell of the beauty of our camp, the abundance of the game, the sympathy of all our party, the fawn we caught, tamed and enjoyed, and left in its native woods, and the fidelity of our guides which made those weeks a green oasis in all our lives. Nor can I describe the subsequent lives of those guides. Wetherby, one of the strongest men I ever knew and of unexceptionable habits, died of a fever in the following year.

My destiny led me far away from the Adirondacks. The last I had heard from Mitchell was when he sent me a draft on New York for considerably more than the balance due upon his mortgage. The locality had become too easy of access—visitors were too numerous. It had so few attractions that I did not visit it for many years. But in 1885 the old feeling came over me, and with such of my family as had not gone out from me into homes of their own, I went to a new and fashionable hotel some thirty miles from Long Lake. From an old resident who knew it thoroughly I had the subsequent history of Mitchell Sabattis. He had never broken his promise to me. He united with the Methodist Church and became one of its leaders, and in a few years was the leading citizen in the Long Lake settlement. In worldly matters he prospered. His wife kept a favorite resort for summer visitors. Their children were educated, the daughters married well—two of the sons served their country with courage and gallantry through the war, returned home unwounded with honorable discharges, and now guided in summer and built the celebrated Adirondack boats in the winter. Mitchell, now a hale and healthy veteran of eighty-four years, still lived at Long Lake in the very house of which I was once the mortgagee.

The next morning I heard a light step on the uncarpeted hall and a knock at my door. I opened it and Sabattis entered. He was as glad to see me as I was to grasp his true and honest hand. But I was profoundly surprised. Had the world with him stood still? He did not look a day older than when I last saw him, more than twenty-five years ago. The same keen, clear eye, transparent skin with the play of the muscles under it, the same elastic step, ringing voice and kindly heart. His eye was not dim nor his natural force abated. We spent a memorable day together—at nightfall we parted forever. Not long afterward he died full of years, full of honors, that noblest work of God, an honest man.

Reader! this is not a "short story" and it is not a novel. It is a true story, and of course has its moral, which is that a kind word or an inexpensive favor may sometimes save a fellow-creature and change him into a useful man. To him who bestows either, I could not wish a more delightful memory than that of my relations with Mitchell Sabattis.

CHAPTER XVII.

THE ADIRONDACK REGION—A WARNING TO THE DESTROYER—A PLEA FOR THE PERISHING.

THE Adirondack region is an uneven plateau, having an average elevation about eighteen hundred feet above the sea-level, in area nearly equal to the three States of New Hampshire, Vermont, and Massachusetts. Its crystalline rocks preceded, its sandstones witnessed the dawn of animal life upon the Western Continent. Its mountains are loftier than any east of the Father of the Waters. Its rivers are numbered by fifties, its lakes by hundreds. Away back in primordial times the forces of nature raised its surface into the dominion of monthly frosts, unfitted it for agriculture and pasturage, and restricted it to the growth of evergreens and deciduous trees, dwarfed upon its peaks but reaching an average height in its valleys and on its sheltered plains. God made it, not for the habitation of man but for that of the natural occupants of the forest, lake, and river. In his economy it was most useful to man when its original condition was maintained. If the great cities of a numerous people were to be built on the waterways of a mighty commerce, all the greater necessity that here should be a great *preserve* in fact as well as in name. It was the natural home of all the land and fresh-water animals of the forty-fifth parallel. The call of the great moose was common in the swamps and marshes—the red deer would have exhausted the grasses and tender shrubs had not their numbers been repressed by the panther and the gray wolf. The black bear fattened upon the beechnuts. The industrious beaver built his dam upon streams fished by the mink and the otter. The fisher, the pine marten, the fox and other fur-bearing animals ranged the more elevated lands; ducks and geese of many species and other migratory birds made their semi-annual visits, and some remained to raise their young. The partridge drummed upon the fallen tree-trunks, flights of passenger-pigeons obscured the sun. The lunge fattened on the fresh-water shrimps, the savage pike and omnivorous pickerel pursued the beautiful brook trout up the silvery streams. The smaller animals and birds abounded. As a rural poet sang in those early days—

"The pigeon, goose and duck, they fill our beds,
The beaver, coon and fox, they crown our heads,
The harmless moose and deer are food and clothes to wear,
Nature could do no more for any land."

In the economy of nature this region had another and an inestimable value. It was the water reservoir for a part of the St. Lawrence and Champlain valleys, but especially for the Hudson River and the great cities which were to rise upon its banks. And it was as complete as the works of the Great Architect always are. The vapors borne against the flanks of its numerous mountains were condensed and precipitated in the daily rains of summer and the snows of winter. The surface was shaded and covered by forest trees everywhere throwing out rootlets, which, penetrated and swollen by frosts, widened the crevices in the rocks below. The decaying leaves of successive seasons spread a soft, thick cushion over the soil. The snows fell to great depths; protected from wind and sun, they remained for a long time, and when they slowly dissolved followed every fibre and rootlet down to the lowest depths of every rock fissure or cavity. The soil became a gigantic sponge, saturated with moisture, expelling its surplus waters, not in destructive inundations, but by slow percolation, into the streams, maintaining them at full banks, and finally creating the noble river which might be navigated for sixty leagues by the navies of the world.

Forty years ago was there no New York legislator who had heard of the Roman marshes, those deadly fever beds where once was grown the breadstuffs of Rome when she was mistress of the world? Was there no student of history who knew that where the Roman farmer bred his son to wield the Roman short-sword he would now perish by a night's exposure? Had no traveller seen the naked rocks after the vineyards of Southern France had been swept into the sea? Was there none who knew of the foresight of Holland when she made herself poor to build her dykes and control the waters of the North Sea? No! no! The pen hesitates to tell the story of their negligence or to record with what silly contempt they spurned, threw away, and refused to preserve the blessings of Almighty God.

The vandalism originated in the Champlain Valley. Far up the Ausable, on a little stream that came down from the mountains, there was a small furnace which used charcoal as a fuel. The country blacksmiths began to use its iron. It was almost as good, they said, as Swedish iron. They made it into horse-shoes; then into nails for the horse-shoes. Then it was made into nails for ordinary building purposes, and there proved to be not an insignificant profit in its manufacture.

The reputation of the charcoal iron spread, new furnaces were built, and the small village of Clintonville became the great nail factory of the north country. The smoke of coal-pits covered the land. The trees were swept away as if some gigantic scythe-bearer had mowed it over. In a few years there was no charcoal to be had at paying prices. Then the furnaces ceased operations, and where the forest had stood were huckleberry plains, where the berries were picked by Canadian-French *habitans*. One may travel now for miles in that region and not find a tree large enough to make a respectable fish-pole.

Next came like an army of destruction the first invasion of the lumbermen. Pine lumber increased in value. These lands could be cheaply purchased at the sales for taxes, stripped of their accessible pines and then abandoned to the State for another tax sale. Only the best trees were felled; their tops and branches were left where they fell. The logs were run down to the mills in the high water of spring.

The pines near the rivers were quickly exhausted. Then some enemy of the region put a scheme into the minds of the lumbermen, which resulted in incalculable injury. It was to dam the outlets—raise the water in the lakes so as to reach the pines upon their shores. The first dam was upon the Raquette River to raise the water in Big Tupper Lake. Dams at the outlet of Long Lake, Blue Mountain, Uta-

DESTRUCTION OF THE FOREST. 163

wanna, Raquette, and many others speedily followed. There was a noble grove of pines on the high west bank of Long Lake just above the outlet. The year after the dam was built their trunks had disappeared. Their tops and branches were left on the ground to die and to decay.

It has been stated elsewhere that the arboreal growth of the lakes quite down to the ordinary water-level constituted one of the principal beauties of the virgin landscape. The lake shores were generally precipitous and the natural rise and fall of the waters produced almost no effect upon the vegetation. The silvery waters everywhere appeared to be framed in a setting of vivid green. But there were places along the rivers as well as the lakes where there were marshes covered with trees, the surface of which was overflowed by a slight rise of the waters. When the dams were constructed the water was permanently raised so as to overflow these marshes and a narrow piece of even the most precipitous shores. This permanent overflow destroyed the life of every tree and shrub where it existed. The setting of emerald green was replaced by dead trees which covered the marshes or stood around the lake, white and deathly, like armies of grinning skeletons, presiding over new sources of contamination and decay.

Great injury to the whole region swiftly followed these obstructions. That caused by fires was the most extensive. The tree-tops and branches left by the lumbermen became dry and combustible. Careless visitors left the fires burning in their temporary camps, which spread over townships, destroying the whole arboreal growth. The fires followed the dry roots deep into the ground and rock crevices, and nothing but continuous rains that saturated the soil could extinguish them. Other fires were caused by lightning. The entire profits of the lumber would not have compensated for the injury caused by these conflagrations.

This elevated region with its pure atmosphere had long been celebrated for its healthful influences. It would have been a great sanitarium but for gross violations of hygienic laws. Not long after the general obstruction of the streams, the scattered residents and their families began to fall sick with typhoid and intermittent fevers. Many died. The local physicians declared that they could not understand the origin of these diseases. The cause was not far to seek. The broad acres covered with slack-water, the masses of organic matter left to ferment and putrefy beneath it, generating poisonous gases to corrupt the atmosphere, were such efficient causes of disease that it would have been a wonder if these fevers had not prevailed. They still prevail. They are epidemic every summer. During the last summer, when the great stream of pleasure travel was traversing the region, it passed many hamlets of fever-stricken patients. And these fearful scourges will continue to sweep off the inhabitants and to be a menace to every visitor until the laws of nature are respected and the causes of these diseases are removed.

The prospect of now preserving the Adirondack country to the uses of its creation, for which it is so admirably fitted, is very remote. The increased demand for spruce and hemlock lumber, for maple, ash, and other woods for the interiors of buildings, and the enormous consumption of wood pulp, are constantly creating new demands upon the forest, making new appeals to human cupidity. But Nature never pardons, never fails to punish a violation of her laws. A time will come when some great calamity will fall upon the people and awaken their legislators to the necessity of protecting what shall then remain of this great preserve.

I may have said enough; but my pen clings to the topic, and I do most deeply regret my inability to present the lessons of human experience in terms which, if they do not convince the casual reader, will at least arrest his attention. If I should say that unless the existing campaign of destruction is arrested the valley of the lower Hudson will become a desert and the site of New York City a bed of malaria upon which human life cannot exist, I should be called a thoughtless, unreliable, sensational writer; yet that is just what I ought to say. With present means of transportation, in eight days I could take the reader to a country once of rare fertility, where agriculture flourished, where stood the famous mart of Populona, where the coast was filled with commercial towns and their surroundings were occupied by a prosperous population, but where the sites of old cities have now not one inhabitant, where the coast is well-nigh depopulated, and where malarious fevers have extended their ravages far into the interior. Yet this region was once the garden of Europe, and but for the same criminal negligence of which our generation is guilty might have been as productive to-day as it was in the reign of Augustus Cæsar. On the shores of Tuscany and the Adriatic —on the banks of the rivers from the Appenines to the Mediterranean Sea, and through the valleys of

Northern Switzerland, everywhere in older Europe, we may read a similar chapter in the book of nature. At first fertile table-lands, hillsides covered with vineyards, everywhere a healthy, prosperous people. Then the mountains first slowly encroached upon, then denuded of their covering. Floods and inundations before unknown came next in succession, sweeping the alluvium, the soil, and finally the gravel down toward the sea, spreading it into swamps and marshes, after which swiftly followed the famine and the pestilence.

Nature is never in a hurry. In her movements she takes all the time that is necessary. One day is as a thousand years and a thousand years as one day. In the Tuscan Maremma where the swallows retreat before the malaria, in Northern Italy where the peasant travels five miles for a back-load of wood, or in the American forests just producing the first crop of fevers, there is one result which follows the destruction of the forest which no observing man can fail to notice. Is there any man of three-score years who does not know that the rivers of New England have diminished one-half in volume since his boyhood? The Connecticut by carrying around the falls was navigable to Hanover, N. H. The Winooski will not float a skiff now over the spot where the *Black Snake*, a fifty-ton batteau, had its fight with the officers of the customs in 1808. During the Revolution a British admiral proposed to anchor his ships of war in the Bronx, now a mere rivulet which forms one of the boundaries of New York City. The poet Bryant once gave a marked instance of this diminution of rivers. He wrote: " It is a common observation that our summers are become drier

DESTRUCTION OF THE FOREST. 167

and our streams smaller. Take the Cuyahoga as an illustration. Fifty years ago large barges loaded with goods went up and down that river, and one of the vessels engaged in the battle of Lake Erie was built at Old Portage, six miles north of Albion, and floated down to the lake. Now, in an ordinary stage of the water, a canoe or a skiff can hardly pass down the stream."

The Hudson, the Mohawk, and the Raquette rivers are already greatly diminished in volume, and the Adirondack region is thickly sown with the germs of febrile disease. Taking things in their present condition, let us turn the mirror of experience so that it will reflect the future, and consider the image. Existing encroachments all around the periphery of the region are continued, clearing the surface, which for a time will yield indifferent pasturage until the thin soil is washed from the rocks, when it will become worthless. New companies of lumbermen will range over the whole, felling every evergreen above ten inches in diameter. They may give some attention to the public demand in felling the trees and disposing of the tops and branches. But they will find it necessary to raise the dams and flood a still greater extent of the lowlands in order to reach forests more remote. Forest fires will multiply as the supply of dry fuel increases. Wood-pulp mills will abound on every considerable stream. Summer hotels will increase with the railroads which will follow the valleys, and as these hotels are built with little regard to sanitary laws, wherever one exists it will be a source of contamination to the water and of malaria on the land. Increasing crowds of tourists, of artists, of persons who think they are sportsmen, will infest the country during the summer, and the poor victims of pulmonary disease will come to it in the winter to sicken and die. How long it will be before the atmosphere of the Adirondack swamps will be fever-stricken like the Pontine marshes is not very material to know, for that time will surely come.

Suppose in the more distant perspective should be seen a great city comprising the New York of the twentieth century and its surroundings. By that time its demands will become peremptory. Unrestricted immigration; huge blocks of cheaply constructed and badly ventilated tenement-houses will have become hives of the lowest orders of humanity. "Unclean, unclean," will be the language of the streets and of the municipal administration. The daily harvest of death will be greater than in the famine, fever stricken regions of India and China. But louder and more imperious will be the demand for a pure water-supply. Then the great crime of 1892, perpetrated without even attracting public notice, will have fructified. The impounding of the precipitation of the Croton watershed in a huge artificial lake, where the waters have no currents and every organic substance sinks to the bottom to and die decay, where every drop of the water will be contaminated, will result in a harvest of death which must continue until the lower Hudson Valley has been abandoned and human negligence has sought other channels of exploitation.

I know only too well that these words of warning will fall upon incredulous and unwilling ears; but they are spoken in all seriousness by one who appreciates their necessity and who ventures a hope that they may yet attract some small measure of public attention.

CHAPTER XVIII.

NOVEMBER DAYS ON LAKE CHAMPLAIN—THE
STORY OF HIRAM BRAMBLE.

ON a recent summer vacation an intelligent bookseller sent to me two very delightful books, written by Mr. Rowland Robinson, of Ferrisburgh, Vt., under the titles of "Uncle 'Lisha's Shop" and "Sam Lovell's Camp." The dialects reproduced by Mr. Robinson—Vermont Yankee by several characters and Canuck-French by Ant-Twine Bissette—are excellent, much the most successful I have seen.

In reading these books, it occurred to me that if Mr. Robinson could imagine incidents enough to make a book out of the experiences of a fishing-camp at the mouth of Little Otter Creek in the out-season month of June, a true relation of some of my own experiences in a neighboring region, on East Creek and Bullwagga Bay, might be equally entertaining to the reading public. For there are few square acres of that creek and bay, including the narrow lake from Chimney Point to Ticonderoga, that I have not been rowed over by one of nature's original characters, more or less in company with one of the best shots and most entertaining companions who ever pulled a trigger or winged a "pintail." Oh, what sport we had on those long-past November days! Here are some of their memories.

Hiram Bramble, or, as his neighbors called him,

"Old Bramble," was an original character. He lived in a log house on the high south bank of East Creek, in Orwell, a half mile above its mouth. He was skilled in wood and water craft—many were the flocks of different species of water-fowl within shot of which he has rowed or paddled an eminent American diplomat and myself in those days of long ago. Bramble loved us well enough to have gone through fire to serve us if we had made such a demand upon him. He gave us great sport and we rewarded him, as he thought, royally. He was himself a successful hunter, but he was disinclined to waste his ammunition upon birds on the wing, a style of shooting in which he became skilful under our instruction.

Bramble had a wife when we knew him—a second Mrs. Bramble. He was poor and sometimes dissipated, but whenever he spoke of his first wife his voice was tremulous, and he had a habit of brushing something out of his eyes. Those who knew them said he always treated her with the affection of a loving husband and the courtesy of a gentleman by nature until she was laid away under the green turf of the Orwell churchyard, under a little mound planted with roses, and even then very carefully tended. When she died Bramble was captured by a masculine widow with a voice like a bark-mill and the temper of a demon. She did not like either my companion or myself. She always spoke of us as "them rascal Burlington lawyers" who paid Bramble to be idle, lazy, and drunk. I think she was impartial, for she abused every one who gave Bramble any employment.

How well I remember the day when I accepted

the invitation of a friend, afterward an honor to his country, to go with him on a shooting excursion to East Creek! He, I am sure, will recall our first visit to this locality—our trip on the steamer through the beautiful lake; our sumptuous dinner; our landing at Orwell, where Bramble was waiting for us, and those two days which followed, of which I hesitate to give, at this late day, the details.

Bramble had made the plans for our afternoon and evening. The teal, both kinds, were just coming from the north. The best stations were on the bank at the mouth of the creek—the best time, the last hour of daylight. One of us, he said, would go with him to his boat, which lay up the creek, where it was nearest to the highway, and he would row us down toward its mouth. We might pick up a stray duck or two on the way. P. would take the short cut through the woods to the mouth of the creek, and in the wood which he would go through scare up one or two ruffed grouse and possibly an English snipe or a gray squirrel.

I went with Bramble. As we came to the bank near the highway bridge, under which he had moored his boat, a mallard drake rose sluggishly from the opposite shore, fifty yards away. He was turned over with a No. 4 Eley's wire cartridge from the right barrel of my muzzle-loader; breech-loaders being then unknown. "He's a goner," said Bramble as he launched his boat. I took my seat in its stern; he rowed across and picked up the duck and said:

"We don't want to hurry. We've two good hours before the ducks begin to come in—two hours at least. Did Squire P. ever tell you about Mr. B., that he brought down here last year? Well, he was a terror, he was. Every time anything with wings got up, bang! bang! went both of his barrels. He never hit anything because there was never anything in front of his gun. When we picked up Squire P. I told him that I didn't think I ought to row his friend any more unless he would be responsible for his accidents, the same as the town was for an accident on a road which was out of repair. Some day his friend would shoot the top of my head off, and somebody ought to be good for the damages!"

We rowed leisurely down the creek. I then knew nothing of Bramble's home or household. As we came around a sharp bend in the creek, I saw on the top of the next high point of land a small house. A person in female dress came out of the door and made an angry stride toward the bank. Her arms were swinging like those of a windmill. She was shouting something at the top of her voice, in which I could only distinguish the words "Old Bramble" and "rascally Burlington lawyers." She was apparently addressing her observations to us.

"Who is that woman?" I demanded of Bramble, somewhat peremptorily.

"Judge," he answered very seriously, "I know all the creeturs that ever lived in these parts—some ov 'em I would not care to meet in the night, but I can truly say that I ain't afeared of none of 'em. Now that there woman" (pointing to where she seemed to have reached the climax of her gymnastics)—"that woman is the only thing on this 'vairsal 'arth that I'm afraid of; that's Mrs. Bramble, my wife!"

"I am surprised, Bramble," I said. "I thought you were a brave man—not afraid of anything."

THE STORY OF HIRAM BRAMBLE. 173

"No more did I. I have choked a bull-dog to death that went mad. I stopped a runaway team, with a man's wife and children in the buggy, and the owner wanted to pay me four shillin' for it, when he knew it put my arm out of joint. I was never scairt by a ghost nor a jack-o'-lantern; but when that woman goes for me in one of her tantrums, the pluck runs out of me like cider out of a cheese of ground apples in a cider-mill. She is a devil—a full-grown, heaped-up, four-pecks-to-the-bushel she-devil, with a tongue like a fish-spear. I don't guess—I know."

"Never mind," I said, "I will manage her!" Bramble looked at me with admiration. I remembered how O'Connell silenced the fishwoman. I could not recall his mathematical terms, but I could try her with linguistics. As the boat neared the house I laid down my gun, took off my coat, and flourishing my arms began with a quotation from Virgil, in the closing words of which I put great emphasis, and, so far as I knew them, the motions of a prize-fighter. The vixen hesitated. This species of warfare was new. Then she resumed: "You drunken, good-for-nothing Old Bramble! Wait till I get you home once more!" "Carramba! Mille tonnerre! Habeas corpus. Ille ego qui quondam!" I shouted. "Sine qua non, sink or swim, I am for Bramble!" I was too much for her. "He's one of them college chaps," I heard her say. "They meet with the devil every week; but when I get you alone, Old Bramble——" Here I took up my gun, and, pointing to the house, fired some other nonsense at her in a sepulchral voice. She retreated into the habitation. Bramble was in ecstasies. He "must learn them words," he said.

He "didn't suppose, until now, that anything but death would silence Mrs. Bramble."

I may as well here record the fact that my companion, "Squire P.," did actually frighten her upon a subsequent occasion. Bramble was rowing him down the creek, when, as usual, she shouted at him her characteristic observations. He directed Hiram to row him up to her carefully, and when within shot he pretended to aim at her and fired. She really thought he was shooting at her and rushed into her cabin. "By Jove! Bramble, I have missed her with both barrels," he said, in a tone of vexation. "I don't understand it. I never had a fairer shot."

"You was too sartin! I saw you was too sartin," said Bramble. "There is more shots lost by being too sartin than any other way." However, the vixen was tamed. She never attacked him again.

CHAPTER XIX.

Duck-Shooting in East Creek.

THERE was a full hour of daylight when we reached the outlet of East Creek. My companion was already there. He had picked up a pair of English snipe and a ruffed grouse on his way from the Orwell Landing. Bramble stationed us on the high bank on the south side where the creek entered the lake, I being nearest to the mouth, where there was no obstruction to the view. "You must hold a long way ahead," he cautioned me. "These birds travel very fast." The teal in small bunches began to arrive. I missed the three and P. his two first shots. "You must either wait until they get past or hold furder ahead of them," counselled the old guide. "You have no idee how fast a teal can travel when he is in a hurry. They have begun to come in so airly that there is liable to be a good many of them before dark. They fly quicker'n pigeons and swallows. You must hold furder ahead or you won't drop a bird." "How far ahead?" I asked. "About four rod, I reckon," was his reply.

A single speck was now coming from the north. I watched its approach and understood the rapidity of its flight. This time I waited until it was well past me. The bird fell at the shot. "I will get into the boat now and pick up the game," said Hiram. "You have got the hang of the creeturs now and we will have teal for supper."

The policy of waiting until the bird had passed was not new to either of us. We had shot passenger-pigeons and swallows. I did not suppose that anything with feathers came any nearer to lightning in rapidity of flight; but these teal surpassed them. However, we had now learned their ways. There were few more misses, and as long as we could see we kept Hiram and "Bang," our Irish setter, busily occupied in retrieving our birds.

We counselled with Hiram whether we should stay over night at Orwell or Chimney Point. The distance was about the same, and we intended to be on the ground at daylight for the morning shooting. Bramble decided upon Orwell Landing. "The last time I was at the other place," he said, "there was a steak so tough that it could not be carved unless both hands and one foot were on the table."

We went to the landing, where a good supper was soon ready, which we insisted Bramble should share with us. He did so, by way of obeying orders rather than from choice. He was a light eater and was drawing away from the table before we had half finished our meal. "Don't leave yet, Bramble," said P. "You have eaten almost nothing. Have another piece of this turkey. He belongs to this generation." Hiram submissively obeyed, remarking *sotto voce:* "I really s'posed I had had enough, but I'm an ignorant man, and what I know is mostly about birds and wild animals good for game; but you have been eddycated at college and know 'most everything. If you say I have not finished my supper, of course it must be so. Now I shall eat till you tell me to stop," he said with apparent seriousness.

Like all good things the supper came to an end.

DUCK SHOOTING IN EAST CREEK. 177

We had left our boots and rubber coats at the hotel where we landed. "I want them long boots of yours," said Bramble. "They need a dressing of neatsfoot oil. I want you to be ready for what's coming. There is more kinds of ducks in the marshes than I have seen in ten years, and not a gun has been fired over them. It will rain to-morrow, I cal'late—not hard, but a kind of drizzle that will keep the birds in the marshes. If you put up a flock of black duck in a clear day they won't stop this side of Long Island. But to-morrow they will lay close. I don't suppose anything less alarmin' than the voice of my wife would start 'em out. I want you to have a day to-morrow that you will remember as long as you live. We ought to be at the mouth of the creek by daylight to-morrow morning."

We surrendered our guns and boots to Hiram, who well knew how to put them in order. By ten o'clock we were enjoying that dreamless sleep which only hunters know, out of which Bramble aroused us with some difficulty at a very early hour next morning. We fortified ourselves with a cup of hot coffee and a light breakfast, and set out, Bramble carrying, as I thought, abundant rations for three days.

As we approached the creek the quack of many ducks came to us through the foggy atmosphere. Hiram declared that they were caucusing whether to go south to-day and "most of the speeches were agin' it." He advised us to take our stands of the previous evening. He said that until the sun came out the ducks would stick close to the creek and we would be able to select our birds. "We don't want no sawbills," he said, "nor coots nor old squaws. Most any other kind will do. Canvas-backs and red-

12

heads come here, but not plenty. They are good, but not a bit toothsomer than a young, well-grown black duck or the little butter-balls. I am going outside into the marshes in my boat. After daylight you will hear my gun, and soon after you will see something fly up the creek, and it won't be stake-drivers neither. Bang will have to do your retrievin'."

We were on our stands before the sun made any effort to pierce the fog which covered lake and creek, and which was so dense that we heard the quacking of the birds long before they were visible. Soon we heard the roar of Bramble's gun far out upon the marsh. It was our signal to watch. A number of dark spots were coming toward us through the mist. They got three of our barrels, and with a joyous yelp Bang dashed down the bank into the water and brought out first one and then another black or dusky duck. We had scarcely loaded our guns before the same flock returned, flying nearly over our heads. Two birds fell on the bank almost at our feet. Bang had brought out a third, making five birds from our opening fire.

With such a beginning so early in the day, we expected by nightfall to have achieved the success of our lives. But sportsmen, like politicians, are sometimes deceived by flattering prospects. The sun was above the fogs struggling to pierce them. First a small white spot appeared in the east. It grew larger and the first sunbeam shone upon the water. In a few minutes, as if a great curtain had been withdrawn, the silvery lake, its green shores and greener islands, the distant Adirondacks with Tahawus towering above them, lay before us like a picture. Then from every little bay and sheltered place the ducks took wing. They circled in the air as if to find their bearings, and then straight as an arrow's flight took their course southward and disappeared from our view. Two little buffel-heads or butter-balls, scarcely larger than quails, started up the creek. They were the last which, on these stands, fell to our guns.

Bramble now came to us with his boat. "What were we to do now?" we asked. "Anything you like," he said, "for you will see no more ducks here until nightfall." We might go over to Ti' Creek, he said, where there had been no shooting. We could also go through a piece of woods which he pointed out, where there were two or three broods of well-grown partridges, and he would row the boat up the lake and meet us at the landing.

We followed his advice. We struck through a piece of first-growth beech and maple, where the leaves had fallen, and as the sun dried the dampness the autumnal fragrance was delicious. We had little time to breathe it, however, for as soon as we entered the wood Bang made a dead point, and, ordered on, he put up a covey of partridges. With that whirring sound that always stirs the blood of a true sportsman, they radiated like the spokes of a wheel from its hub. I got the line of one, but was not quick enough for a second. My companion was more deliberate. After the fall of his first bird, he turned and caught the second by a sixty-yard shot in the opposite direction. Within a half-hour the rest of the brood, six birds in all, were in our bags. As we came out of the woods to the lake shore, Bang at once informed us that we were near other game-birds. He was an intelligent and thoughtful animal. His language was not vocal, but was as well understood as if he had been able to speak. He began to quarter a belt of rushes, so tall that we could follow him only by the waving of his bushy tail. As he crossed an opening he came to a point before a tussock of grass. "What is it, Bang?" I asked. He looked back, saw that my gun was ready, made a step or two forward, when with the note, "seep—seep," so seldom heard, two English snipe were flushed and one of them fell. Then followed what I have only seen upon one other occasion. Instead of going off at a tangent the remaining bird rose in a circular flight, uttering his "seep—seep." He was answered by others, which rising described similar circles until there were a dozen in the air. We got in our four barrels upon those that were within range, when the whole flock started together in a southerly direction. We well knew that snipe-shooting for the day in that locality was ended.

We reached the hotel in time for the twelve-o'clock dinner, after which we laid out our work for the afternoon. P. with Bramble was to go to another creek just below the old fort at Ticonderoga, where no guns had been heard, and whence if any ducks were started they would probably fly down the lake to East Creek. I, with a French neighbor of Bramble's, was to take my chances under a point which projected into the lake from the Vermont shore about half-way between the two creeks.

We left the landing, going in opposite directions. P. had passed out of view around a bend of the lake, when my Frenchman, who was rowing with his face to the south, exclaimed: "Voila! Canards! canards!" Turning, I saw a small flock of broadbills coming from that direction, and two of them fell before I heard the report of P.'s gun. The four remaining birds came on, flying well apart. Standing in the boat, I dropped the only one that came within reach. The Frenchman exclaimed: "Load him you gun so quick you nevaire can. Maybe he come back dis way." And come that way they did, two birds flying so high that I scarcely supposed they could be reached. But one fell with a broken wing, and Bang caught it in the water after a lively pursuit. The other was killed by P., making the entire number of that little flock.

There were no birds in Ti' Creek, though P. managed to pick up a couple on his way back to the landing. I remained at my post until nightfall and was beaten by one bird. For supper we had some of our young birds roasted. We retired early, for we were very weary and had planned for an early start, so as to reach Bullwagga Bay in the morning as soon as it was light enough to see a bird on the wing.

CHAPTER XX.

A Cold Morning on Bullwagga Bay.

WE loved the sport in those days of youth and vigor, or we would not have endured the hardships of the next day. We were called at three o'clock in the morning. It was so cold that the falling rain threatened to turn into snow. Bramble and P. looked after themselves. I was seated in the stern of the little Frenchman's boat. His teeth were chattering and he observed that "le matin vas leetle beet froid, vat you say cold, but the sun mak' more hot bam-by." Sharp work at the oars restored his circulation, and vigorous use of the paddle did the same for mine. The bay lies between the peninsula of Crown Point and the New York shore. We landed well south of the extreme point. For the last half-mile the loud quacking of the ducks across the peninsula indicated that they were holding a debate in unlimited numbers. Suddenly Frenchy stopped. "I tink I be fool pretty bad," he said. "Dat all one famlee, les canards noir." "You mean black ducks?" I asked. "Dat ees eet, dat ees eet," he exclaimed. "Black duck—canards noir. He fly all one way, all one time. Bam-by quand le soleil, le sun come—zweet, he all gone quick, you don't see no more dis day."

I gathered from his jargon that at daylight the flock would all leave. Bramble was of the same opinion. We decided to land and draw our boats over to the bay. Then we could at least get in all our barrels when they rose. We crossed the land and were fortunate enough, in the darkness, to find a shelter of rough boards covered with branches which some one had constructed for a blind to shoot from. There we shivered, Bang the coldest of the party, and waited for the dawn. The noisy quacking of the ducks indicated that they were not more than forty or fifty yards away. It was loud enough to render our steps inaudible and indicated their presence in great numbers. Their proximity stirred our blood so that we did not quite perish with the cold.

The antics of Frenchy were amusing. "He's got more as ten tousan' black ducks on de bay," he whispered; "mais, he's de meanes' duck for stay you never see it. You shoot one tam—he's gone for Wite Hall, you don't nevaire see him some more. He's got one sacré ole duck on de watch-out dis minute—more as feefteen year old. He know so much as man, dat ole duck—he see, he hear, he smell. Af de wind blow nudder way he smell you an' pff! he go quick. You shoot queek's yer see one duck. Put you gun on dis leetle hole—da's de way; you get one shot—no more, aujourd'hui."

Did you ever see a flock of ducks asleep on the water? It is a very funny sight, especially when the wind blows their bodies in contact and wakes them to an angry quacking. As the light slowly increased we first made out a piece of open water infront of the blind, surrounded by rushes; then dark patches upon the water came into view which seemed to be moving. These were the ducks asleep, notwithstanding the quacking all around them. We arranged to fire the first barrel from the inside of the blind, then to step outside and fire as they rose. It was now light enough and we gave them the first two barrels. When we stepped outside it was a land rustling, if not shadowy with wings. All over the bay there was a sound like the rushing of a storm through the branches of a forest. I never heard the like before, I have never heard it since. As arranged, we stepped outside and fired our second barrels into the thickest of the risen flock.

Bang had obediently waited until he got the word. He now dashed into the water to retrieve the dead and wounded birds. I thought the Frenchman had gone crazy. He was leaping about and almost screaming: "Load you gun! load you gun! Don't you see! Les canards he's start for Canada. He's mak' meestake. He come back. Ah, mon Dieu! Ah, load you gun two, tree, six times! you get more ducks, plenty more!"

We had shot from the southward of the entire flock, which had consequently first moved northward. What Frenchy meant was that they would return and go south. Then a breech-loader would have been invaluable. Return they did, but not before we had charged our barrels. We let the single birds pass, and when the thickest of the flock was almost over us we again fired the four barrels. "He is rain some snow, much more black duck," shouted the Frenchman. "He's got no more black duck to-day," he said as the last of the flock went past. Bramble agreed with him. The last duck had risen from the bay and departed. Our duck-shooting for the day was over.

A COLD MORNING ON BULLWAGGA BAY. 185

We had left directions at Orwell that our game and traps should be put upon the steamboat going north that afternoon. When Bang had brought in all the dead and wounded we pulled over our boats and were rowed across the bay to Port Henry. There we dismissed Bramble and Frenchy liberally compensated and happy. On the arrival of the steamboat our game was exposed upon the forward deck, to the wonder of the surprised passengers. We reached our homes after an absence of two days and a few hours.

How many birds were there collected in the two days? I have not mentioned the number for several reasons. Even two-score years ago, when game-birds of every species were thrice or four times as numerous as they are now, they were the most successful days of all my shooting. My companion has since risen to eminence and I would not like to have him annoyed by inquisitive correspondents or personal inquirers, although I know that if called as a witness he is too true a sportsman to desert his friend. Finally, the shooting in every bay and around every marsh on that beautiful lake is now preserved at great expense, and the sportsman who haunts these preserves from morn till dewy eve, fortunate if at nightfall he can feel the weight of the birds in his game-bag, would find it difficult to believe that it required two porters to carry our game ashore from the steamer. Whether the story is attractive to them or to any member of the present generation, it warms my heart to know that there is one man living who will read with a thrill of delight this brief sketch of *two November days.*

CHAPTER XXI.

Quacks and Quackery.

From ducks to quackery is an easy transition. "Quack" is said to be an onomatopoetic word, but I am unable to discover the slightest resemblance between a boasting medical pretender and the language of the duck-pond. The duck is an honest fowl, conservative in his ideas, using the language as well as preserving the habits of his ancestors. There is no justice nor propriety in associating him with a mountebank because of the sound of his mother tongue.

It is amazing that quackery should not only survive, but flourish in New England, where there is a newspaper in every family and an educated physician in every hamlet. I am not now referring to that form of it which finds expression in patent or proprietary medicines, for in most of those which attain any popularity there is some merit. I have in mind the more disreputable class which deals in charms, commands, and superstitions, the natural bone-setters, the seventh sons of seventh sons who claim to inherit the gift of healing; who suppose that those are most capable of repairing the delicate machinery of human life who are the most ignorant of its structure and functions. It is incredible that such pretentious ignorance should be able to secure a foot-hold in an intelligent community. That it does, goes far to prove the good old Presbyterian doctrine of the total depravity of the human heart. An occurrence with which I was once invited to have something to do professionally will illustrate the impudence of the quack and the credulity of his victim.

A farmer of average intelligence, in good circumstances, was thrown from his wagon and suffered a compound fracture of his thigh-bone. An experienced country surgeon was called, who restored the parts to their places, dressed the limb in proper splints, and, with a suitable weight and pulley, arranged to keep it extended until there was a firm union of the fragments of bone. He gave to the patient and his family very positive and emphatic instructions. The reparation would take a long time and involve some pain. Unless the farmer wished to leave his bed a cripple for life, with one leg some inches shorter than the other, he must endure the pain without taking off the weights or handling the limb in any way; that if the extension was once relaxed the cure would be difficult, perhaps impossible. As the surgeon lived several miles away, he should not visit him oftener than once a week, nor would more frequent visits be necessary if his instructions were obeyed.

On his second visit the surgeon saw that his directions had not been followed. After denials and prevarications, the family confessed that the weights had been removed and the position of the body changed several times because the pain was greater than the farmer could endure. They had therefore relieved the pressure, removed the bandages, and bathed the limb with hot water and "Pond's Extract," which was popularly known as the "universal painkiller." The doctor was indignant. He ridiculed the pretended inability of the patient, a strong man, to bear a pain which children could endure without complaint, repeated his directions with greater emphasis, and declared that unless his advice was followed his farther attendance was useless, and that if upon his next visit he found that it had been disregarded he would abandon the case and leave the patient to become a permanent cripple.

Just at that time, drawn by a pair of the celebrated Morgan horses driven by a colored servant in livery, a very remarkable person, according to his own estimate, appeared and took a suite of rooms at the hotel in the county town. He wore a long cloak of dark velvet, with a crimson collar and trimmings, buckskin trousers, a vest of figured satin covering a ruffled shirt, made fast in the bosom by an enormous yellow diamond pin. Thus equipped and ornamented, he appeared before the modest dwelling of the farmer ready to guarantee his cure. His rule was "No cure, no pay," but this case had been so mismanaged by the country surgeon that he would make it an exception. If the wounded farmer would execute and give to him his promissory note for twenty-five hundred dollars as an advance payment in the nature of a retaining fee, he would not only promise but would guarantee his cure.

Of course the farmer accepted the conditions and signed the promissory note. There is a hypnotic control which these quacks can exercise which for the time is stronger than the judgment of their victims. He did not even remove the dressings of the wounded limb. He made various motions over it, recited formulas in unknown tongues, declared that the cure would shortly be complete, pocketed his promissory note, and went in search of new victims.

The poor farmer had a distressing experience. The directions of the surgeon were no longer obeyed; the splints and dressings of the limb were removed; ulceration began, promoted by bathing the leg in hot water; there was no union of the fractured bones; new joints were formed at the fractures, and when he finally hobbled from his bed he was a permanent cripple, with a useless limb, condemned to the use of crutches for the remainder of his life. The quack visited him a few times, assured him that his directions as a natural bone-setter had never failed, and that in the end his cure would be perfect.

The promissory note was made payable at the —— Bank. On the day it matured it was presented, payment was demanded, and the note was protested for non-payment. Suit was commenced upon it, and, as the unjust statutes of the State then permitted, all the horses, cattle, and personal property of the farmer were attached and about to be removed by the sheriff, when his neighbors volunteered and gave an undertaking to pay any judgment which the quack should recover in the action.

When the issues in the action came on to be tried the farmer was represented by one of the most skilful advocates at the bar. The quack would not pay counsel and intrusted his case to the attorney who had commenced the action. Instead of proving the execution of the note and resting his case, as he might have done, the attorney called the quack to the stand and proved by him the demand of payment and the farmer's refusal to comply with the demand.

His personal appearance on the witness-stand suggested a combination of a dancing-master and a mountebank. His velvet coat with scarlet ornamentation, his broad expanse of shirt the ruffles whereof were transfixed by the diamond pin, his velvet knee-breeches, silk stockings, pink gloves, and patent-leather shoes; his hair bleached to a sickly yellow; his long, waxed mustaches curled at the ends, suggested a comparison which would have been to the disadvantage of a monkey; his compressed mouth, pointed nose and chin gave him the expression of a rat, which did not at all comport with the air of lofty dignity which he attempted but failed to assume. Without waiting for a question, he launched out upon a story of his tremendous professional successes, the kings and great persons who had been his patients, and of his excuses for treating the farmer for so small a compensation, his regular .fee for a broken leg being five thousand dollars! When he had damaged his case as much as he could by these improbable statements he was turned over to the farmer's counsel for cross-examination.

"I will trouble you, doctor," said the counsel, "to name some patient who ever paid, or promised to pay, you a fee of five thousand dollars."

"Must I answer such an insulting question?" said the doctor, appealing to the judge.

"I think you must," said the judge, "unless you plead your privilege."

"Then I plead my privilege," he said promptly.

"What do you mean by your privilege?" demanded the counsel.

"I mean my privilege to answer such questions as I choose."

"Are you quite certain that you know what is the meaning of the privilege of a physician?"

"I know everything that any doctor knows."

"That being the case, I will not pursue this inquiry. Now will you kindly tell us what kind of a doctor you are?"

"I am a universal doctor, sir. I cure all kinds of cases."

"That is not precisely what I mean. To what school of medicine do you belong? I should have asked."

"I don't belong to no school. I don't believe in no school. I'm a born doctor. I am a seventh son."

"Now, doctor, pray gratify my curiosity and tell me whether you are a botanic, a hydropathic, an allopathic, or a homœopathic; what kind of a doctor you call yourself."

"I don't know nothing about no *paths*, sir. I'm a universal doctor, only I don't use no *markery*."

"I see; you would be understood by your professional brethren as an eclectic doctor, what the Japanese would call a very high-class doctor?"

"Yes, that's it. I didn't understand you. I'm an eklektik doctor!"

There was a hesitation, a slight pause after his pronunciation of the first syllable, which gave to the word the sound of "ecolectic," and proved to be the rock on which the quack was to suffer shipwreck. In his very gentle and kindly tone the counsel said:

"Doctor, please give us the orthography of the word you have just used. I wish to be certain about the professional position of a gentleman so eminent as yourself. Kindly tell us how you spell the kind of doctor you claim to be—an *eclectic* doctor."

The wily impostor hesitated, demurred, finally objected. He did not claim to be a teacher of spelling; he never was a very good speller. He appealed to the court. Was he under any obligation to tell the counsel how to spell hard words?

Judge Pierpont said he would be pleased to accommodate the witness, but, unfortunately, the counsel was insisting upon his clear legal right. If he pressed the question, the witness must tell the jury how to spell the word which described his profession.

The counsel insisted. If he was to pay $2,500 for the information his client wanted to know what kind of a doctor he had employed.

"Then I'll be d—d if I tell him," burst out the doctor. "I will not be put on exhibition by any pettifogging attorney!"

"As you please," observed the judge. "Since you refuse to answer a proper question on cross-examination, it is my duty to direct the jury to return a verdict for the defendant."

"No! no! Don't do that!" exclaimed the mountebank. "I'll spell her—she's easy enough." He hastily muttered some unintelligible sounds, and said, "That's the way I spell her, sir."

"Please stop, sir!" said the counsel in his gentle, but very decisive style. "Pronounce each letter and syllable distinctly so that they may be written down."

The fellow stammered, hesitated, but determined to rely upon his impudence, which had so often carried him through difficulties.

"I can spell her, sir," he exclaimed. "She goes this way: E, k, ek, k, o, ko, l, e, k, lek, t, i, k, tik —ekkolektik!"

He was at the end of his exercise before the court and the spectators appreciated the ludicrous exhibition of his ignorance. The court made no effort to suppress the roar of laughter which followed.

The witness was very angry. "I am entitled to three guesses," he said, "if I have not fetched her the first time."

"Go on," said the counsel. "I have no objection."

"E, c, k, ek, c, h, o, ko——" The applause now completely stopped him. His colossal impudence gave way—it could not survive such ridicule. He rushed from the witness-box foaming at the mouth and cursing the court and jury. His attorney had nothing to say, and the jury without leaving their seats returned a verdict for the crippled farmer.

I encountered an illustration of the celebrity which some of the so-called "patent remedies" attain in one of our Western Territories. It was in a stage crossing one of the illimitable sage-brush deserts of Nevada. Far away, at a right angle to our course, we discovered a horseman firing his revolver, waving a white piece of cloth, and approaching at the top of his horse's speed. Our driver decided that "them dog-goned Shoshones had broke out uv their reservation," and this messenger had been sent to turn us back. At the road crossing we halted. As the courier approached he, shouted his message: "Jesus Pacheco wants a box uv er little liver pills, and his gal Meta wants er bottle uv Ayer's Hair Vigor for the fandango ter-morrer night!" The driver nodded assent, and the horseman turned back with an air of an important mission executed.

The earliest pages of profane history are records of

the most incredible quackery. "The Mistery of the microcosme or little world which is man's body and the medicinal parts belonging unto man," written by Basil Valentine, Monke of the order of St. Bennet, is a storehouse of medical science. It was comprised in his will, "which he hid under a Table of marble, behind the High Altar of the Cathedral Church in the Imperial City of Erfurt, leaving it there to be found by him whom God's Providence should make worthy of it." In this learned treatise the physicians of the first years of the seventeenth century learned how "the Stone of the Philosophers was made and perfectly prepared out of true Virgin's milk," and how it "transmutes the base metals into good and fixt gold." Here are described the miraculous properties of the shining, glowing, leaping, striking, trembling, falling, and superior rods—the *aurum potabile* and the fiery tartar. Here, too, was the manual whereby he prepared his medicines which never failed to cure. Perfect faith in all the statements of the monk of Erfurt is somewhat difficult. But it involves no such tax upon human credulity as the medical portion of the great Natural History of Pliny.

"Humanity," said Adam Smith, "is very uniform." In the first, as in the nineteenth century men who exercised calm judgment and common sense upon all other subjects, in dealing with their own healths and lives cheated themselves by the most atrocious quackery. Æsculapius and Pythagoras founded the medical science for Cicero and Julius Cæsar, who in that behalf were not as well provided for as the Indians of North America are by their medicine-men in our time. For the doctors of the

Piutes and the Sioux do acquire some practical knowledge in the use of medicinal plants which is valuable. But the most inferior of these medicine-men are not credulous enough to believe that acorns pounded with salt and axle-grease constitute a certain cure for bad habits, or that the toothache is cured by biting a piece of wood from a tree which has been struck by lightning. In Pliny's time the human race must have been fearfully afflicted with disease. Just how many remedies are given in the thirty-seven books of his great work, I have not taken the trouble to count. In seven of these books, which comprise those derived from forest trees, wild and cultivated plants, living creatures, and such aquatic products as mineral waters, sea-mosses, salt, etc., there are no less than six thousand two hundred and sixty-five of these remedies described. Of these the most fruitful source is salt, and the bramble and creeping ivy respectively furnish fifty-one and thirty-nine. The witch-hazel was probably unknown to Pliny. If he comprises it under the general word hazel, it by no means possesses the magical qualities attributed to "Pond's Extract." On the contrary, it produces headache and increase of flesh and is really good only for catarrh.

If Pliny is an authority, the surgery of his time was as extraordinary as its pharmacopœia. An expeditious union of broken bones was accomplished by bruising the ashes of burnt field-mice with honey, and burnt earth-worms were extremely useful for the extraction of splintered bones. To extract arrows, pointed weapons, and other hard substances from the body, the Roman surgeon applied the body of a mouse split asunder, or in special cases the head of the same animal pounded with salt, and the same practitioner cured his drunkard with the eggs of an owlet in three days. We cannot pursue the historical accounts of this great authority in natural science. He was a close observer of the scientific progress of his time. But for Pliny, the works of Diocles of Carystus, of Hippocrates, Praxagoras, Herophilus, and Erasistratus would have been lost to science and the remedies of Cleophantus and Asclepiades would never have been preserved.

In the records of the earliest explorations of the New World are found illustrations of the medical uses of plants by the native Indians of great interest. Jacques Cartier of Saint Malo, that enterprising French explorer, first ascended the St. Lawrence River in May, 1535. Arrested by the rapids above Montreal, he found the rich alluvial soil along the river carpeted with wild flowers. His men sincerely believed that they had reached the Flowery Kingdom. They exclaimed, " La Chine! La Chine!" and gave a name to the locality which it bears to-day. They landed, and, ignorant of the changes of temperature to which the region was subject, determined to remain there while expeditions were sent out to explore the surrounding country. Suddenly the cold of December gathered them in its embrace. They had none but salted provisions, and they were quickly attacked by the scurvy. Said the historian of the expedition: " We were stricken by a disease previously unknown—the legs were swollen, the muscles turned black as charcoal and seemed spotted with drops of blood. The disease involved the hips, thighs, shoulders, arms, and neck. The gums became rotten, the teeth loosened so that they fell from the jaws. Of one hundred and ten men from our three ships, by the middle of February there were not ten who were strong enough to take care of the sick, and there were not fifty who had any hope of life." In this desperate condition the Frenchmen were visited by two Indian women who made a decoction from the bark of a tree and made the sick men drink it. The effect was almost miraculous. As soon as they drank it the disease was arrested, and within two weeks every sick man was cured. The species of the tree is given only by its Indian name, but it was probably the black cherry or a species of the willow. "Tous ceulx qui en ont voullu vser ont recouvert santé et guerison, la grace a dieu," is the conclusion of Cartier's record of the incident.

CHAPTER XXII.

Essex Junction.

THERE is no term in American lexicography the mention of which raises the indignation of so many travellers to a white heat as "Essex Junction." The reasons for this will hereafter abundantly appear. As I had some connection with its monstrous birth and a thorough knowledge of its earlier growth, perhaps a sketch of its history may be, in some sense, a duty.

Away back in the early forties two lines of railroad from Boston were constructed *pari passu* toward Burlington, a common terminus. We may call them the *Rutland* and the *Central*. No one then supposed that they would extend farther west, for Lake Champlain was thought to interpose an impassable barrier. Later, and before either road was constructed to its terminus, the Vermont and Canada was chartered from Burlington north to Canada line, and this road was leased to and became permanently identified with the Central. Still later an application was made to the legislature in the name of the Vermont and Canada to bridge Lake Champlain at Rouse's Point so as to secure an unbroken line toward the West.

Then commenced a contest famous in the legislative annals of Vermont. The Rutland, supported by the towns south and west of its line, supposed it could stay the progress of the railroad westward. Burlington, ambitious to become a railroad terminus on the lake, took an active part in the contest. The bridge was opposed on grounds which now seem absurdly untenable. It was claimed and proved by experts that the bridge would obstruct navigation, that it would raise the water and overflow the low lands along the lake shores, and that great public and private damage would inevitably follow its construction.

But the Central won and the bridge was authorized. Then the Rutland wanted to participate in its advantages, and after another fierce contest in the legislature it procured an amendment of its charter which authorized it to build an extension from Burlington north to Rouse's Point.

There was a lawyer who, by indorsing for a friend, had at that time become interested in a paper-mill at Hubbell's Falls, near the present Essex Junction. We will call his name Jacob. He lived at Stanton's Tavern, a hostelry on the river road convenient to the Falls. He was a diminutive creature about four and a half feet high, with an enormous head, which contained cunning and mischief enough to stock the Third House or fit out the students of a university. He was employed by the Central as counsel to prevent the construction of the Rutland railroad north of Burlington, and he entered upon his work *con amore*. He discovered and forthwith purchased the services of one Stevens, who lived in Essex, and who was an original subscriber for five shares of the capital stock of the Rutland Railroad Company, not then worth the same number of coppers. The Rutland was about to make a new issue of bonds secured by a mortgage of its entire line, with the proceeds of which it intended to build from Burlington to Rouse's Point.

As unexpected as thunder from a clear sky, Jacob came down upon it with an action in favor of Stevens for an injunction against the building of the extension, on the ground that the extension was an infraction of his (Stevens') vested rights as a stockholder in a railroad the terminus of which was at Burlington.

Jacob's motion for a preliminary injunction came on to be heard before Judge Milo L. Bennett at Burlington—a judge whom no inducement could swerve one hair's breadth from his judicial duty. No lawsuit had ever arisen in Vermont which caused greater excitement. The leading lawyers from the southern and western portions of the State were present at the hearing. They protested against the outrage of permitting a traitor to the Rutland company, who had sold himself to the enemy and whose paltry five shares of stock were worthless, to obstruct a great public enterprise in which three-fourths of the State were interested. Capitalists from Boston whose money had built the Rutland railroad offered an enormous price for the Stevens shares. Everything that legal ability and ingenuity could devise was done to resist the granting of that motion. But Jacob was inflexible. He appeared alone, without associate counsel. He wasn't "selling shares then," he said. "Some other day, perhaps; but just then he was after an injunction."

And he got his injunction. In spite of all the opposition, his motion was granted. In the opinion of an inflexible judge he was entitled to it, and it was not withheld. I may as well say here that that injunction was never dissolved, and the railroad was never built north of Burlington. The excitement was so unreasoning that it took the form of personal hostility to Judge Bennett, because he did not find some way of defeating or denying the motion. At the next session of the legislature his re-election was defeated. It was the first time in Vermont that a judge was opposed because he had made or not made a decision which the public wanted. Before the year had passed the Vermonters were thoroughly ashamed of their conduct. Judge Bennett was restored to the Supreme Bench by the unanimous vote of the legislature, and remained there by annual re-election until he died.

And this mischief-making attorney made another discovery of what I always regarded as an intended fraud. It was that while the charter of the Vermont and Canada road connected with the Rutland in the village of Burlington, it had the option to connect with the Central at some point in the county of Chittenden. Very soon the report was current that on account of the steep grades of the line into Burlington from the north and east, the engineers were prospecting for a line to connect the Vermont and Canada with the Central somewhere in Essex. Even then it was not believed that any needless injury to Burlington was contemplated. Burlington was the largest town or city in the State or the Champlain valley, located on a sheltered harbor at the widest part of the lake, and midway between its two ends. She had water communication south with New York, north with Montreal and Quebec, and west with the St. Lawrence, the Ottawa, and the great lakes. She was almost the largest lumber market in the Union. Her manufactures were flourishing, her private residences beautiful, and her people hospitable. It seemed as if nature and art had combined to equip her with every quality for the natural lake terminus of three railroads, and to make her an attraction to travellers upon whose memories she should leave the imprint of a pleasant dream. She was the Queen City of Lake Champlain.

But an accident which placed the control of the Central where it could be made to minister to a very small local prejudice exposed Burlington to grave and lasting misfortunes. Six miles from anywhere, there was a barren sand plain that would not subsist one jack-rabbit to the square acre. The region round about it had not one attraction, and its general features could only serve to prejudice the passing traveller, and to deceive him as to the fertility of the soil of Vermont, the beauty of her valley, and the grandeur of her mountains. On this dreary spot a little brief authority decreed should be planted a public nuisance—an irritating obstruction to the traveller, which he would never, except upon compulsion, encounter a second time.

Said the piping voice of that attorney: "Build me here, out of the culled hemlock or the cross-grained spruce, a shanty, through which the rains of summer may drizzle and the storms of winter whirl the blinding snows. Along its walls plant benches hard and uncomfortable enough to give the rheumatism to a foundered tramp, should he be so unfortunate as to be obliged to sit upon them. In one corner build a stall, and place along its shelves the stale doughnut, the deadly pie, and the vinegar-rotted cucumber. Let a cold decoction of burnt corn be prepared and call it coffee. Arrange all trains so as to condemn many travellers to four hours of starvation and imprisonment there, in the din of ringing bells and screaming whistles, until they shall be thoroughly prepared for suicide, and let it be called *Essex Junction!*"

And it was so. As an abomination of desolation it was an early and a conspicuous success. In 1852 this dreadful place was a possession unto the residue of the heathen, taken upon the lips of talkers, and an infamy of the people. Men thought it then a superlative type of misery. But Essex Junction possessed a reserve force of discomfort unsuspected by its inventors. It has become worse with the rolling years. The only thing which has prospered in that vicinity during these almost forty years is the graveyard.

A place so noted, which has ploughed such deep furrows of misery upon so many memories, which, disregarding age, sex, or condition, has imperilled so many human lives, has naturally attracted the attention of many American poets and prose-writers. Some have abandoned it after a cursory examination, satisfied that it was beyond their powers and a subject to which they could not do justice. Others have persevered until they became convinced that any adequate description of its detestable attributes involved the use of profane and wicked expressions punishable under the penal code and prohibited in polite society. Only one native poet has had enough of the *divine afflatus* to enshrine Essex Junction in immortal song. All who are familiar with the English poetry of the last half of the nineteenth century will at once understand that I refer to that celebrated classic which (I quote from memory) runs after this wise:

> "With saddened face and battered hat,
> And eye that told of blank despair,
> On wooden bench a traveller sat,
> Cursing the fate that brought him there."

I hoped to be able to give to my readers the whole of this admirable poem, for I know well that no account of Essex Junction can be complete without it. But my way has been beset with many difficulties. All known copies of the poem have been bought up and suppressed by those whose hard fate anchors them to Essex Junction. Applications to the author for a copy have been met with invective, reproach, contumely, obloquy, and objurgation. Attempts to reproduce it from memory against his will have developed the fact that it is so thoroughly protected by trade-marks, design-patents, and copyrights that the inventor could at once enjoin its sale should its publication be attempted *in invitum*. After thorough investigation, I am convinced that but one consolation remains to the public. The line of this writer is so obviously poetry, not sacred but profane, that he may be expected hereafter to devote himself exclusively to its composition. In the first edition of his collected works we may therefore confidently expect to read with a sympathetic thrill the only great ballad of Essex Junction. I feel that I have in a perfunctory manner done my duty to the place and its proprietors, and that I may say of it as Uncle Toby said of the fly when he carefully put it outside the window: "Go, poor devil! In all this wide world there is room enough for both thee and me!"

CHAPTER XXIII.

The Humor and Mischief of the Junior Bar— Our Annual Bar Festival.

> "Send out for all the lawyers,
>   Collect the jovial crowd,
> To gather 'round the tables
>   With mirth and uproar loud.
> Call those whom we so long have known—
>   Squire Seymour, Linsley, Starr,
> And also all the devil's own—who?
>   Of course the junior bar!"

THE term applied in the foregoing verse did not inaccurately describe a class of lawyers who in those early days were known as the junior bar. We did not have many clients nor much income. But we had abundance of leisure and were given to mischief as the sparks fly upward. There was one occasion on which the safety-valve was thrown wide open and the dangerous pressure of humor was relieved. It was the annual supper of the bar at the winter term of the Supreme Court, held by all the judges at Middlebury, in the county of Addison. There we laid Coke and Blackstone on the shelf and sung with great fervor—

> "O dear brothers, may the time be distant, far,
> When the first one shall be missing from the gathering of the bar."

That was a company of men with hearts and consciences which this festival annually brought together. Our oldest brother of threescore and ten years we always called "Squire Seymour." A member of the celebrated Seymour family of Connecticut and New York, his kindly heart and amiable character secured not only our respect but our affection. There was an expression in his clear blue eyes which without exaggeration we called lovely. Our Starr was a deacon who could take a joke and make one, if necessary; others were Linsley, with a saturnine expression which was only skin-deep, and his stock song of "The Hunters of Kentucky;" John Prout, who seldom spoke above a whisper, and was consequently accused of making all the noise; Tucker, with his thirty-two degrees of Masonry and his eloquence in behalf of injured females; Needham, our Falstaff, with all the wit and weight but none of the grossness of his Shakespearian prototype; Geo. Chipman, the born gentleman from the mountain wilds of Ripton; Barber, the poet of love and free-soil! Our leaders in song were the brothers S., whose annual programmes always comprised "The McGregors' Gathering" and *imitation* opera. One of our most active members already gave promise of the eminence in diplomacy which he afterward attained, by his skill in the use of language to conceal ideas. Woodbridge and Grandey wore the honors of the largest city in Vermont, which was also celebrated as the smallest in the world. These, with occasional visitors from adjoining counties and worthy representatives of the names of Pierpont, Briggs, Beckwith, and Wright, always furnished abundant material for a feast of reason and a flow of soul.

We were officers of the court, bound to obedience to statutory law. Our State had adopted the " Maine liquor law," and under the maxim in equity which presumed that to be done which ought to be done, the use of all beverages stronger than cider and spruce beer no longer prevailed. The only fluids upon our *menu* (we called it bill of fare) were Ripton mineral water, cider fermented and unfermented, and metheglin. Our judges, qualified as experts by long experience, were of opinion that the Ripton water had a delightful "blue-grass" aroma, that the cider in flavor and consequences was undistinguishable from a product of French vineyards imported in baskets, and that the metheglin closely resembled a complicated mixture known to our remote ancestors by the name of "rum-punch." These opinions were undoubtedly imaginative, though it must be admitted that the liberal absorption of these fluids softened the sternness of the judicial countenance and produced a change in its visual organs which once led our most venerable judge, pointing to our deacon, to break out with the nursery ballad, "Twinkle, twinkle, little Starr." The conclusive evidence that there was no deception in our bill of fare was the fact that no lawyer or judge was ever known to be absent at the opening of court at ten o'clock the next morning.

The wit of these festivals was much too personal for publication. It was always good-natured, never malicious. When it was raised to concert pitch, it was our delight to send out committees to bring in all the judges. Our invitations were never declined, for they knew that while our exercises promoted good feeling among the lawyers, they were never permitted to diminish our respect for the bench. But we did sometimes call upon them to explain their opinions in cases recently reported. One of them, naturally too realistic to appreciate a joke, had in a recent opinion defined a "heifer" as a "calfless bovine two years old." This opinion we considered misleading. A committee secured the presence of the judge and formally demanded that he should explain whether or not a *male* bovine two years old, being calfless, was a heifer. He certainly was as the judge defined the word. We insisted that the opinion was an innovation calculated to disturb the certainty of the law. His explanations were much confused and we made the occasion very lively for him. He rather turned the laugh upon us, however, by the admission that his use of the word was inaccurate and "must have been induced by the increasing number and constant presence before him of sucking members of the bar." He offered to compromise by the order of a basket of something, and his explanation and compromise were accepted as satisfactory.

I recall one of our sentiments which worried another of our judges. The action of "book account" had been in use from the adoption of our constitution. It was originally intended for a case of mutual accounts or of an account with many items difficult of proof except by the oath of a party. In an action of this kind the parties had been permitted to testify long before the general statute which made all parties to an action witnesses. This action had been favored by the court and greatly extended. In a recent case it had been maintained in what looked much like a case of trespass, for carrying away a flight of *cellar stairs*, the judge observing that one stair could not, but a flight might be recovered for in this form of action. The sentiment to which he was called to respond was:

"*The action of book account.* Like necessity it knows no law—like the area of freedom it is constantly extending its limits—like the peace of God it passeth all understanding."

There are lying before me the manuscript notes of several of these festivals. In them I recognize the handwriting of nearly every one of those I have named. I might transcribe, for the amusement of the casual reader, some of their sharp, bright words, but, alas! I have not the heart. For of all those dear brothers, judges as well as lawyers, I can count the survivors upon less than the fingers of a single hand. The others have all preceded us to that Higher Bar which we are very near. Only *four* will read these lines. There is no need that I should express to either of them the memories which fill my heart as I write. For we loved one another with a love which will never grow cold in the bosoms of the survivors on this side of the grave. I would like to hear the few who remain, with voices not so clear as they were forty years ago, once more uniting in the stanza:

"Now swell the parting chorus as the lamps grow pale and dim,
And fill each man his goblet till it circles round the brim;
Let our hearts glow with the feeling that like lambent flame burns bright,
As we drink the toast of the evening, 'To the absent ones to-night.'"

Echoes of the feast sometimes mingled with the proceedings in court on subsequent days. Our briefs were not printed—we made seven copies, one for each judge. One of our number, who seldom smiled, an able lawyer, afterward an honor to the bench, prided himself upon the neatness of his papers, which were always folded to an uniform width. He was to open the argument in the first case the morning after one of these suppers. He walked up to the bench in front of the Chief Justice, brought his pack of briefs down upon the bench, and as if his mind was upon a *pack* of another kind said, "*Will your Honor please cut?*"

"Mr. P.," said the judge with great dignity, "you must use language which the court understands!"

"Excuse me," said the sober P., "I did not suppose that your Honor had forgotten over-night!"

Another incident had its origin at one of these suppers in a promise to pay off one of the judges for a joke perpetrated at my own expense. He was a perfectly pure and upright judge, but disqualified by nature for the trial of criminals. He was unable to overcome his natural presumption that every man brought before him for trial must be guilty until he had affirmatively proved his innocence. "Mr. Attorney, *can't we get hold of a criminal?*" I heard him ask one morning when there was no civil case ready for trial. This inquiry indicated his temper of mind. Obviously a criminal against whom there was any evidence did not have much chance of escape when Judge B. in his charge had the last argument to the jury.

At the jury term following the bar supper a melancholy, disconsolate, worthless scamp was indicted for the crime of selling intoxicating liquor without having a license therefor. He said he had no counsel and no money, and he might have added that he never expected to have any. With a wicked expression in his eye, Judge B. assigned me as counsel for his defence. I refused peremptorily, but the judge said I was an officer of the court and could not disobey its order without incurring the penalties of a contempt. I then pleaded engagements and endeavored to beg off. But the judge was inflexible. I saw that he was determined to make me endure the infliction, and then insisted that two lawyers of my own age should be assigned to assist me, who assured me that they were willing to share the responsibility with me. The judge hesitated, for he evidently suspected mischief. But he finally made the assignment, at the same time remarking with emphasis, "None of your deviltry, gentlemen!"

I promptly said that "I did not quite comprehend the scope of his Honor's observation. · Were we to defend the fellow in earnest, to get him acquitted if we could, or were we only to go through the motions in a formal and perfunctory manner? I was indifferent which course should be taken, but I would like to understand in advance which his Honor preferred."

"Oh, no!" said he. "No formality. You are to get the fellow off if you can. You are to do your best. I do not think you will find it an easy matter," he said very significantly.

The jury was impanelled and the trial proceeded. I should think the prosecuting attorney proved about two hundred offences, and might easily have proved a few hundred more by the same witnesses. He then rested his case. I arose with a perfectly serious face and read out a long list of witnesses, comprising several physicians and some of the most dignified members of the bar.

"What do you intend to prove by these witnesses?" demanded the judge.

I replied, with solemnity of speech and expression,

that my witnesses were principally experts. "I am instructed, sir," I said, "by my unfortunate and persecuted client that he is a law-abiding citizen, innocent of any intent to violate the law; that the fluid vended by him was not intoxicating; that it was purchased from a dealer in Whitehall, who watered it so as to remove its intoxicating properties before it was permitted to enter our State. In order to be perfectly safe, my unfortunate client watered it again. He instructs me that no one was ever intoxicated by it. He says that in some cases where his patrons had purchased at the town agency a glass of beer in the early morning, they will testify that they came to his place and drank of this fluid all the day long—that the more they drank the soberer they grew, and when at bedtime they severally retired to their virtuous couches, they were not only perfectly sober, but inspired by a firm determination in future to live upright and temperate lives. I intend also to have liberal samples of the fluid brought into court, and its non-intoxicating effects demonstrated in the person of the sheriff or other officer of the court."

"You will do nothing of the kind!" exclaimed the judge. "The impudence of your offer alone prevents my punishing you for making it. Positively it is the most impudent proposition I ever heard made in court. Your *unfortunate* client sold this stuff for whiskey, and whiskey it will be taken to be for the purposes of this trial. I rule against your offer. If you have any other witnesses call them!"

"Very well," I said. "If the court rejects my evidence I must submit. I have no other witnesses."

The State's attorney said that he did not wish to

argue the case to the jury—that there was nothing to argue. The court agreed with him and was about to direct a verdict of guilty, when I interposed and insisted upon my right to address the jury.

"What questions do you wish to argue?" asked Judge B.

I replied that this was a prosecution against the respondent for a high crime. It was a case in which the jurors were judges of the law as well as of the fact. That I had recently made a thorough examination of the authorities, and I was prepared to show by a very large number of cases, beginning with the "Year Books" and ending with a very recent case in Texas, that it was the duty of the court to instruct the jury that in this case the jury had the right to determine the law.

"The question is one of great interest," I said, "and I hope by an exhaustive discussion of the cases to satisfy the court that my view of the law is accurate and sound."

"No, sir! No, sir!" exclaimed his Honor. "Do you ask me to sit here and hear you tell the jury that they know what the law is better than the court? Your proposition is an insult. I think you know better. I have a great mind to commit you for contempt in making the offer."

"Oh, no!" I said. "Do not do that. In the first place, instead of entertaining a contempt for this court your Honor knows how sincerely I honor and respect the court. In the next, when I go to jail it must be for a client who can pay. I submit to your Honor's ruling and take my seat. With your Honor's permission I should be pleased to withdraw from the case."

"Where is the prisoner? Where is your *unfortunate* client?" suddenly demanded the judge.

One of my associates now rose and said that he had been waiting a long time for an opportunity to address the court, but he thought it would be improper to break in upon the instructive and interesting colloquy between the court and one of the counsel; that he understood that in the English courts, whence we derived our common law, when the plaintiff's case broke down and he was permitted to withdraw a juror, it was the correct practice for his leading counsel to rise and say to the court:

"M' Lud, I see only eleven jurors in the box!"

"Mr. B., if you know where the prisoner is, you had better say so and omit all this rigmarole."

"Oh! very well. If your Honor does not wish to hear me, I will resume my seat. I was about to make a communication to the court, but perhaps the court can improve my language," said B. with perfect imperturbability.

"Oh! go on! go on in your own way. Only get to some point in the course of the day," said the judge, now becoming irascible.

"Then, sir, I will resume. Using a similar formula I was about to say, or rather if I had not been interrupted I should have said, 'Your Honor, I see no prisoner in the box!'"

"Well, sir! Well, sir! and what then?"

"Then it occurred to me that while my attention was absorbed by the discussion between the counsel and your Honor upon the much-debated question whether in this State the jurors in a criminal case were judges of the law, the respondent pressed me with the inquiry whether 'the judge wasn't agin' him.' I insisted that my position as his counsel, under the order of the court, did not require me to answer such an inquiry. He was persistent, however, and to get rid of him I finally said that I was on the whole inclined to the opinion that *the judge was agin' him!* Then he remarked that he 'guessed he would go out and see a man,' and he went—that is, I think he went, for I have not seen him since."

"Why did you not instantly inform the court of his escape?" sternly demanded the judge.

"Because I did not know that he had escaped. The only information I had was that, *animo revertendi*, he had 'gone out to see a man.' Observing that he did not return, I caused inquiry to be made, and learned that when last seen he was following a wagon in the direction of the boundary line of an adjoining county."

"Sheriff, go instantly in pursuit of the prisoner!" said the judge. Then addressing the counsel, "I think the court will give you some instructions in the line of your duty," he said very significantly.

"Your Honor is quite right," rejoined the lawyer, coolly ignoring the threatening nature of the intimation. "Your Honor will readily appreciate my dilemma. My first impulse was to break in upon your Honor's very interesting observations upon the rights of jurors and the court, and shout: 'The prisoner has skipped!' But I was restrained by three powerful considerations. If the prisoner was caught and convicted, he would be imprisoned, clothed, and fed at the expense of the county, thereby imposing an expensive burden on the tax-payers, of whom I am one, and if left alone he would carry the burden into some other county; secondly, was I certain enough of my premises to conclude that he did not intend to return? and, thirdly, your Honor had told us in so many words *to get him off if we could!* On the other hand, was I under any obligation to give information to the prejudice of my unfortunate client? Before I could clearly see my way through the labyrinth of these conflicting duties the fellow had got such a start that the sheriff could probably not overtake him. Being in doubt I thought the safer course was to do nothing, and I did it."

The judge supposed we intended to ridicule him, when nothing was farther from our purpose. He became very angry, said that he would give us a lesson profitable to us in future; that the sheriff would take us into custody, and after the mid-day intermission he would fix upon the term of our imprisonment for contempt.

I observed that the court "must indulge me in an objection. We severally and seriously disclaimed any intentional disrespect to the court. No contempt whatever had been committed in the presence of the court. If there had been a technical contempt it arose out of our omission to communicate certain facts touching the prisoner's movements outside the court. For such a contempt we could only be adjudged guilty upon evidence taken after interrogatories had been filed which we had had an opportunity to answer; that nothing would give us greater pleasure than to answer such interrogatories."

I did not finish my remarks. The bar began to appreciate the absurdity of the performance and to see that my objection was well founded. Father Needham, the sight of whose broad, sunny face was a cure for despondency, as *amicus curiæ* took our side. He said that this court was in no doubt about the respect entertained for it by every member of the bar; and if the boys had gone too far, he knew they would apologize. The side judges, two goodhearted, hard-headed farmers, argued with their chief in an undertone; a more genial expression began to steal over the face of his Honor, and we were saved. After a brief consultation the presiding judge said the court had decided that we were not guilty of contempt, but advised us that it would be very unsafe to repeat the experiment. "The court itself is in fault for giving you such an opportunity to conspire. Do you never meet without devising some mischief?"

"Very seldom, your Honor," said B. in an undertone.

"Seriously, then, gentlemen, it is a grave offence to countenance the escape of a prisoner. It is a graver one to do anything to lower the dignity of the court. A time will come when you would no more do it than you would commit a felony—when *you* will uphold the dignity of the tribunal which even the judges may fail to maintain."

To-day I realize the truth of these observations. I have told the story, for it gives me an opportunity to say that an upright and a pure judiciary, such as long existed and I hope still exists, of which the highest court in the republic is and always has been a model, is the hope of our republic. When it ceases to exist the republic will perish. No lawyer young or old should trifle with its dignity or lower it in the respect of the public. In the case cited our conduct was inexcusable and reprehensible.

I have wandered a long way from the bar supper.

I return to it to say that it would be better for everybody—the court, the bar, and the public—if such festivals were more common. Nowhere have I met a local bar where there was less of jealousy and envy, more of hearty good-will and desire to assist each other, than among those who annually sat at our table in Addison County. Here is one of their characteristic illustrations. One of our number, a man of a great, generous heart, a gentleman by birth, instinct, and education, could not succeed in the profession and became poor. We seldom met him without putting into his empty pockets something from our own, which were but scantily furnished. He had an old case on the calendar which was to be tried or dismissed. We saw that he was in great distress and ascertained the cause. His client had betrayed him to his adversary. If he did not recover, or if the case was dismissed, he would lose his own costs and charges and have to pay the costs of the defendant for which he was bound. We examined the case and decided that he was entitled to recover. I think about ten of us volunteered to assist him on the trial. Two were to be the active counsel; the others were to look wise, smile upon us, and frown upon the defendant. *We recovered*, and our friend got his money. We would not permit him to share it with us or give it away, and it gave him a couple of happy years. I recall with a thrill of delight his blue, moistened eye, his thin lips tremulous with emotion, when with clasped hands, seated around our table, all sang—or if they could not sing declared—that

"He is a jolly good fellow—good fellow—good fellow!
Which nobody can deny."

But now the hour of separation comes. Again H. N. shakes his 350 pounds avoirdupois and the very foundations of the hall with the last story from the mountain hamlet where he reigns. If there is a lull the three B.s or S. will fill it with a new verse to the old song, while the venerable judges in unison declare:

"We won't go home till morning, till morning, till morning."

"And Linsley still contributes
From his stock a single leaf,
And reads with deep emotion
From old Judge Keyes's brief.
And if the cars don't leave meantime,
We shall be very lucky;
For he'll stay and sing his favorite song—which?
The Hunters of Kentucky—O! Kentucky!
The Hunters of Kentucky."

And now the gray dawn is creeping over the valley; we know that the top of Ripton mountain is already aflame and that the court-house bell waits for no man. The judges in their easy-chairs may close their eyes, and while apparently buried in deep reflection may go to sleep. But we must clear the dust from our eyes and the cobwebs from our throats and be prepared to argue our cases when they are reached in their order.

Our chairman rises—the gavel falls for the last time. It is the signal for every guest to stand upon his feet. The rich voice of one of the brothers S. leads and every one joins in the well-known words which always unite our hands in a strong and cordial grasp:

"Now here's a hand, my trusty fiere,
  And gie's a hand o' thine;
An' we'll tak' a right guid willie-waught
  For auld lang syne!
And surely ye'll be your pint-stoup,
  And surely I'll be mine,
And we'll tak' a cup o' kindness yet
  For auld lang syne.

"For auld lang syne, my dear,
  For auld lang syne,
We'll tak' a cup o' kindness yet
  For auld lang syne."

The last note of the good old song dies away. We have had our "uproar long and loud," but it is ended now. Our hearts are very full of friendship and goodwill one to another. We say good-by and go away to our several duties, warmer friends, better citizens, and better lawyers. Honored and cherished be the memories of the festival for the pleasure it gave me at the time and for the satisfaction which this slight notice of it has given to me after these many years.

CHAPTER XXIV.

Owls, Falcons, and Eagles.

WHEN Minerva selected the owl as the chief attraction of her aviary, she must have judged him by his face rather than by his character. For no biped or quadruped was ever created so profoundly wise as he looks to be, and none ever established a character more questionable. From the little wretch whose fearful screech stirs the blood of the hunter in the wilderness to the big fellow in snowy plumage with the surname of *Nyctea*, all are thieves, and some are bold robbers with the silent movements of the burglar. There is a female of the *Virginianus* family that looks down upon my library table from the top of a book-case, whose first acquaintance I have permanent cause to remember. She is nearly one-third larger than her spouse, she was mistress of the family, and was very sure to be quartering the country on some marauding excursion while her mate in the dark forest was frightening children with his dreadfully mournful "Hoo-hoo-hoo! Ho-hoo!" which gives him the Indian name of "ooloo," or the devil, and the common one of the "hooting or great horned owl." The only good I ever heard of him is that his brain cures fits in children, especially those into which they are frightened by his funereal wail.

I made the acquaintance of the Madame Strix of my library after this wise. I had killed a full-grown mallard which fell upon the river bank, and had reloaded my gun, when a large object passed over me as noiseless as a shadow. It swooped down toward the ground, and when it rose in an ascending curve I saw that it was this female robber, and that she was carrying off my mallard before my very face. I sent a charge of number six shot after her, and some of the pellets must have collided with her shoulder-blade or *ulna*, for she sailed gracefully to the ground, releasing the duck from her talons as she fell.

I first secured the duck—a large one weighing, I suppose, over three pounds, and measuring two feet in length, apparently larger and heavier than its rapacious captor. As I noticed the ease with which Madame Strix carried this great bird in her flight, I queried for a moment whether there might not be some color of truth in the annually recurring story of the carrying away of unregenerate babes by the white-headed eagle. With this thought in my mind I approached the owl, which, instantly throwing herself upon her back, presented what the prize-fighter would have called her "fives" with such dexterity that she appeared on her under side to be made of claws. I carelessly touched her with the tip of my right foot, when, presto! in an instant there was a sensation as though the calf of my leg had been seized with hot pinchers. Madame had struck her sharp talons through the hard leather of my hunting-boot deep into my leg with a grasp of intense energy, producing a very painful sensation. Had it been practicable I would have compromised by a surrender of the duck, for although I might crush out the life of the bird I knew that fierce grip would be maintained, though it might tear out the very muscles of my limb, which could have been done without much increase of the pain. Fortunately there was in my game-bag a bottle of chloroform, which I used to destroy the life of the specimens I wished to preserve without injury to their plumage. To saturate a handkerchief with the anæsthetic and throw it over the head of my temporary captor was the work of a moment. Relaxation of the fierce grasp and cessation of the pain speedily followed, and Madame Strix fell into the sleep that knows no waking. I never allowed her to return to this life. I believe she carries fiercer weapons, operated by a more powerful muscle than any rapacious bird of my acquaintance.

The Osprey, or Fish-Hawk.

No rapacious bird possesses a character so unexceptionable as the fish-hawk. The largest of our falcons except the eagle, provided with powerful pinions and fierce talons and with an appetite which is seldom satiated, he never invades the poultry-yard or any of the possessions of the farmer. He subsists wholly upon fish, preferably upon species which the fisherman would willingly have exterminated. No sportsman ever injures the fish-hawk, and to destroy one of their nests is supposed to be a certain way of incurring bad luck and heavy misfortune.

The fish-hawk is the only bird which constructs its nest in the most prominent and conspicuous localities, where it cannot fail to attract attention. A dead tree of large diameter, with a few branches capable of sustaining great weight, standing on a point formed by an Adirondack river, visible for miles in every direction, is the favorite nesting-place of this splendid bird. Here both male and female labor in the construction of the nest. It is made of dried branches, some of them as thick as the wrist, with grasses or any soft material in the centre. It is occupied by the same pair year after year, and as they annually make additions to it, it sometimes reaches the dimensions of a small haystack. The young never leave it until they are full grown and each one is able to "go a-fishing" on his own account.

There was for many years, and I hope still is, one of these nests on the outlet of the beautiful Raquette Lake. As we passed it late one September afternoon, two young and nearly full-grown birds showed themselves, sitting upon its edge. We had reached the lake and were slowly moving along its bold southern shore, when I noticed the female fish-hawk sailing high above our heads on the lookout for the evening meal of her family. Through a strong field-glass, by lying on my back in the stern of the boat, I had an excellent opportunity to observe her movements. Using the trees on the shore for comparison, I estimated her elevation to be not less than two hundred feet above the water. She suddenly dropped like an arrow, her talons downward, and struck so near the boat that the water dashed over us. She had some difficulty in rising, and only did so after a considerable struggle. When she succeeded, she carried with her a four-pound pickerel which she held in both her claws, one stuck into its shoulders, the other just above its anal orifice. She was slowly moving upward uttering her screams of triumph, when a reverend gentleman, my accidental companion in the bow of the boat, fired both barrels of his gun in her direction. Fortunately he was not marksman enough to hit a barn-door, and the hawk was untouched. The brave bird would not drop her prey. She continued to ascend, screaming her contempt at the pot-hunter, until she had attained her former elevation, when she sailed away in the direction of her nest. I watched her until she reached it and deposited the pickerel in the midst of her hungry family.

The reader who is unacquainted with the word-picture by Wilson, the ornithologist, of the robbery of the fish-hawk by the white-headed eagle has yet to enjoy a fine example of descriptive writing. These robberies are not infrequent, and I witnessed one of them which was not a successful experiment. It occurred on the shore of Long Lake.

At the time of which I am writing, on a point which extended into the lake from its western shore under Buck Mountain, there was a grove of white pine trees. In the largest of these was the nest of a pair of eagles. They had nested there for many years. Sabattis, then a man of fifty, could not remember a year when it was not so occupied. By annual additions it had grown to an enormous size and was visible for miles. These eagles were masters of the lake, and it was not often visited by the ospreys, even upon a fishing excursion.

One morning, from my camp at the outlet, I noticed a pair of ospreys with two young but full-grown birds in the trees on the eastern shore. The old birds were training the young ones in capturing small fish, which I thought were yellow perch, near the shore. One of the young birds made a circuit farther up the lake and struck a lake trout. He had some difficulty in rising from the water, but slowly succeeded. Before he took his course toward the place where the parent birds were on the watch, a young eagle dashed out from the point and with a fierce scream started in pursuit. At the same moment the old ospreys started to defend their young. They were not in time. The eagle had almost reached the young hawk, when it dropped the fish. The eagle did not seize it before it struck the water, and in four or five similar cases I never saw the fish caught in its descent. While the eagle was struggling to rise after it had seized the fish, and before he was twenty feet from the water, one of the ospreys made a swoop and struck his claws into the eagle with such force that both went into the lake, where they separated. As the eagle rose a second time it was struck by the second osprey and again forced into the lake. I think he was struck in this manner four times, when the old eagles came to his rescue and the ospreys retired, screaming defiance, and one of them carrying the fish which had been the cause of the contest. But the eagle was disabled and could not rise. One of the guides went for him in a boat, but before he could reach him he was drowned. His back was found to have been so torn by the talons of the fish-hawks that the wounds would have been mortal if he had fallen upon the shore.

In the early days of March in a subsequent year I was in the shop of Mr. Hurst, a taxidermist in Albany, when he received by express from some place in the Adirondacks two young eagles which had evidently been killed a few days before. They were covered with a cream-colored down and only a few primaries and tail-feathers had just commenced their growth. They were probably about a month old. The period of the eagle's incubation cannot be less than thirty days, consequently the eggs in this case must have been laid in December or January. How they could have been protected from the cold in a locality where the mercury often fell below zero is a question for every one to settle for himself. Obviously the male must have taken a part in the process of incubation.

The eagle is a mighty hunter. The remnants of half-consumed fish, rabbits, ruffed grouse, and other birds were so numerous about the nest that the carrion stench sometimes floated to our camp, a mile below. The quick digestion and rapacious appetites of such a family must have been liberally supplied when the remains of the feast were so abundant.

The pines are no longer to be seen. The lumberman has invaded Long Lake, and with the pines the nest of the eagles has gone, thus establishing another crime for which the invaders of what ought to be a preserve are responsible.

CHAPTER XXV.

NOVELTIES OF OFFICIAL EXPERIENCE.

I CANNOT expect my readers to get as much entertainment as I did out of some of my early experiences in the Treasury, which were not provided for in the regulations. But I will describe two or three of them on the chance that they may be found worth reading.

One morning within the first month of my official life I found upon my table a box of mahogany, inlaid with silver, bearing a tablet on which was engraved my name with "Honorable" conspicuously prefixed. When opened, I found, reposing upon a velvet-lined interior, a pair of revolvers, silver and ivory mounted and decorated in a very exquisite style. There was a note requesting my acceptance of the box from the agent of a corporation which had constant dealings with the department. Inquiry of my colored messenger disclosed that the box had been placed upon my table by a clerk whose duty it was to enter checks for the payment of accounts in the order of their receipt from the Secretary, and to present them to the Register for signature, after which they were sent by mail to the payees. It was a matter in which the clerk had no discretion. But he could, by violating his instructions, occasionally advance the payment of a check for a few days, and by a manipulation of his books conceal the irregularity. Some of these checks were for large amounts, so that a few days saved would be a great convenience to the payees as well as a considerable saving of interest. This clerk had held the position for many years, and found it very difficult to maintain his family on a salary of only $1,400 per year.

The clerk was summoned, and entered with that fawning obsequiousness which was common between clerks of a higher and a lower grade, and which was so offensive that I put an end to it with the first opportunity. Bowing and scraping, he began to speak as he advanced. He begged my pardon for his assurance, but the agent of the —— corporation had presented every in-coming Register with a pair of the revolvers made by the company. He had left the box with him, with a request that it might be laid, with his compliments, on the Register's table!

I told this clerk when he next addressed me to remember that he was an officer of the Treasury and a man—not a menial; to stand upright and look me in the face.

"Now tell me," I said, "do you say that this presentation was made in pursuance of a custom?"

"Oh, yes, sir! It has always been. At all events, ever since I have been in the bureau, whenever a new Register was appointed. No objection was ever made to it."

"Have you received such presents?" I asked.

"Yes, sir," he answered. "And so have others. The agent has said to me that the corporation had so many drafts coming through the Treasury that it was very important to them to have their business done promptly. They would consider it a favor if I would accept a little present occasionally. It is difficult, sir, to live upon our small salaries."

I told the clerk that out of consideration for his family I would not remove him for this grave offence. But he must return my present, and that thereafter any employee of the bureau who accepted any present from any one having business with it would be instantly removed when the facts came to my knowledge.

This treatment broke up the custom of accepting presents. But it was felt to be a great hardship by the old employees. It was regarded as depriving them of a legitimate means of adding to their income.

I wish I could write a sentence of such power that it would induce Congress to make for these poor clerks in the department such compensation as they deserve. I have no words strong enough to express the views on this subject which I entertain. There were several hundred of them in my bureau. Their salaries were fixed long ago, when money had double its purchasing power in 1860. When the war came on these salaries were made subject to a heavy internal revenue tax, and they were paid in currency, which once fell to a discount of sixty per cent. Yet they served the Government with such fidelity that there was absolutely no loss by their error or fraud. A more industrious, faithful body of public servants could not exist. If their compensation were increased fifty per cent from its present rate, no injustice would be done the country and only scant justice to them.

In the first year, and in fact through the whole war, there were in Washington many *chevaliers d'industrie*, who were well dressed and preserved the bearing of gentlemen, but who had no visible means of support. I was to learn from a peculiar and not very agreeable experience how one of them managed to meet the demands of the butcher, the baker, and the candlestick maker.

I have always been conscious of a personal defect which through all my life has been a great obstacle to my success. It is a positive inability to recognize the names or the faces of gentlemen whom I ought to know. No year has passed in which I have not offended good friends by passing them in the street without recognition, or in some way giving them the impression of my deliberate intention to slight them. As the defect was one which I could not remedy, I have endeavored to atone for it by invariably seeming to recognize every one who first recognized me.

At a Presidential reception one evening, early in 1862, when I was in conversation with the Marshal of the District, a well-dressed gentleman bowed to me with an air of familiar recognition, and I naturally returned his salute. After he had passed, but while he was still within view, I asked:

"Marshal, who is that gentleman? He always bows to me. Evidently he is some one whom I ought to know; but I am wholly unable to recall his name or where I have met him. What is his name and position?"

The marshal's face assumed a look of unmistakable surprise. "Well, now, that is excellent," he said. "Do you tell me that you do not know that gentleman, and ask me his name and occupation? Come, now! You don't mean that. You cannot be serious. You must know him much better than you do me."

"I assure you that I was never more serious. I

have met him in the street, possibly in my office; but I cannot remember that I have ever spoken to him or had any business with him. I think I must have had, for he always recognizes me with the air of a familiar acquaintance."

"Well, well!" he said. "This is very rich. If anything could astonish me your statement would. That man is Major G., of New York. He is understood to be not only a very old friend of the Register of the Treasury, but a species of business adviser. That officer is supposed frequently to avail himself of the major's long experience in Washington and his knowledge of affairs. He has the *entrée* to the department at all times and access to the Register. It is rather unkind of you to say that you do not know such an old and influential friend."

"I shall have to do it, nevertheless. I now, upon reflection, do remember that I have seen him in the bureau, where I supposed he had some business. However, I can leave him to enjoy his supposed relations, since they do me no harm."

"You do not quite understand the pecuniary value of such a relation," said the marshal. "The major contrives to make money, and a considerable amount of money, by it."

"How is that possible?" I asked.

"The city is thronged with contractors and men who have claims which are constantly passing through the Treasury. It is a good thing for them to have a friend at court who can get their claims taken up and passed upon out of their order—who can ascertain just when they will be paid or assist in procuring their early payment. Such services are valuable. Contractors are willing to pay for them.

The major is understood to earn a very fair income out of his close relations with you."

"That cannot be possible. There is not a man living who could advance the payment or allowance of a claim by so much as one hour. The regulations prohibit all such favoritism."

"No doubt such is the fact, but strangers are not aware of it, and Major G. is not the only man who does business here on the capital of his influential position. He has some facilities for obtaining information from your office. How otherwise could he tell on what day a check for an account would be drawn?"

"That is possible by co-operation with a clerk. But this could only happen when accounts to a large amount had been liquidated, only a certain proportion of which could be paid daily. Such information would be restricted to two or three days in every case and could not be of much value."

"It is of value enough to trade upon," said the marshal. "If you make inquiry I think you will find that much of this business is transacted and that it is regarded by many as legitimate."

I was disposed to do Major G. no injustice. I asked a city friend who had claims passing through the Treasury to look into the matter in his own way. Major G. rose to the first cast of the fly. For a moderate per cent on the amount of his collections the major agreed to give my friend all the advantages of his intimacy with the Register, and hinted that when it became very important to his principal he could procure the payment of a claim by increasing the pressure. In such cases the commission must be increased, for it *must be divided with others.*

The next morning a written order was delivered to the doorkeeper and posted upon the doors of all the rooms in the Register's office which had any connection with payments, to the effect that under no circumstances would Major G. be permitted to enter that office or any room under the Register's control, except upon the written order of the Secretary of the Treasury. This order was the subject of much comment, and the authority of the Register to make it was fiercely disputed. It had the effect to convert the major into a watchful spy upon all the official and personal conduct of the Register. But it broke up his business, and I never heard afterward that any one trading upon his acquaintance with the Register of the Treasury was able to make it profitable.

We all had to watch the balances of our bank accounts very closely when our salaries were paid in notes which were at a discount of sixty per cent and subject to a large internal revenue tax in addition. In the beginning of 1862, for the first time in my life, when my bank account was written up, it showed a balance in my favor fifty dollars greater than I was able to make it. This balance increased monthly until it amounted to two hundred and fifty dollars, an amount as unexpected to me as if it had fallen from the sky. I wanted it so much that I was quite contented to accept it without very close inquiry.

In due time the explanation came. An old, a poor and very worthy friend had asked me to do what I could to secure for his son an appointment to a clerkship of the first class, with an annual salary of $1,200. I had recommended him, he had received the appointment, was assigned to duty in my own bureau, and the matter had passed from my mind. One day the clerk solicited an interview. He was very much troubled, he said. Illness in his family and the inability of his father to assist him had so increased his expenses that *he found it very difficult to make his payments to me. Would I not oblige him by postponing a part of the amount due to me and permit him to pay it out of his salary for the second year?* He had paid almost half of the debt, but it was almost impossible for him to continue the payments!

"What are you talking about?" I demanded. "You owe me nothing. Why do you ask me to postpone the payment of a claim which has no existence?"

"You were to know nothing about it, I understood," he said; "but I wished to comply with the custom, which I was told was to pay for an appointment—one-half the salary for the first year! You procured the place for me, and I assure you I will pay the balance just as soon as I can save the money. There are $350 still your due!"

I repudiated the implied contract and sent him a check for the $250 he had paid into the bank to my credit. This check he refused to present. Years afterward the bank wished to close the account, and the amount was used by me. It is the only profit I was ever conscious of making out of my connection with the Treasury. Instead of gaining any credit for not collecting the balance out of the poor clerk, I learned that I was regarded as a very foolish man who had neglected his opportunities.

CHAPTER XXVI.

THE DEATH OF ABRAHAM LINCOLN.

I ONCE thought that nothing could induce me to recall the events of the 16th of April, 1865. It was a day of national mourning such as the Republic never saw before, such as I devoutly hope it may never experience again. There was no doubt of its sincerity. A stranger would have said it was universal, for the few who did not participate in the general sorrow did not show themselves after an early hour in the morning. For there was a desperately savage element in the grief which pervaded all classes. The servants in the breakfast-room of a large New York hotel refused to take another order until the housekeeper was out of the hotel. She had said that "Old Lincoln had got what he deserved." At an early hour on Broadway a person had said "he was glad that Lincoln was out of the way." The crowd, by a common impulse, set upon him like ferocious animals. He was kicked, buffeted, and stripped almost naked before the police could rescue him. The same feeling seemed to pervade all classes—sorrow for the death of the President, a fierce thirst for vengeance upon his assassins, some fears for the future, and a general wish that the gloom of that day might speedily be replaced by brighter hopes and never again be recalled.

But time, which in the end makes all things even,

THE DEATH OF ABRAHAM LINCOLN. 237

will blunt the sharpest grief. When, recently, a highly valued lady friend placed at my disposal a letter written only one day later by the graceful pen of a veteran observer at the capital, I learned that I could read of our great President's taking-off without pain, and even with a kind of chastened pleasure. I have learned that a very general desire exists among the thoughtful of the generation born since the Civil War to read accounts of its incidents truthfully written by those who saw or participated in them. I am permitted to gratify this desire by the publication of Mr. Blair's letter, and I will add to it some recollections of my own.

Only the savage elements in our nature find their gratification in war. Probably there never was a war in which there were not in each of the contending nations or parties some who were wicked and reckless enough to be willing to employ against their adversary the secret skill of the poisoner and the knife and bullet of the assassin. But their judgment is grossly at fault who would impute to a people or a nation the responsibility for sporadic cases of this kind or for individual cases of cruelty. If threats of assassination had controlled their conduct many of our eminent men in civil as well as military life would have been hampered by a very constant restraint. But these threats, even when communicated by our representatives abroad, were but slightly regarded. It was scarcely possible to defend the President or members of his Cabinet against assassination. Therefore these threats were not noticed. Mr. Seward, to whom was attributed much of the wickedness of the Administration, rode almost daily in his open carriage. Very late at night, and many nights in succession, Secretaries Chase and Stanton were met on their way, on foot, from their official labors to their often sleepless pillows. The President walked or drove all about the city. It was only when he went out to live at the Soldiers' Home, when he knew the city swarmed with desperate men, that he could be persuaded to have a small escort of cavalrymen. We did not even then really believe that he was in danger. The threats against him were regarded as the idle vaporings of disordered brains.

We all knew that the war was approaching its end. The hope was dawning of a brighter future for the country. The members of the Cabinet were men of cold rather than sympathetic natures. They were appreciated and esteemed, but they were not loved. It was otherwise with the President. None who were near enough to be witnesses of his incessant labors, who knew how heavily his responsibilities bore upon him, could look upon the sad face of that earnest man without a wish for his happiness. Just then a great personal tenderness for him began to fill the hearts of the people. The colored race had no doubt of his supernatural character. To each of them he was a personal redeemer. He had given them freedom; he did not despise, he loved them. The personal affection of four or five million individuals, albeit of an inferior race, is a great possession. Its influence was extending over the white race. The pressure of the imperious duties of every hour was relaxing; we were having more time for reflection. We were beginning to know how great and how good a man our President was, and to reproach ourselves because we had not long before made the discovery.

THE DEATH OF ABRAHAM LINCOLN. 239

If he would gain even a moderate comprehension of the affection of the people for Abraham Lincoln and of the shock produced by the announcement of his death, the student of history must study his public addresses, from his departure from Springfield, and he should commit to memory his memorable words spoken upon the field of Gettysburg. He should pause over the weighty counsels of the second inaugural address. Its closing sentence will show in what a spirit the President addressed himself to his remaining duties. The student will not pass by the impromptu speech on the 17th of March on the presentation of a captured rebel flag, in which there was no note of triumph, but the thoughtful deduction that our "erring brethren," as he called them, had drawn upon the last of their resources when they asked the negro to fight for them, and we could now see that the end was at hand. Follow him on the 25th of March to the Army of the Potomac and his interview with Grant and Sherman at City Point; read his dispatches to Stanton on the last day of March and the first two days of April. They have no sound of conquest; they close with the message: "All seems well with us; everything is quiet just now." In the early dawn of the next morning he announces that "General Grant reports Petersburg evacuated, and he is confident that Richmond also is."

Follow him in his *incredible* entrance into the rebel capital on the day following its capture. Within sight of its spires, he asks the admiral of the war-ship if he will permit his sailors to gather the wild flowers which his young son has discovered on the river bank, "for the boy loves flowers." See him with his son leave the war-vessel with the admiral and row in the open boat a mile up to the landing. See his leisurely walk up the street to the house just left by the President of the Confederacy, now the headquarters of the Union commander. Multitudes of the emancipated crowd around and seek to touch the garments of their benefactor, as with streaming eyes they shout their thanksgivings. Truly, as he said, "it is a great thing to be responsible for the freedom of a race." Note the historic picture as he removes his hat and bows in silence to the old negro who exclaimed: "May de good Lord bless you, President Linkum." Truthfully did one write at the time: "That bow upset the forms, customs, and ceremonies of centuries. It was a death-shock to chivalry and a mortal wound to caste."

Let the student follow him when, with eyes of the loyal people upon him, he returns to the capital. He had endeared himself to the soldiers, to the whole people, by innumerable acts of kindness and love. Once only was his voice again heard in public. It was a speech of thanksgiving, of care for the captured, of justice to all. There was in it no exultation over the fallen. Then with what joy he dictated the order to stop drafting and recruiting, to curtail all war expenses, to remove all restrictions upon trade and commerce consistent with the public safety. Even then the student will have but a faint idea how the people loved their President in the hour when he fell.

I had left Washington on the afternoon of April 14th, not strong in body but rejoicing in spirit, for although neither rebel army had surrendered, we all knew that the end of the war was near. Washington was shadowing with the Stars and Stripes. I went to the Executive Mansion to take leave of the President. So many were waiting, the President seemed so much occupied with pressing business, that I came away without sending in my card. Salutes were being fired. A regiment, the term of service of which had expired, crowded the station. They were going home! They were like boys abandoned to the pleasures of the hour. I mingled with them, I heard their stories of the camp and the battle, shaded with tender memories of the fallen. There were crowds at the station and the sounds of saluting cannon. It was a happy contrast to the scenes at the same station four years before when I was on my way to Washington.

The Hoffman House, on Madison Square, had just been opened by the brothers Daniel D. and John P. Howard. There I met my family. Weary in body I retired to my apartments. I could not sleep. The excitement was too intense, too universal.

At an early hour, long before daylight the next morning as I lay awake in bed, I heard voices in the hall. "Revolution in Washington—the President murdered. They are killing everybody!" I bounded to my feet, hastily dressed, and, clearing three or four steps at a time, reached the office, which was already filled with an anxious and excited crowd. There was a bulletin board on which was written: "Murder of the President! Secretaries Seward and Stanton assassinated! Terrible excitement at Washington! The President dying!" too soon followed by the words, "The President is dead!"

The mind acts quickly under great pressure; mine leaped to the conclusion that we might have a day of bloody revolution. Counselling my family on no account to leave their rooms until I returned, I called a carriage and told the driver to take the back streets and drive to Pine Street as rapidly as possible. It was not yet daylight, and yet the open space on the west side of Madison Square was filled with excited people. We drove rapidly to the Assistant Treasury in Pine Street, which was not yet open. Here I dismissed my carriage and made my way on foot down William and across Wall Street to the Custom House. As I ascended the stone steps, forcing my way through the crowd, some one exclaimed: "He can tell us about Lincoln!" It was Prosper M. Wetmore. "Speech! Speech!" roared the crowd as I sought to make my way into the building. Then the thought flashed over me that I might say something which would allay the excitement. I turned and, standing on a narrow ledge of stone that formed the ledge or sill of a window, faced such a crowd as I have never since seen in Wall Street. Up to Broadway, down toward the ferry, filling William Street in front and Broad Street as far on my left as I could see, was a crowd of excited men, shouting, groaning, and demanding "Speech! Speech! Tell us about Lincoln! Lincoln!" Standing upon that very narrow space, where I was held in place by Mr. Wetmore and others, I spoke a few earnest words.

There was no introduction. I was unknown to most of the audience. "Who are you?" they shouted. "You may read his name on your greenbacks," exclaimed Wetmore, and in a moment busy Wall Street, with its twenty thousand spectators, was so silent that I sincerely believe my voice could have been heard at Broadway.

I would not record them if I could recall my

words. The thought which I endeavored to enforce was that the Confederates had no hand in the murder of their best friend—of the friend of a great people about to be reunited in a great Republic. "You will soon know that he fell by the hand of a madman," I exclaimed, just as some one at a window below me read out a dispatch that *Wilkes Booth* was the assassin.

Then a change swept over that multitude of men. They had been furiously, dangerously angry. They had charged their loss upon an enemy already crushed in the field. They were ready to fall upon the disloyal and tear them limb from limb. The knowledge that the public calamity was the act of a madman relieved them. A wave of grief swept over the crowd beneath which the very stones seemed to tremble with emotion. As rapidly as it had collected, the crowd melted away, and silence fell upon the theatre of speculation.

The following letter, written two days after the death of the President, throws a vivid flash-light upon the situation at the capital. It was written by Francis P. Blair, a veteran editor, observer, correspondent, and friend of the Union, and addressed to a lady whose graceful pen and sterling qualities have secured for her the warm friendship of so many of our public men. The kindness of Mrs. Cornelia W. Martin, of Auburn, N. Y., enables me to give this letter to the public:

WASHINGTON, Monday, April 17th, 1865.

My dear Friend:—Since your letter was received, our city has been transformed from the gayest and brightest to the gloomiest and saddest. All the houses were illuminated from within, and on all the walls and peaks without floated our flag rich in its color and stars, and for more than a week the salutes of cannon shook the air with glad tidings—when in an instant the pageant sank down and the lights were extinguished when the pistol-shot put an end to the life that had brought the peace and deliverance we were celebrating. A grand torch-light procession was actually marching, with banners flying, through the avenue at the very moment when the assassin struck his victim. The whole city stalked about in its gloom while the President was dying. His spirit fled as the morning dawned. My family would not wake me to witness this sad change of scene, although it was known to them; the military having surrounded my house at daylight, to protect its inmates from what was supposed to be the beginning of a sort of political St. Bartholomew. One of the assassins, who was to have killed the Vice-President, occupied the room adjoining his at the Kirkwood House, where he lodged after his return from Richmond. A card sent to him by Booth was carried by mistake to the Vice-President, who did not understand the admonition given by the principal to his accomplice until the tragic scene in the theatre explained it.

The message did not give the clew to the person to whom it was addressed, whose heart, it seems, failed him, and he left his room locked the night of the catastrophe; but his bowie-knife was found concealed in his bed the next morning. It is wonderful, but the man who stabbed Mr. Seward, his son and servant, though well known, has not been arrested.

The horse on which Booth fled has been found, but no clew to his rider. It is thought by many that he remains concealed in the city. Letters found in his trunk show that the scheme was long meditated and all the means for its execution and the escape of the actor well prepared. General Grant was expected to be with the President, and the knife that the murderer brandished was for him. I have this moment returned from an interview with General Grant. He showed me a dispatch just received from General Sherman, containing one from General Johnson, proposing a suspension of hostilities to arrange matters through General Grant, which, Sherman replies to Johnson, may be effected upon like terms as those arranged with Lee. So you see the "wild war" is over and gentle peace is returning. Grant, too, has just received a special from Wilson, commanding the army in which Andrew moves, confirming the rumor of his taking Selma, a great body of prisoners and of munitions, provisions, and the machinery which was established at that depot. Grant also told me that Hancock was on this very day compounding matters with the guerilla chief, Mosby. This is the fellow who has led all the raids into Maryland and to whom all the danger to me and mine at Silver Spring was attributable. His band of troopers could in two hours reach my house from their lurking-places near the fords of the Potomac. They could have taken me from my bed on any dark night and carried me off as a victim for any of their gang, and during the last four years I have had some secret intimations that they could avenge themselves if their will inclined them or any exigency prompted them to use such means. I am, dear madam, yours very cordially,

F. P. BLAIR.

P. S.—Mobile is taken.

CHAPTER XXVII.

SAVANNAH IN WINTER AND IN WAR.

SHERMAN had driven his army like a wedge of steel through the body of the Confederated States, from Nashville to Atlanta, from Atlanta to the sea. Hazen had stormed Fort McAllister. Hardee had evacuated and General Frank P. Blair had led the seventeenth army corps into the city of Savannah, and Sherman had made of that city, with its many thousand bales of cotton, a Christmas gift to the President of the Republic.

With this present came northward a wail of famine and of suffering. When Hardee with the Confederate army marched out of the city into the morasses of South Carolina, there followed him every wheeled vehicle drawn by every horse and mule, transporting the last barrel of pork and beef and flour and the last bushel of rice. He had left nothing for the subsistence of the people, and they were starving. So ran the report which was almost universally believed.

Straightway the people of New York City, without distinction of party, sect, or condition, forgot the firing upon Fort Sumter, the horrors of Andersonville, the almost four years of bloody war, and remembered only that the people of Savannah were Americans and that they were hungry. In a single morning a large committee was named by the Chamber of Commerce to receive contributions of provisions; the committee was organized, named a depot where supplies might be sent, and before nightfall there were contributed provisions enough to load a steamer, the owners of which made her charter their own contribution. She was loaded in the night and the next morning was ready to be cleared for Savannah.

Her clearance involved a difficulty. The War Department objected. "To exhaust the supplies of the enemy," said Secretary Stanton, "is one of the objects we are trying to accomplish; it is one of the most effectual means of making war. To feed him, or to feed the families of soldiers who are in the field fighting our own armies, would prolong the war and make us the butt of other nations. Why do you ask me to do what you would not do yourself in my place?" he demanded when at the request of friends in New York I asked him to permit the steamer to be cleared. "I will not do it. If the people of New York City want to feed anybody, let them send their gifts to the starving prisoners from the Andersonville stockade. They shall not with my consent send supplies to the rebels in the very State in which the enormities of that hell are perpetrated!"

I could not answer the Secretary and I wanted to accommodate my friends in New York. I was in a strait betwixt two, and I had learned what to do in such a situation. I went to the President and laid the case with Secretary Stanton's objections fairly before him. "Stanton is right," he said, "but the Georgians must not be left to starve, if some of them do starve our prisoners. However, I will not offend Stanton unless I can make something by the transaction. I will compromise. If you will go on the steamer and make a report upon the actual condition of the people, I will do better than Pharaoh did by the Israelites—I will let the steamer go."

I accepted the condition and the mission, went to New York the same evening, and as soon as the Custom House was open the next morning submitted the President's order, obtained the clearance, and by twelve o'clock the vessel was ready to sail.

The manifest of the steamer's cargo was not suggestive of famine nor even of destitution. It was midwinter, when fresh provisions could be transported without risk. The hold was filled to the deck-beams with barrels of flour, barrels and other packages of salted and canned beef, fish, and vegetables. Smoked hams and bacon were thrown into every crevice. Between the decks in close proximity were suspended on hooks the carcasses of fat beeves, calves, pigs, and sheep. All the staterooms unoccupied by the committee and the commissioner were crowded with layers of dressed turkeys, geese, ducks, and chickens. From manifestations after our arrival I was led to believe that there were fluids on board of higher proof than mineral waters.

The captain or skipper of the steamer was an original. He was a native of the eastern shore of New Jersey and was about fifty years of age. He stood six feet high, and carried a back and shoulders broad enough and a backbone stiff enough for two ordinary men. His face was intensely red—his hair bleached from dark brown to a straw color by long exposure. His whole life had been passed at sea. He had risen from boy-of-all-work on a coal-carrying schooner, through all the grades, to the command of a three-master, from which he had been transferred to a small steamer as mate, and had attained to the captaincy of the largest in a considerable fleet of coasting steamers.

He began by driving his passengers ashore to their homes after what he called decent winter clothing. "You are going around Hatteras in January," he said, "an' that ain't no summer excursion. I don't want to report you frozen to death on my hands. You had better put on all the flannels you've got in your chists, two or three pair of thick trowses, and as many coats. Clap an oilskin suit a-top of them, with a buffalo or a fur coat for real lively stirring weather, and you may be happy off Hatteras. Better to lose an hour now than to send you, frozen mummies, back to the bosoms of your families."

We were glad enough of the captain's foresight before we passed Sandy Hook. It was very cold in New York City and it grew colder every hour until we entered the mouth of the river at Fort Pickens. The red-heat of the coal-stove in the cabin was all absorbed by the circle of shivering landsmen gathered around it, while the captain danced and roared his orders above the howling of the wind in the very exuberance of his animal spirits.

The next day was one of uneventful cold. We were principally employed in keeping warm. At nightfall, when we retired to the seclusion of the cabin, the captain informed us that we were off the capes of Virginia. We passed the evening in games of whist and chess. About ten o'clock the captain rushed into the cabin exclaiming, "There's merry h—l to pay in-shore. I think it is another attack on Fort Fisher. I have half a mind to run in and see. It will not cost us more than four or five hours' delay."

We went on deck in a body, the captain not stopping until he reached the mast-head. He declared that he could see the flashes of the guns on the southern horizon; we could only hear a dull, heavy roar, now swelling and again falling, but never quite dying away. The flashes of the guns soon became visible from the decks, and in a couple of hours the whole magnificent spectacle was imprinted in flashes and curves of fire upon the southern sky. The curves of fire must have been made by the burning fuses of the shells, one of which occasionally burst in its transit, lighting up the whole scene. The fire from the ships was constant; we were not near enough to see whether it was answered from the fort. We pursued our voyage until the light fell below the horizon, for we had no knowledge how long the bombardment might continue. The dull roar of the guns was heard long after the lines of fire had disappeared.

The next morning we were off Cape Hatteras and the low sandy shore was no longer visible. Mighty seas overtaking us threatened to swamp our steamer, but a little in advance of the top of the wave her stern rose gently, the sea rolled under her, and rushed to break into masses of white foam over the shallow bottom that seemed directly in our course. Our captain said there was a channel very narrow and very crooked, and he was bound to follow it. Glass in hand he went up to the mast-head. From his perch he shouted his orders to the two men at the wheel, turning the bow of the vessel now this way, now that, always keeping it in the narrow space marked by the green unbroken wave. There he stood for three long hours, until our good ship was ploughing the unbroken sea; the white foam lay behind us, and we knew the danger was passed.

"You must know this coast well, captain, to be able to pilot your ship through that crooked channel," I said, as he came down to his post on the bridge.

"I reckon I ort to," he replied. "I've known her for more'n forty year. I know her bottom better'n I do her shore. Wake me in any watch and show me a bit of her bottom and I'll tell you whar we are!"

"Do you coasters take observations and ascertain your position by the science of navigation?" I asked.

"Sartin!" he replied. "I shall take the sun at twelve o'clock an' show you how it is done!"

He took his observation and proceeded to explain to us the whole science of navigation. His short legs as solid as two iron bars were planted well apart, sustaining his square figure with its big head and well-tanned face. Between the short, stubby thumb and finger of his big right hand he held a shorter and more stubby lead-pencil; in the other hand a well-worn copy of Blunt's "Coast Pilot." With some difficulty he found the margin of a page not already covered by the figures of a former example. "You git the sun," he said, "and then you set it down and go into the book and git the logarithm for to-day. And then you multiply and divide and subtract, and then you add fourteen more, and there you are. It's as simple as falling overboard."

"But why do you multiply and subtract and divide in this way?"

"Because them's the right figgers. It's all down here in the "Coast Pilot," all a-taunto!"

In short, he had not the slightest conception of the

reason of any part of the process. But I presume he would have navigated a ship to any part of the world in perfect safety, without any doubt whatever of his own power as a navigator.

Before the voyage was over our confidence in the capacity of our captain was settled. As we approached the mouth of the Savannah River he kept the lead going until we reached a point some miles off shore where there was not more than a half-fathom in excess of the steamer's draught of water. Here he anchored and set his signals for a pilot. No pilot came. He got out his chart of the river and harbor and spread it on the post of the windlass, and began to survey the shore and soliloquize. "It's risin' three year sence I was here last. The bottom hasn't changed, I reckon. But the derned rebs have put out every light, cut loose every buoy, and cut down every tree on the shore. What for did they bite off their own noses, I wonder? There used to be a live-oak on that point. You steered for the flag on Fort Pickens until that tree bore; then you opened another tree and steered straight for it until you laid your ship well into the river, opposite the fort. Now there ain't no tree nor no flag on Fort Pickens. Yes, there is, and they have just sent it up for some reason. It's our flag, too." Thus he went on until it became evident that he must lie on the bar all night or make his own way into the river.

He gave the order to raise the anchors and place one on either bow ready to be let go on the instant. A man was also placed on either side forward with orders to keep the lead going. He put the vessel under a low steam and she began to move slowly forward. Answering her helm quickly, she moved right, left, forward, stopped and backed at his command. Often there was not more than a foot of water under her keel. But before sunset he had worked his steamer safely into the river almost up to Fort Pickens, when he roared loud enough to be heard on shore:

"Let go them anchors!"

They dropped into the muddy bottom and brought up the steamer under her slow motion in one-third of her length.

"Look there and see what a d—d rebel can do," he said, pointing over the steamer's bow. We looked and saw nothing but a small spar one end of which appeared to be floating abreast of our vessel. He sent a boat with a line to take a turn around it and haul it on deck. Then we saw that its larger end was anchored at the bottom, while the smaller was shod with a steel point. It was then left, the smaller end to float with the tide ready to pierce the hull of any vessel which struck it. We did not wonder at the captain's indignation. If he had known how they had planted the river, the city would have had a seven years' famine before he would have risked his steamer to bring its people supplies.

Just at nightfall a very respectable colored man came on board, and a few minutes later an officer and boat's crew from the fort. The officer informed us that it would be impossible to ascend the river. The torpedoes were supposed to have been removed, but there was a dam of cribs of timber filled with stone a couple of miles below the city, which our engineers were removing and would have cleared out within a few days. Until that obstruction was removed no steamer could go up the river to the city.

The colored man, who was a fisherman, said he knew of a channel with a bottom of soft mud which entered the river above the obstruction, and through which he thought he could take the steamer in the daytime. We therefore lay at anchor all night and in the morning our colored pilot took command. He told the captain that there was not a rock, a snag, nor a bit of hard ground in the channel through which he would take us, so that the worst that could happen would be to stick the nose of the steamer into the mud until she was released by high water or a tug. He was as good as his word. He carried us through beds of reeds into places where the mud was level with the surface, but our headway was never entirely stopped, and we passed the dam, turned into the river, and under a good head of steam moved up alongside a wharf in the business part of the city. Our pilot wanted one of "dem turkeys," but his fees would not come to so much, and he thought he ought to have a dollar and a half in good money. We thought so too. He went ashore a very happy colored man, for he carried a market-basket heavy with a good cut of beef and a Rhode Island turkey, and one of Uncle Sam's golden eagles in his pocket. On the day of our arrival an opening was made through the dam broad enough for vessels to pass, and a fleet of steamers loaded with military supplies which had been waiting below came up to the city. One of the steamers, which came in that morning proudly bearing the British flag, carried a captain with a rueful countenance. He had his own pilot on board. He had run the blockade, his pilot had evaded all the torpedoes and steel-pointed spars, and finding an opening in the dam he had steamed up to the city and dropped his anchor between two vessels the commanders of which at sunrise hoisted the Stars and Stripes not only on their ships, but on his own.

The first call I made was upon General Sherman. He did not think there was much occasion for our expedition, but since our steamer had come he proposed to see to it that our provisions went to those who were truly in want and not to those who were able to pay for their own supplies, a proposal which met with my hearty co-operation.

* The chief of the commissary department of Sherman's army was an old acquaintance and a fellow-Vermonter. Colonel, afterward brevet Major-General, Amos Beckwith had a deceptive face. He looked much like a minister who had failed of success as a preacher and given himself up to idleness and regret. One would have said that he was a quiet, modest man who had no harm in him, who would have made a fair chaplain of a regiment in which there were no hard cases and of which no severe service was expected. In fact, he was a man full of resources, of tireless energy and tremendous force. He had fed Sherman's army under conditions which would have appalled ordinary men—which he himself could not have overcome if he had not been able to impart his own energy to many others. He hated cant and humbug. Lazy men were afraid of him. "Beckwith never requires any orders," said General Sherman. "Let him know where the army or any part of it will be at any time, and the supplies will be there. He is the only man I ever knew who always does the right thing at the right time. He thinks quick and acts quicker!"

Beckwith received me with cordiality, and, busy as I knew he was, pressed me to be seated and tell him all the news. I was about taking myself away, when a committee of the citizens of Savannah was announced and invited to enter.

"Your business, gentlemen?" was the colonel's crisp military demand.

The chairman, a dignified cotton factor, portly enough for a Dutch burgomaster, with many words expressed his high estimate of General Sherman and his staff, and his thanks for their preservation of life and property. He opened a river of speech that might have flowed on forever.

"Yes! Omit all that. Come to the point. You want something—what is it?" demanded the colonel.

The speaker began a long way from his conclusion. General Hardee was short of transportation; he had taken with him all the horses and mules when he evacuated the city; the negroes would no longer work unless they were paid in good Northern money —they would not touch Confederate notes. The United States had taken possession of the movable steam-engines used in discharging vessels. A steamer had just arrived from the North with provisions. It was necessary to discharge her cargo and cart it to the public market. Would Colonel Beckwith be so kind as to send a force of men and wagons to unload and transport this cargo?

There were premonitions of a convulsion before this speech was half delivered—they materialized with a crash as it ended.

"No! A hundred times no! You, traitors, taken red-handed, fighting against your flag, permitted to go at large when you ought to be hung or imprisoned —you asking that brave soldiers be sent to unload provisions contributed by charity to save you from starvation! What lazy, miserable curs slavery made of men! A few years more of it and you would have had a nigger to open your eyes in the morning and to work your jaws at breakfast. No. I'll see you d—d first, a thousand times, as you deserve. I may want that steamer any day. If by twelve tomorrow she is not unloaded I will discharge her and distribute her cargo to the families of men who are willing to work and not too lazy to live. I have a great mind to do it now. Now get out, all of you! This is a business office and no place for bummers!"

They left without ceremony. The colonel turned to me with an apologetic air. "D—n them!" he said. "I have respect for a fighting rebel, but for these lazy, cowardly curs—bah! They will complain of me to General Sherman. If you want amusement go over to his headquarters."

A member of his staff who was present took me into the quarters of General Sherman by a private entrance. In a few minutes the committee appeared. The chairman was eloquent over their wrongs; he wished to complain of Colonel Beckwith. They had asked him for a detail of men to unload a vessel, and he had abused and threatened them. They wanted him reprimanded and taught how to treat gentlemen in future.

"Are you quite certain that he threatened you? It is the first time I ever heard of a threat from Beckwith," said the general.

"He may not have threatened us personally. But he did say in his brutal language that if we did not unload that vessel d—d quick he would unload her and distribute her provisions himself. We ask you particularly to prevent that outrage, general!"

"Then you had better get to work on that cargo at once," said the general. "Beckwith seldom tells what he is going to do, but if he told you *that* he will do it without the slightest doubt."

"But you will at least reprimand him for insulting the committee?" insisted the chairman.

"There is some question about that," said the general. "Beckwith is the best commissary I ever knew. All through the campaign this army of mine has looked to Beckwith for its rations. He has never failed them. He has never interfered with my duties nor I with his, and we agree perfectly. Then before I could reprimand him I should have to know that I would not have said just what he did under the circumstances. Was it not a trifle cool of you to ask that men from my army be sent to work for you?"

"I see," said the chairman, "the heel of the conqueror is upon us. We must submit. It is useless to remonstrate!"

"I have no time to waste with you, gentlemen," said the general. "When you are able to appreciate the gentleness with which you have been treated by my army, you may come to me for advice, not for complaint. Until then you will not do better than to follow Beckwith's advice and go to work."

Two hours later a crowd of citizens were unloading the steamer. Twenty-five of them on a rope which passed through a snatch-block were marching forward and back to the song and chorus of a darky, whipping barrels out of the steamer's hold. She was discharged within twelve hours. Beckwith had got good work out of the citizens and their committee.

I sought every opportunity to converse with the

private soldiers in the city. There was a general appearance of rugged health and strength and of personal cleanliness which surprised me. I stood by a window in his headquarters when the division of General Geary began its northward march. Every man carried his gun, his forty rounds of ammunition, his shelter tent, and rations for five days. Each one had some articles which contributed to the common comfort, axes, bill-hooks, spades, gridirons, frying-pans with long handles. Yet with all this burden the soldier's step was elastic. Instead of slowly striding over a pool of water or an obstruction in the highway each line actually bounded over it, as I had seen sheep bound over a low fence in a hill-pasture. Geary himself was a general worthy of such a force. Over six feet high, his body straight and strong as the trunk of a forest ash, with the bravery of a lion, he was every inch a soldier.

"What a splendid body of men you command, general!" I said to him as the last regiment was passing.

"My friend!" he exclaimed, "I will tell you a short story. I crossed the Ohio River with that division when it numbered twelve thousand five hundred men. They were good, strong, brainy men from the city and country—no better average was ever enlisted. To-day there are present for duty only a few more than three thousand, and yet I think the fighting strength of the division was never greater than it is at this moment. Many good men have fallen upon many battle-fields, others have been sent home permanently disabled. Of the others, every one with a defect, physical or mental, has been sifted out. Those that remain are in perfect health, used to hard service, brave, disciplined soldiers, who have faith in their officers, believe themselves to be invincible, and are as nearly so as it is possible for men to be. Every man knows how to take care of himself. Halt the division for twenty minutes and each man will be eating his hard tack with a cup of hot coffee in his hand." His eyes sparkled as he said, "There is no reward for the soldier equal to the consciousness that he commands such men!"

Very soon afterward I learned what General Geary had in mind when he spoke of men who knew how to take care of themselves. I had spent the night in the upper part of the city. About eight o'clock in the morning as I was crossing Bull Street, a broad boulevard, on my way to the steamer, a large division of men had just entered the street and stacked their arms. They had been encamped on a rice-field from which the water was excluded by tide-gates. Some rebels hazing about in the night had destroyed these gates, and when the tide rose the field was flooded and the division had literally been "drowned out," some individuals saving their baggage with difficulty. Five hours later I visited the division by invitation. The boulevard had undergone a magical change. Unoccupied buildings had furnished the lumber. Four posts firmly set in the earth were closely boarded for about six feet from the ground. A ridge-pole was raised, over it shelter tents were stretched, forming a roof. From the bales on the dock cotton had been brought for the mattress, over which a blanket was stretched and pinned to the earth, and here was a dry, comfortable house and sleeping-room for six men. Kitchens and cook-rooms were provided for each squad, in which a hot dinner with the indispensable hot coffee was in the process of preparation. These men knew how to take care of themselves!

There was a sad procession of negroes in the rear of every division. The owners of plantations had abandoned the sick, the young, and the infirm, in many cases leaving them destitute. They had been told horrible stories—that the Yankees put the able men in front of every battle, that the old men, women, and children were thrown into the rivers or burned in the factories and storehouses.

But these stories produced no impression upon the colored race. They knew the Northern soldiers were their friends. They would follow them to the ends of the earth. An old white-headed man, his body crippled by neglect and hard work, said to me: "I don't speck to see the land of freedom, but I's gwine to follow dat flag ontwell I jest fall an' die in de road." I turn away from any farther description. The black followers seemed to me more numerous than the army. One of them, a white-haired man of eighty years, crippled and almost doubled by ill-treatment, said to me as he painfully limped after Geary's division, "I will follow it ontwell I drap. I is goin' north to de land of freedom."

There were tragic events caused by these ignorant colored people. "Will you come to my quarters, where I have to dispose of a case of some difficulty?" said a general of division to me one morning. We found lying there a man who was said to be a prisoner, a typical butternut-colored Georgia cracker, with his chest riddled with buckshot. A negro named Sampson, in chains, was seated near him, charged with his attempted murder.

It was a long time before I could get Sampson's confidence. He had decided that he would be hung and that it was useless for him to attempt any defence. I succeeded in convincing him that I was his friend and he finally gave way.

"Yes! He had shot the man," he said, but he was not a rebel prisoner. He was a Confederate who had changed his clothing with a prisoner, and who was to have two hundred gold dollars for killing General Geary. He had followed him for four successive days, he said, and had not interfered with him until he saw him with his Winchester fire at the general, who was passing on horseback. Then he dropped him. He would do it again if he had to die for it every time.

"Why do you keep so close a watch over General Geary?" I asked.

"Why, because he is one of President Linkum's men, God bless him, and he gave us our freedom," he responded. "I knew this fellow was trying to kill General Geary. If I could save the general's life I didn't care what became of mine. I watched him four days and nights. Four times he raised his gun to kill the general, and four times I was ready to send a buckshot cartridge through him. The last time he fired. So did I. If I have killed him and saved the general, all right. It's no matter about their hanging me." He was not hung; his fidelity to his deliverers proved to be a common affair.

One night I was sleeping in the house of a citizen. I was dreaming that Hardee and the rebel Wheeler had surrounded and were bombarding the city. I dressed myself and rushed into the street, intending to go to our steamer. Strong hands arrested and forced me back into the house. "Look," said an officer, pointing toward the western horizon, where the air seemed full of bursting shells.

"What is the matter?" I finally asked.

"The armory is on fire. There are 20,000 loaded shells in it. Every street near the armory has these shells buried in it, and they are connected with the armory by a fuse. These shells are exploding every minute. No one knows the arrangement; every one may take his chance in the destruction of the city now going on."

I shrank back partially under a porch and began to reflect upon the situation. The arsenal fronted upon a street only one block to the left, at the head of which stood my friend's residence. South of this line the air was filled with bursting shells. There was a lofty tower, to the top of which the water was carried by force pumps for distribution over the city. A shell opened the side of this tower almost at the top, and a great column of water rushed through the opening and descended in a curve to the ground.

But for the courage of Union soldiers, the whole city must have been destroyed. The fire department was cowardly and powerless. The soldiers formed a line around the blocks which seemed to be in danger. This line was contracted foot by foot until the area where the shells had been planted was defined. It proved to be the square on which the armory stood and two adjoining squares north of it. Water was abundant and these squares were speedily saturated with it. The illumination, and with it the alarm, was speedily suppressed. Now and then a solitary shell burst with a grumbling, discontented sound, but its particles fell upon the wet ground and were extinguished. In another hour the danger was over.

General Sherman named a military governor for the city, gave him a provost's guard of disabled men, and with his army commenced that magnificent march northward which terminated at the triumphal review in Washington in the following spring. Colonel Beckwith ordered our steamer into the service, as her powerful engines and small draught of water eminently fitted her for coast work. Upon my representation of the importance of making an early report to the President, he released the steamer and loaded her with compressed bales of Confederate cotton for New York City. Her captain was directed to coal her from schooners just arrived. The captain reported that there was less coal than slate in the fuel, and before we were out of the river announced that he could not get coal enough out of that stuff to keep the vessel off shore in a decent breeze. I therefore took the responsibility of ordering the steamer into Hatteras Inlet, where I knew there was a supply of fuel.

For three days I now laid aside all thoughts of the war and gave myself up to physical science. An immense school of porpoises was waiting for us just outside the bar of the Savannah River, and kept us company all the way to Hatteras Inlet. They seemed to get great enjoyment out of the trip. They had no difficulty in keeping pace with the steamer. Scores at a time shot out of the water in the form of a bow, turned a somersault in the air and all came to the surface of the water, headed northward. As far as we could see in every direction the sea was alive with porpoises. Two big fellows, one on each side of the stem of the vessel, not four inches below the surface, kept pace with the movement of the steamer. Lying upon the bowsprit I watched them for hours. I was not able to see that they changed their position relative to the vessel. I went to my stateroom for a Winchester rifle. As I walked forward to the bow my eye swept the horizon, and the whole surface of the sea appeared to be alive with porpoises. I sent a bullet into the body of one swimming at the vessel's bow. It must have passed through him, but he plunged downward at an angle of thirty-five degrees and disappeared. Again I swept the ocean with my eye, and not a porpoise was visible. Every one had disappeared and we did not see another on our homeward voyage. Why they disappeared, what the communication was which so promptly advised each of his danger, I leave to the reader's imagination.

The channel into Hatteras Inlet was very intricate, but our captain threaded it without difficulty. Two three-masted schooners which went ashore only a few months previously were now fifty yards inland and high above the water-level. The tide ran out with a strong current which the poor coal would scarcely make power enough in our steamer to overcome. After some time we got well inside the inlet and the steamer swung gently at her anchors.

Two companies of soldiers encamped at the inlet had made a seine not more than fifty feet long and some ten feet broad. They declined to fish for us, but offered us the use of their net. Two men held one end of it on the shore while two others walked out the length of the net into the swift tideway. They had no sooner straightened the net than the two men in the tideway exclaimed that they could not hold the net, while the soldiers shouted to them to bring the end ashore. They did so, describing a small half-circle, but when they hauled in the net it carried more than three barrels of fish, almost all of them being the young of the striped bass, about ten inches long. A more savory fish never came out of the sea.

With coal of a better quality we made better headway, and in due time were moored alongside the dock at the foot of Wall Street. We were not inclined to say much about our voyage. If there were starving people in Savannah we did not encounter them. The citizens we met were quite willing to accept our benefactions, but they seemed to think they were foraging on the enemy, and gave me the impression that they were still unreconstructed rebels.

Writing after so many years, two incidents of this mid-winter voyage are very fresh in my memory. One is the vigorous and stalwart carriage of "Sherman's men" and their faith in their general-in-chief. There was no trace of the braggart in their bearing or conversation. They did not appear to know or very much care whither they were going, so long as it was northward and in the direction of the Confederate army. They called their leader "the old man," but there was no trace of disrespect and much of affection in the term. "We are going," said one, "wherever the old man wants to go. He always takes the shortest route to the camp of the enemy." General Sherman, too, seemed very fond of moving about from corps to corps among his men. He could not always be identified, but he could be followed by the cheers which followed him everywhere. Whenever there was unusual activity and the disciplined cheers of thousands of strong voices, one usually saw a tall, sharp-eyed man, with long boots and a quick movement—that was Sherman. This army believed its general to be invincible, he believed that his men were unconquerable.

I saw none of the "bummers" which I had understood always followed the army. I did see men with fine horses who did not seem to be attached to any particular corps or divisions and whose movements were free and easy. They used to come riding into camp, almost buried under a very miscellaneous cargo, principally of an edible description.

The usual followers of the camp were replaced by the long procession of the colored, with their faces turned toward the land of freedom. It comprised all ages, from the white-haired old uncle or mammy of ninety years to the baby upon its mother's breast. It was very pathetic to see how they were treated by the soldiers and the teamsters. I heard no rough, I heard many kind words spoken to the pilgrims in these processions. The black faces of young children, the sad ones of their mothers, looked out from under the canvas of the army wagons, the mules in harness contentedly carried others, and many were assisted by the soldiers. These poor creatures had been abandoned to starvation and death in winter by those who claimed to be their owners. I thought, as I saw and conversed with them, of the words of Abraham Lincoln: "Slavery is wrong; slavery is unjust; slavery is cruel!"

The most thoughtful, conservative men whom I met on this journey were the colored clergymen. One of our generals had told me of an interview which had been held with these clergymen during a recent visit of Secretary Stanton, when the Secretary, General Sherman, and all the generals present had been surprised by the intelligence and good sense they had exhibited in discussing the complicated questions touching their own race which had to be immediately dealt with by the general of the army. My informant said that after the close of the interview the Secretary declared that the discussion of these subjects by a dozen of these clergymen would have been creditable and would have excited interest in a meeting of the Cabinet, and it gave him new hopes for the future of the colored race. The conduct of the colored people of Savannah, also, was most creditable. Sherman's army brought them freedom. If their joy had been manifested in some excesses, no one would have found fault with them. But they knew how to govern themselves. They were civil, respectful even, to their old masters. For the soldiers, or any who came with us from the North, they were quick to perform any service. They even consulted the military governor (if I rightly remember, it was General Getty [?]) before they decided that they would not work for the Southerners except under a promise of payment in good Northern money. One of the most extraordinary occurrences of the war was the manner in which the colored race received its freedom.

CHAPTER XXVIII.

TEACHING SCHOOL ON HOG ISLAND—ITS ADVANTAGES AND PLEASANT MEMORIES.

IF a census had been taken fifty years ago of the men who, unassisted, had successfully fought the battle of life, a large majority of them would have said that their first money was earned by teaching a district school. I have never happened to know one who did not remember his experiences as a teacher with pleasure, and as a very important part of his own education. To govern a school he had first to learn how to govern himself, and from the little men and women in whom he could not fail to become interested, he took his best lessons in the study of human nature. Teaching is less popular now, and the same necessity which existed in my boyhood is not so prevalent as it was then, and yet I should not hesitate to predict more successful lives for those who are teaching school this winter than for the more apparently fortunate ones who are devoting themselves to athletic or other sports on a liberal allowance from the fortunes of their ancestors.

An uncle who was a leading lawyer in Franklin County was kind enough not only to give me a place in his law office, but to take me into his family in the last half of my eighteenth year. He lived in the village of Swanton Falls, a community which, on account of its sympathy with the Canadians in the

Papineau rebellion and its resistance to the President's proclamation of neutrality, had acquired the name of "the Kingdom of Swanton."

Hog Island, a part of the township of Swanton, is a portion of land surrounded by the waters of Missisquoi Bay and River. Its divisions were the "North End" and the "South End." The "North End" comprised an extensive marsh, a part of which was covered with a first growth of pitch-pine and a very limited area of farming lands. It was inhabited by large families of the Honsingers, the Donaldsons, and the Carleys, great fishermen and mighty hunters of muskrats who disdained all such useless expenditures as for "skoolin," and no school had been maintained among them within the memory of man. The "South End," separated from the "mainland" by Maquam Bay, about two miles in width, was good agricultural land, occupied by a number of farmers, who were rough and unpolished, but good-hearted, excellent people with large families of children, for whose benefit they desired to maintain a school during the winter months of the year. The "North-enders" were litigious, and their numerous lawsuits before a justice of the peace against their neighbors of the "South End," which were defended by my uncle, had made me acquainted with most of the farmers on the southern part of the island.

One afternoon in November three of these farmers visited the office. I explained that my uncle was absent, when to my surprise they said that their business was with me. They were the "prudential committee," and wished to hire me to teach their district school. The term was three months; the master was to "board round," that is, he was to board with each family in proportion to its number of pupils; the wages were to be twelve dollars per month or thirty-six dollars for the term. They said the school was a small one, there were only about twenty scholars, and the district had voted that twelve dollars a month was all they could afford to pay.

I explained that I had had no experience in teaching, but if they thought I would suit them I would accept their terms. I then asked them why they had waited until the last week in November before engaging their teacher, and was informed that two teachers had opened the school already that season, but both had left, one at the close of the second, the other of the fourth day. The fact was, they said, that the large boys were a "leetle bit onruly;" they had smoked out the first teacher by climbing on the roof of the school-house and stopping up the chimney with pieces of turf. The second teacher they had stood on his head in a snow-drift; he was dissatisfied and left. The previous winter they had entirely broken up the school. Now the committee had determined to have a school, and if I would take the place, one of the committee would come to the school and "help me lick any boy who undertook to cut up any monkey shines. The boys had all been licked at home by their fathers," he said, "but it didn't seem to do no good. If they were licked every day at school the deviltry could be licked out ov 'em." They were greatly surprised when I told them that I should decline the assistance of the committee, that I did not believe in "licking," and if I taught the school it would be without assistance and without flogging.

We closed the contract, but the committee were all despondent. They did not believe I could keep the school a week unless the larger boys were "licked." One of them said that his own boy was about the worst of the lot—the very devil must be in him, for he had licked him until he was tired and it only seemed to make him worse.

Bright and early on the following Monday morning I was on hand. A roaring fire had warmed up the log school-house, and all the scholars were present to see the new master. The girls were bright and pleasant-faced, but four of the boys, each heavier and older than myself, looked very unpromising, and I saw at once that my trouble was to come from them.

I used the first two days in getting acquainted with my pupils, in pleasant conversation and dividing them into classes. For a day or two afterward all went smoothly. But on Thursday night one of the older girls said she wanted to speak to me after the school. After the other scholars had left, she told me that the boys had decided to send me home to Swanton the next (Friday) morning. Three of them were in the plot. One of the four said he liked the master; he believed he was "square" and he wouldn't try to drive him out. But he had agreed to stand neutral. Mart. Clark had undertaken alone to stand the master on his head in a snow-drift, and on the first trial the others were not to interfere. She had told them that she should tell the master; they had abused her and called her a tell-tale and said they would never speak to her again. But she didn't care; she thought it was real mean, and so she had told me. She hoped I would get a club and beat out their brains if they touched me.

I was the proprietor of a walnut ruler, two feet long, and one of its edges was bevelled. It was very heavy, and when in school I carried it constantly in my hand. The next morning the school was in a high state of expectation. It was nearly an hour before the champion appeared. He swaggered into the room to his place on one of the high seats which had a plank desk in front of it, and sat down with his cap on. I walked up to his seat and said in a pleasant tone, "Martin, take off your cap!"

"I shan't take off my cap for no Swanton Falls pettifogger!" was his emphatic reply.

A moment afterward his cap was sailing across the room, and still holding the ruler, I had seized his collar with both hands and drawn him out of his seat with such force that the bench in front was carried away and he sprawled over it on to the floor. He was on his feet in an instant and seized my collar with his right hand. His arm was extended, the large muscle strained to its utmost tension. That muscle I struck with the sharp edge of the ruler with all the force of my right arm. With a roar of pain like a wounded bull he relaxed his grasp and half fell to the floor.

"Goll darn ye! You have broke my arm!" he exclaimed, grasping the place where the blow fell, and limping about the room with a groan at every step. I let him groan for a short time, and then said:

"Your arm will feel better when it stops aching. Now I think you had better pick up your cap, go to your seat, and behave yourself. Don't you?"

He stood for a moment looking down upon the floor in a brown-study. Some idea seemed to be struggling into his mind. Then with the observation, "By Goll! I guess I had," he picked up his cap and went to his seat. I went on with my exercises. Soon a very subdued voice asked, "Master, can I speak to you alone?" "Certainly," I said, and called him to my desk. There in a whisper he said: "My arm hurts so that I can't study nor do nothing. I wish you would let me go home and bathe it with some liniment. If I stay till school is dismissed the boys will laugh at me."

I told him that he might go home, but first I wanted him to hear what I had to say to the boys. Turning to them I said: "Martin and I have settled this matter between us. Any boy that speaks to him about it will have me to settle with." To Martin I said: "Come down to Colonel Benjamin's, where I am boarding, and see me this evening."

He came to see me as I requested. In a few minutes I got his confidence and found that he had probably never had any one take any interest in him or speak to him kindly. His mother had died when he was an infant. I told him I had come there to teach that school. I was going to do it and I wanted him to help me. If he would, we would have no trouble with the other boys; he could make my work easy and I hoped to be able to teach him a great deal in the next three months. I told him not to make any promises then, but to think over what I had said to him.

The next morning he came early and said he didn't wish to make any promises, but I would see. And I did see. He became my warm friend. He always came and built the fire and had the school-house warm before my arrival. He told me that the boys had all decided that it was better to make me their friend than their enemy. But they could not understand why I didn't use the whip. Every teacher did that they had ever heard of; they expected it, and if they had not, they would not have thought of resisting me.

In that school I never struck another scholar. The larger boys were ready to do anything for me. They found that I wanted to go to Swanton every Saturday and to return on Monday morning. I had intended to skate two miles across the bay and then walk nearly two miles to Swanton. I was to return in the same manner. The boys arranged for one of them to take me home and another to come for me Monday mornings. Every Monday morning the team was at my uncle's door at daylight, having already been driven five miles from Hog Island.

The reader may think that "boarding round" was a hardship. It was anything but that. The best bed and the best room were for the master. The nice things they used to have cooked for him—the doughnuts, the sausages, the spare ribs roasted, the mince pies! their memory is fragrant. I would rather have them now than a dinner at Delmonico's.

There is one article of the Hog Island *menu* which I must perpetuate in history. In the months of October and November there is a fish caught off the Island called by the Islanders the white fish or the frost fish. I think it is a land-locked shad with its form and flavor modified by its new conditions. The Islanders select those which are in the best condition, dress and corn them. In the winter they cut a hole through the ice and sink the fish in the pure cold water and leave it there until it is freshened so that only just the suspicion of a saltish flavor remains. Then properly broiled with butter and pepper, it is a breakfast fit for a gentleman or the school-master, and too good for any but very honest men.

There was not another disagreeable incident in the school. I took a personal interest in every scholar, and if they did not learn it was no fault of mine. Every one of them grew up to be my friend. Poor Martin Clark became a sturdy, honest farmer and lost his life in a heroic and partially successful effort to save the lives of a party whose boat had been swamped in a storm. Many years later I met on Broadway a gentleman whose face wore a familiar look. "Come into my store," he said, and took me into a large establishment over which the sign bore his own name. "I know you," he said, "if you do not know me. I was one of your scholars on Hog Island."

I received my thirty-six dollars in new and crisp bank-notes with great satisfaction. It was almost the first money I earned, and I loaned it to my uncle at ten per cent interest. The first money I ever earned was my salary as clerk of a militia company. It was paid in an order on the treasury of the State for five dollars, which I promptly exchanged for Leverett's "Latin Lexicon," which now, after hard usage by two generations, stands upon a shelf in my library. Nor was this all the profit of my Island experience. In the following October the committee of the school district at Swanton Falls, hearing of the satisfaction I had given on the Island, offered me the position of teacher for four months, with board at the hotel and the munificent compensation of fifty dollars per month.

I accepted the offer, and I taught, or tried to teach, the school. At its close, in an exhibition to which the public was admitted, I received a vote of thanks and a beautifully engrossed certificate from the com-

TEACHING SCHOOL ON HOG ISLAND. 277

mittee attesting my success as a teacher and the satisfaction I had given to the district.

The reader will be able to estimate the measure of my actual success when I inform him or her that the average attendance of scholars was *above one hundred* and that I was supposed to be the only teacher. I am happy to say that the introduction of graded schools and a better system has since made education more practical. I appointed under me a number of subordinate teachers, who taught themselves by teaching others, and I thus secured enough time to be of some service to the rest of the school.

This winter's experience again was of great service to me, while it had no incidents of so striking a character as that with the ruler on Hog Island. It taught me self-control and economy of time, and it was the source afterward of many pleasant and some very sad thoughts. I heard from time to time of my Swanton scholars. There were two affectionate, excellent little white-headed boys. Their names were Elisha and Valentine Barney. The last time I saw them was when they received their prizes at my hands at the ages of about eight and ten years. When I next heard of them they were officers, bravely fighting for their country. One of them led his regiment of four hundred and forty-one men into the bloody Wilderness in the battle summer of 1864. The regiment never retreated, and when it again advanced *one hundred and ninety-six* of their number remained dead or wounded on the field. Among those wounded to death was their brave, loyal colonel, my scholar. His brother was another soldier with an excellent record who survived the war. Two ministers, a lawyer, two physicians, and two wholesale merchants were also in my school. I remember two sons of a Canadian Frenchman, on account of their intelligence. I believe their father bore the noted name of Richelieu. He was very poor, but he must have had a good wife, for the boys were known by their cleanly appearance and courteous manners. Within two years I met the agent in charge of the old and justly celebrated line of steamers on Lake Champlain. I had heard him spoken of by many as a business man of known integrity who had been a popular captain of one of the steamboats he now controlled. "I have long wished to see you," he said. "I was one of your scholars at Swanton Falls. My name is Rushlow." It was my bright little Canadian boy grown to be a business man of great ability and respected by all who knew him. His brother is a successful farmer in the West. Those who think I was not glad to meet the captain, and did not feel that I had done something toward directing him into the paths of integrity and success, I am sure have never taught a district school. I have, and I am proud of it. I should have been a better man if I had had more experience as a teacher.

CHAPTER XXIX.

The Book Chase—Non-Existence of Unique Copies — A Hunt for "Sanders' Indian Wars" and "The Contrast," the First American Play—Stolen Engravings and Drawings.

THE pleasures of the chase are almost coeval with the sinfulness of man. A great-grandson of Noah enjoyed them, for "he was a mighty hunter before the Lord." They are common to man without "reference to race, color, or previous condition of servitude." They may vary with climate and race, but from Eskimo to Tasmanian all men at some period of their lives are hunters. The game varies with time, place, and opportunity, but all living and some fossil animals of the air, the forest, and the ocean have been objects of the chase. Some *men* seem to have experienced a keen delight in hunting their own race. In the border to the rare map in the "Novus Orbis" of Grynæus, of 1555, engraved by Holbein, there is a picture of a party of these man-hunters. One leads a horse with two youths, their limbs trussed together, and thrown across the horse's back, in the manner of the Highland gillie with his pony carrying the stags which have fallen before the rifle of the deer-stalker; another is hanging the human limbs which he has carved, upon the projections of his hut. From latest advices something of this kind may be still going on in the heart of the "dark continent."

But we may turn from all the savage, cruel, and offensive pictures of the chase to a species of its diversions in which no butchered bird or animal is the quarry, but books and engravings are its nobler game. The chase of the well informed and equipped book-hunter has pleasures as keen, excitements as thrilling, moments as anxious, successes as gratifying, as any kind of sport, ever since Nimrod's time, practised or pursued by man. It is the object of the present article to sketch some of the requisites for success in this species of the chase and some of the dangerous pitfalls which constitute its chief obstructions. Nothing more than a sketch is proposed, for the limits of this chapter preclude any attempt at an exhaustive treatment of the subject.

The successful book-hunter, like the poet, must be born, he cannot be wholly made. He must have some natural qualifications which may be cultivated by education and matured by experience. He must learn to exercise and abide by his own judgment. If he does not he will be the subject of constant and cunning imposition. He must learn the haunts of his game, where it is not, as well as where it is to be found, for the earth is too broad to be hunted all over. He should not be discouraged by any number of failures. He should not begin the hunt until he knows that its object exists, but once started he should follow it with the scent of the bloodhound and the persistence of the beagle, if necessary, through a score of years, to final capture. The longer and more troublesome his pursuit, the more valuable will be his success when it is finally attaineed.

There are a few things upon which the experienced book-hunter will never waste any time. One of these is a *unique* copy of a book or a print. They have no existence. I do not say that such a thing is impossible, but I venture to assert that it is at the present time unknown. One or two copies of a book may have been printed upon vellum or on a peculiar paper, one or two impressions of a print may be taken from a plate which is then changed, but these are not unique in the book sense of the term. When the enthusiaistic maker of catalogues, after exhausting the vocabulary of such superlatives as "most excessive rarity," "of unheard-of scarcity," speaks of a copy as *unique*, he means that the book was published regularly, and that by use, destruction, or otherwise all the copies except the one in question, of the particular dimensions and edition, *have ceased to exist*. In this sense, while I know of a score of books which have been sold as unique, I know of none actually existing. I do not believe in unique copies, and I think the general experience of collectors justifies my incredulity.

"Made-up" copies are a continuing and increasing nuisance to the collector. The only satisfying object to his soul is the perfect book in its absolute integrity, untouched by the vandal knife of the binder, just as its signatures were assembled when they came from the press. A made-up copy, created by taking leaves from a half-dozen imperfect copies, with its defects mended by the pen or by the type of to-day, is a fraud. Such a thing of shreds and patches is like the patched garment which a gentleman, instead of wearing himself, would give to the first beggar. The imposition has reached enormous proportions and increases daily. It is but a few months since that I received from a German city a booksellers' catalogue which described *as perfect* the first edition of the "Heures" of Geoffroy Tory, a rare book, for which a full price was named. The booksellers were informed that if the book was all right I would buy it, but I would not purchase it without first collating it. They sent it to me. Its most interesting quality should have been a double or folded engraving called the "Angelic Salutation." At the first turning over the leaves I found this print *a modern counterfeit*, and the volume made up of not less than four imperfect copies. It was an impudent fraud, not admissible into a genuine collector's library, not worth a twentieth of the price demanded.

Without further generalization let me say that the actual incidents of the chase for books and prints are always the most instructive. I will proceed to describe some of my own experiences in this species of diversion. Many years ago I began to collect books relating to Vermont printed before 1850. In the early years of Vermont history a violent controversy existed with New York, which, as there was no newspaper in the State, was wholly carried on by pamphlets. They were nearly a score in number written by Ethan and Ira Allen and Stephen Roe Bradley. These had become excessively rare, and yet I never knew of one which I could not capture in a chase of a couple of years. My first real difficulty was in the hunt for a book printed in 1812 of the following title:

A HISTORY OF THE INDIAN WARS, ETC.
(*Written in Vermont*)
Montpelier, Vt. Published by Wright & Sibley, 1812.

This title stood high up in my list of *wants* for many years. I knew that such a book had been written and printed. Its author was the Rev. Daniel Sanders. It was a small duodecimo of about three hundred pages, in form closely resembling "Watts and Select" hymn book. There was a copy of it sold at the auction sale of the books of Mr. Fisher about 1866, where it was described as of "most excessive rarity," and brought an enormous price, some two hundred dollars. I had held this copy in my hands. There was no doubt whatever of its existence. But no second copy ever appeared in commerce. Why had a book published as late as 1812 become so rare that only one copy of it was known, which had already gained the reputation of a unique copy? Why should it be more scarce than even the Boston edition of "Hubbard's Indian Wars," with the genuine map, published in 1677, almost a century and a half earlier? Such a book must have a history which would give some account of its disappearance. I gave up the chase for the book and commenced a determined search for its history.

The booksellers, who knew upon what subjects I was collecting, frequently sent me books relating to Vermont, on approval. In a package sent by one of them I found two octavo volumes called "The Literary and Philosophical Repertory," published in numbers, issued at irregular intervals, the two volumes, of about five hundred pages each, covering the time from 1812 to 1818. It was "edited by a number of gentlemen" and printed at Middlebury, Vermont. There was no index, but upon a careful reading of its contents, at page 349 I found a review of "Sanders' Indian Wars" which put me upon the track of its history.

It is a mistake to suppose that the monthly magazine originated in the present century, or in any American city. As early as 1795, one was published in Rutland, Vt., as large as Scribner's, without its advertisements, and perhaps of equal literary merit. "The Literary and Philosophical Repertory" was another, the origin of which will be found in Vermont history. In the early part of the present century Burlington and Middlebury each established a college, which two institutions have ever since been maintained in a competition with which that between Harvard and Yale bears no comparison. Both colleges were orthodox. Their professors were scholars, ministers of strong intellectual powers, but the first and indispensable qualification of a professor or tutor in either was that he should be a disciple and follower of John Calvin. A candidate might be deficient in his mathematics, his literature, his languages, and his athletics; such defects could be supplied. But unless his theology was unexceptionable he was rejected. The other qualities related to the present state of man. His theology touched his future condition. If there was any flaw or defect in that, Satan would be sure to detect it and promptly take him into his camp.

Now 1812 was just about the time that Unitarianism was experiencing a revival, and the Rev. Daniel Sanders was a captive to it. Perhaps it would be more appropriate to say that he had caught the infection and had a slight attack of the disease, something like a man who takes the small-pox by inoculation. But it left some scars upon his mind, and these were more or less apparent in his literary productions. He had been appointed President of the University of Vermont at Burlington. How his Unitarian tendencies came to be passed over, we do not know. Shortly after his appointment he had written "The History of Indian Wars."

Mr. John Hough was a professor in Middlebury College. He was a Calvinist of the straightest sect. In his opinion a Unitarian—one who rejected the doctrine of the Trinity—was an awful man. He would have been a Good Samaritan to a criminal of any other kind, but he regarded a Unitarian as the enemy of the race—*hostis humani generis*.

Professor Hough wielded a very sharp pen. Carlyle himself could not have compressed into a literary criticism any more caustic contempt. Judged from his writings he must have had an analytical intellect and extraordinary felicity of expression. When, therefore, some enemy of the Rev. Daniel Sanders put it into his heart to write a "History of Indian Wars," print it, and send only four or five copies to his friends before the book was ready for sale, one of these copies, by accident, fell into the hands of Professor Hough; and the Rev. Daniel was undone. The Lord had delivered that Unitarian into orthodox hands. Professor Hough wrote a criticism of the book and published it in the number of "The Literary and Philosophical Repertory" for November, 1813. It occupies twenty-five octavo pages. He not only criticised the book, but he extinguished the literary aspirations of its author. It was indeed a cruel piece of work. He flayed the author alive, he bound him to the stake and burned him with a slow fire, he tortured him to his literary death. He gave him elementary instruction in grammar, rules for English composition. He showed that his facts were not true, that there was nothing new in the book except that which was false, as every one but the author knew. But the brilliancy of the criticism appears when the critic reaches the author's theology. He revelled in this part of his work; he speared the Rev. Daniel with his pen, and held him up to exhibition like an insect transfixed with a pin. He shot more arrows into him than St. Sebastian bears in his body. The criticism concluded in this language of excoriation: "This work then is adapted to create in the minds of the young, the uninformed, and the unwary, for on others it can have no influence, the most mischievous and unfounded associations. It is plainly suited to lead them to associate hypocrisy and corruption with the appearance of piety, and the most dire malignity with zeal for divine truth. The author richly merits the severest detestation of every individual who values public virtue, who reveres the religion of Christ and who prizes the eternal happiness of his fellow-man. That parent is lost to his duty, and regardless of those whom God has committed to his charge, who allows this history to be within reach of his children, to corrupt their principles, poison their minds, and lay the foundation of irreligion and guilt, of their misery and perdition."

Professor Hough decapitated the author, broke him on the wheel, crucified him head downward, pulverized him and scattered his dust to the winds. I know of no other piece of criticism in the language more fierce and effective. It is not to be wondered at that the author gave up without a struggle. He used every possible exertion to suppress the book, and honestly believed that he had committed every copy of it to the flames, including the four or five sent to his friends.

After this book had been on my list of wants for more than twenty years, in the year 1874 I was in attendance upon the Circuit Court of the United States, at Windsor, Vt. Windsor was the residence of Alden Spooner, the brother and successor of Judah Paddock Spooner, the first Vermont printer. While waiting for my case, I strolled into a book-store kept by an elderly gentleman named Merrifield. In answer to my inquiries about Alden Spooner, he informed me that Spooner was his ancestor, and that he now occupied the house in which Spooner formerly resided. He gave me leave to explore the garret of his house. It was neat and orderly, but literally filled with the clothing, furniture, and implements of past generations. At the very bottom of one of the numerous barrels which it contained I found a copy of a "Treatise on Prayer" by Nathaniel Niles, the author of the famous Sapphic ode, beginning,

"Why should vain mortals tremble at the sight of
Death and destruction in the field of battle?"

and also, *mirabile visu*, a perfect copy of "Sanders' Indian Wars." It was just as it came from the press, except that unfortunately it was not "*uncut*." I honestly told the old bookseller the story of the book, paid him a liberal price for it, and became its owner.

But rare books are like sorrows, they come "not single spies, but in battalions." The story of my "find" got into the newspapers. Very soon I began to receive letters announcing the existence of other copies. One turned up in the Vermont State Library; two others in as many different towns in Vermont; so that, although the author supposed every copy of the book was not only suppressed but actually destroyed, not less than six copies are now known to exist. I do not know that I ought to feel gratified, but I believe all these copies except my own and one other are *imperfect*. I must add that the finding of these copies has lowered the value of the first or Fisher copy, which had sold for over two hundred dollars. It has since been sold at auction for about one hundred dollars. And yet, if a perfect copy of "Sanders' Indian Wars" were now offered for sale at public auction, there are collectors by the score who would pay for it possibly the price of the Fisher copy and make a profitable investment by their purchase.

A Long Hunt for "The Contrast."

In the early days of my chase after books "relating to Vermont," I encountered many disappointments. Omitting the pursuit of the numerous pamphlets touching the controversy between New York and Vermont, relating to the New Hampshire grants, which are now worth more than their weight in silver, as shown by the prices paid for them at the Brinley sale, I will come at once to a legend which has ripened into a fact, in the history of the American theatre. The legend was that the first play written by an American author ever represented upon the American stage was written by a Vermonter, named Royal Tyler. He was known to have been a lawyer, a justice of the Vermont Supreme Court, a celebrated wit, a well-known contributor to the "Farmers' Museum," published at Walpole, N. H., by Isaiah Thomas. Tyler had made an accidental visit to New York City, where he had formed the acquaintance of Thomas Wignell, a leading comedian, who wished to introduce to the stage the character of Brother Jonathan. Judge Tyler had accordingly written the comedy of "The Contrast," in which Brother Jonathan was a principal character. It had been performed with great *éclat* in New York, Philadelphia, Baltimore, and Washington, to crowded houses. It was a part of the legend that the play, under the name of "The Contrast," had been printed and published in New York City about the year 1790.

A play with such a history, written by a Vermonter, would be a veritable *nugget* in the literature of the Green Mountain State. The title stood at the head of my list of "wants" for almost twice fifteen years. But the chase for it was never hopeful. No copy of it was ever discovered, nor any evidence, except the legend, that it had been printed. If it had ever been published, it must have been in a pamphlet form. Pamphlets are invariably short-lived. The respect which insures preservation cannot be secured without covers. Put covers upon any pamphlet and it becomes a book, to be protected against the waste-basket and the rag-bag; it secures the respect of the housewife and the servant, those peripatetic and most dangerous enemies of the treasures of the book-collector.

In the chase for "The Contrast," I had employed all the recognized means of getting upon the track of a rare book. I had patiently examined all the auction and sale catalogues for years. I had standing orders for "The Contrast" with all the booksellers. I had handled many, possibly hundreds of cords of the trash in Gowan's and other second-hand dealers, and the result had been *nil*. Not only had no copy of the play been discovered, but I had not found a particle of evidence that it had ever been printed.

The play could scarcely be a century old. If printed, its date could not have been earlier than 1790. Surely a book of a date so recent could not have wholly ceased to exist. I was finally forced to the conclusion that the legend was erroneous; that "The Contrast" had never been printed.

This decision of mine was published in some newspaper and came to the knowledge of a lineal descendant of Judge Tyler, a reputable citizen of Boston. To convince me of my error, he sent me one printed leaf of the play, comprising pages 45 and 46. At the top of each page was the title, "The Contrast." In the dialogue were the characters "Brother Jonathan" and "Jenny," and the former sang the song "Yankee Doodle." These pages settled the fact that the play had been printed. The printing was proved; the disappearance of the last printed copy I was compelled to regard as impossible to be accounted for by the rules which commonly determine the life of a book.

The wheels of time rolled on to the year 1876. I had given up all hope of "The Contrast;" the mystery continued unexplained and grew darker with age. One day I received a catalogue entitled "Washingtoniana, Books, rare plans and maps, a part of the library of General George Washington. Many of the books contain his autograph. To be sold in Philadelphia, on Tuesday afternoon, November 26th, 1876, by Thomas & Sons, auctioneers."

No. 35 of this catalogue contained this title, "The Contrast—A Comedy in Five Acts. Frontispiece, 8vo, morocco, Phila. 1790. Has autograph."

Was this the *Contrast* which I had hunted so long, or some other? It was printed in Philadelphia, the genuine was supposed to have been printed in New York. Yet the date 1790 was about correct. But why was it in the library of General George Washington? This was a very suspicious circumstance, after the forgery of his motto, *exitus acta probat*, and his book-plate, which had imposed upon so many collectors. But it was unsafe to attract attention to the title by correspondence. Slight as the chance was, I determined not to lose it. I employed a well-known bookseller and bibliopole of New York City to attend the sale, and, if this was the genuine Contrast, to buy it without limit of price. I was very confident that, after so long a chase, the genuine comedy was worth as much to me as to any other collector. I also gave him moderate bids upon Numbers 101 and 104, the folio volumes of maps, paged by the hand of General Washington, and as the catalogue stated, supposed to be the maps used by him during the Revolutionary War. These bids were given without any further investigation.

My order proved a success. It secured the genuine "Contrast," which was purchased for a few dollars, and my agent returned with it in his possession. Its inspection showed that it formed no exception to the rule that every *published* book appears in commerce once in fifteen years; for this play had never been published. It was printed for a list of subscribers, which appeared with the comedy. "The President of the United States," was the first subscriber. This copy had been bound in red and green morocco, tooled and ornamented in the highest style of the bibliopegistic art of the time, for General Washington, who then filled the exalted position of chief magistrate of the republic. The title-page was adorned by his well-known autograph. The volume now lies before me, perfect in every particular, with a frontispiece engraved by Maverick, one of our earliest engravers on metal, from a painting by Dunlap, containing the portraits *ad vivum* of Wignell as Brother Jonathan, Mrs. Morris as Charlotte, and three of the other principal characters in the play as represented. It would be difficult to imagine a volume possessing more elements of attraction to a collector than the first play written by an American, which created the stage character of Brother Jonathan, was once owned by the Father of his Country, who had written his own name upon the title, and which was withal of such excessive rarity.

One would suppose that a volume which had so long evaded the most exhaustive and comprehensive search would be properly called *unique*. And yet it was not. Collectors know that it is a rule to which exceptions seldom occur, that the discovery of one very rare volume is followed by the discovery of its duplicate. I was not therefore much surprised when, a few weeks after this volume came into my hands, I was informed by that careful and intelligent collector of portraits of actors and other material connected with the stage, Mr. Thomas J. McKee, that he, too, had just secured a copy of "The Contrast," at the end of a search which for length and thoroughness almost rivalled my own. He had secured it by the merest accident. A catalogue sent to him from some small English city, Bristol, I believe, contained its title priced at a few shillings. He ordered it, and in due course of mail received a copy of this rare and long-hunted play. From his copy "The Contrast" has recently been reprinted. That copy and the one above described are the only copies so far known of the original edition.

The first one hundred and thirty-eight numbers in the catalogue of the Philadelphia sale were books which unquestionably once formed a portion of the library of General Washington. Many of them contained notes in the careful chirography of their illustrious owner, in addition to his autograph. They had passed to a relative under the provisions of his will, whose descendant, the last owner of the collection, had been impoverished by the war, and compelled by his necessities to sell them. The larger folio of maps bears evidence of the regular, methodical, business habits of its former owner. It comprises over one hundred maps of North America and the West India Islands, with detailed plans of the defences of the principal cities. There are also many plans of battles, sieges, etc., four of Braddock's defeat, for example. Each of these was issued separately. To arrange them in their proper order for binding, was a work which required historical and geographical knowledge. It had been most carefully done by General Washington himself. He had paged every map in figures a half-inch in length so carefully outlined and then filled in with ink, that every figure appeared to have been engraved. Some of these maps are of great historical interest. No. 22, for instance, a map of the Province of New Hampshire, published as early as 1762, would have been very powerful, perhaps conclusive evidence, that in the controversy with New York concerning the New Hampshire grants, the right of the case was with the province last named. It extends the western boundary line of New Hampshire to Lake Champlain, instead of restricting it to the west bank of Connecticut River, as claimed by New York. According to this map, the governor of New Hampshire had the exclusive right to make grants of land within what are now the limits of Vermont, and New York had no jurisdiction over it. The crown officers would have been bound by it, since it was prepared for the use of the war department and dedicated to Charles Townsend, at that time the British secretary of war.

My agent represented to me that a gentleman who was then collecting "Washingtoniana" very much desired to possess the smaller collection of maps, catalogued as No. 104, and as I had secured the three "nuggets" of the sale, pressed me to permit this purchase to be transferred to his customer. To this I consented. The two folios were delivered to the agent, who sent the smaller to the collector. Not long afterward, the agent advertised for sale one of the most interesting memorials of Washington which existed. It was a detailed plan of the Mount Vernon estate, showing its division into large lots, the portions under cultivation, the forests, the residence and grounds, its location on the river, its gardens and orchards, meadows, pastures, fields, etc. The dimensions of each field and its area were given, and each of its qualities was described. The survey was made and the plan drawn by Washington, who was a practical surveyor, and the descriptions were written by his own hand. The price demanded was two hundred and fifty dollars, which was readily obtained. I was assured by the agent that this plan was found in the smaller folio which I had given up to his customer. But it was a little remarkable that its folds should have exactly corresponded with the dimensions of the larger folio which I have described, and not at all with the smaller which I had surrendered. This fact was one of those little things which have no explanation. I mention it to show that the experiences of the book chase are not all pleasures, but like the pursuit of larger game they are tempered by annoyances and disappointments.

Turning now from the unavailing search for "*uniquities*" which do not exist to *iniquities* which do, the conclusion of my experience as a collector is, never to purchase a rare book or print from a stranger. The collector will profit in the end who makes all his purchases through one of the reputable, established houses in the trade. These houses have an interest in dealing honorably with collectors and in protecting them from frauds and annoyances.

If a rare book or engraving is offered by a stranger it is safe to assume that there is some iniquity connected with it. Theft is the most common. Although no one can say why, it is still the fact that many frequenters of libraries and book-stores will carry away a rare volume or picture who would be horrified at the thought that they were thieves. It is not many years ago, when the fever for "Washingtoniana" was at its height, that the autograph letter written by General Washington to the Common Council of New York City, acknowledging the receipt of "the freedom of the city, in a gold box," appeared in the catalogue of an auction sale of books and autographs. This letter was a public document of the city. It could no more be sold or given away by authority than a volume of the public records. Yet it produced a fierce competition at the sale among a number of collectors, to one of whom it was struck off for twenty-five hundred dollars. The buyer bought the experience he deserved. He was sued in replevin by the city and compelled to surrender the letter. I believe he afterward recovered his money from the executor of the seller. He deserved to lose it, for it must have been as well known to every one connected with the sale that this letter was stolen property, as if it had been inscribed "stolen from the city."

In the following instance I volunteered to act in the interest of the owner. I shall not be much surprised if the publication of this article enables him to recover his property.

Some years ago a fresco painter of foreign birth was sent by his employer to do some work on the ceiling of my library. There were a few early etchings by Durer and Marc Antonio on the walls, with which the painter appeared to be singularly familiar. After mentioning some marks, not generally known, by which experienced collectors identify a print with the different stages of the plate, he observed that he had a portfolio of early etchings and original drawings which might interest me. Upon inquiring what they were, he made the apparently extravagant reply that the portfolio comprised original drawings by Martin Schoen, Durer, Cranach, Burgmaier, Marc Antonio, Raphael, Michael Angelo, Mantegna, and others of the early German and Italian schools, with early etchings of many of them. In answer to strong expressions of my incredulity, he said with some spirit that he knew an original from a copy; that the portfolio was at his home, a certain number in Bleecker Street, where, if I would call, his wife would show me the drawings and prints and I could satisfy myself of their authenticity.

I passed the place daily and could make the examination without inconvenience, or I should not have regarded the prospect of results as worth the trouble. I had not the slightest expectation of seeing one original he had named. I made the appointment and kept it. I found on the first floor a very small shop kept by the painter's wife, in which there was a stock of toys, cheap stationery, and newspapers, the whole value of which could not have amounted to two hundred dollars. They lived over the shop in two rooms cheaply furnished. I was taken to one of these by the painter, who unlocked a long, wide, but thin wooden box, and took from it a thick portfolio large enough for Marc Antonio's Massacre of the Innocents. Opening this he took from it and laid on the table and floor before my astonished eyes a most surprising collection.

It consisted of etchings, engravings, and drawings in pencil, ink, and sepia, by all the masters he had named and some others. They possessed every indication of genuineness. Some of the drawings were sketches for a larger work, others were half completed.

Two sketches I recognized as portions of M. Angelo's famous fresco of "Roman Soldiers Attacked while Bathing," conceded by Da Vinci to have been superior to his "Fight for the Standards." There were several by Raphael, some unmistakable Andrea Mantegna's, there were Durers, Cranachs, and Van Leydens. Of etchings there was a superb impression of Marc Antonio's "Massacre" with the fir tree; a fine copy of "The Crucifixion," the masterpiece of Lucas van Leyden; specimens of the "little masters" by the score. Without farther enumeration I may say generally that I thought then, and still believe, that the contents of that portfolio would have netted more than two thousand dollars at auction.

"Where did you get this collection?" I asked.

He answered without hesitation or confusion, that his father and grandfather had been fresco-painters like himself in Germany; that love of the arts was hereditary in his family; that his ancestors had been employed to repair many of the old monasteries on the walls of which many of these drawings and prints had been pasted; that the monks did not care for them and had given them to his father and grandfather, who had removed them with great care. He showed indications on some of the drawings that they had been so detached. In this way during three generations the collection had been made.

"But," I said, "here is a drawing by Rosa Bonheur, here are others by living English artists, which could have scarcely found their way on to the wall of ancient monasteries!"

These he said he had obtained by exchange with a collector in Belgium whose name he gave. He bore a sharp cross-examination well; he was prepared with a ready answer for every question. His familiarity with the history of engravers and of valuable prints rendered his answers appropriate. He pointed out several marks of identification of Durer's and Martin Schoen's which were new to me, and which I have not met with in any book; he knew more about some of the prints than I did, and I claim to be able to identify a genuine Durer by a very brief inspection.

At the close of the examination I selected four pieces: A head of Wohlgemuth in pencil with Durer's monogram and the date 1489, on the back of which was written in German the words "Portrait of M. Wohlgemuth, my art teacher. A. Duerer." This date I remembered was during the three years of Durer's apprenticeship to Wohlgemuth; the paper was hand-made, old, and bore the watermark of the elephant's head. The second was a pen drawing, half length, of Charles the Fifth by Cranach. It had no inscription, but there was no more mistaking the projecting chin and heavy jaws of the German ruler than the double shields and flying dragon of the artist. The easy grace of the lines of this drawing was marvellous, surpassing anything in Durer's illustrations of the Prayer-Book. The third was the head of a monk in crayon, marked "H. B., 1520." I was in some doubt about this, but it strongly resembled the work of Burgmaier. The fourth was a drawing of two young cattle in India ink, one animal standing, the other lying down. It bore no mark or monogram, but the lovely expression of the face and eyes of the female, and the splendid vigor of the male, unmistakably declared it to be the inimitable work of Rosa Bonheur. I had not the slightest doubt of the genuineness of either, except the one by Burgmaier. When I asked him how much money he wanted for the four pieces he turned toward me a face if not "like Niobe, all tears," it was at least equal to hers, in the grief of its expression. "Sell them!" What could have led me to imagine that he would sell them? They were an inheritance from a loved father, the light of his eyes, the joy of his life. Such priceless treasures were not for money. He would as soon sell his wife.

I restored the drawings to the portfolio and took

my leave, reflecting that here was a novel and extraordinary experience in the chase for prints. A journeyman painter, working for day wages, living in poverty over a small mean shop, with a collection of prints and drawings in his possession which could not be rivalled on the continent, which were worth thousands of dollars, and yet who would not part with one of them for money. Was this the expression of artistic love, or was it fear? My diagnosis was that this collection was associated with something undisclosed, probably with a crime.

For more than a year I heard nothing of this unique proprietor of artistic treasures. One evening toward the close of the year, a certain 24th of December, my door-bell was rung and I was informed that a man wished to see me who declined to give his name and for that reason was left standing in the hall. The gas was not yet lighted and in the gloom of approaching darkness I did not recognize him, but when he spoke I knew it was the fresco painter. He said he had brought something to show me. I invited him into a lighted room, where he laid a portfolio on the table, opened, took from it and spread out the four drawings I had selected, in the same condition as when I last saw them. He positively represented "the knight of the rueful countenance," as he told me of his errand. He had been working and saving for years, that he might at the coming Christmas make his wife a present of a savings-bank book with a certain sum to her credit. He could not quite make up the sum upon which he had set his heart. What should he do? Fail of his present or part with some of his heart treasures? Here was a divided duty, but rather than disappoint a faithful and hard-

DEALING WITH A FRAUD. 301

working wife he had decided to part with these drawings to one who would appreciate and preserve them. He had therefore brought them to me; he could not bargain about them. I could have them at my own price.

I mentally summed up the situation and the fellow's character thus: He was a first-class fraud; his whole story was false. He was selling stolen property, probably rifled from some foreign collection. Should I call a servant and order him kicked into the street; or should I offer him a small sum which the owner would willingly pay to redeem his property if he ever appeared?

I decided upon the latter course. I offered a sum so insignificant that I will not name it. He remonstrated like "Oliver asking for more," but I was flinty-hearted, although the sorrow of his parting from his treasures was almost enough to excite my compassion. But he took his money, left his drawings, and tore himself away.

Then the purchaser of the stolen goods had a short season of self-communion. Was he quite sure that he had not himself been sold? It would not be interesting to discover that the drawings themselves were frauds. He gave them a searching investigation, and, while every indication favored their genuineness, he placed them in a drawer, never to be shown until some unchallenged authority had attested their authenticity.

Before the new year, the police reports one morning disclosed a true case of desertion and destitution. A fellow whose wife had supported both, by keeping a small shop, while she lay sick in bed had sold out the shop, taken every cent of money from the clothing of his sick wife while she was sleeping, abandoned her in utter poverty, and absconded with a woman of no doubtful character, leaving his own creditors in the lurch. The wife had no relatives, for they were foreigners. She was starving. They lived at No. — Bleecker Street, and the name of the rascal was —— that of my fresco painter.

The wife was assisted by a small sum which the owner will have to pay if he redeems his property, and on my next visit to Paris the drawings were exbited to the experts in old drawings at the Louvre, who pronounced them all genuine. Rosa Bonheur solved all doubts of the drawing attributed to her by writing her artist autograph on its margin. The drawings were then framed and have ever since awaited the coming of their owners. As the leap of the boy from the sixth-story window uninjured was proved because the window "was still there!" so it may be said to any who question the foregoing account, "It is certainly true, for the drawings are there to prove it."

CHAPTER XXX.

SOME MEN WHOM I KNEW IN WASHINGTON DURING THE CIVIL WAR.

JAMES S. WADSWORTH.

IN an old note-book of 1864 I recently found this dispatch from Acquia Creek in May, 1864, the day of the month omitted:

"Wadsworth fell yesterday. He is in the hands of the enemy, either dead or mortally wounded."

I remember now the sharp pang of sorrow that went through my heart when this dispatch was laid on my table; for James S. Wadsworth was a *lovable* man, my model of the very best type of the citizen of a free republic. I first knew him in the Peace Conference. He was then in the prime of life, with a magnificent physique, an open, frank face, a kind heart, and a fearless soul. After our call upon President Buchanan, he regarded our mission in the Conference as ended. He said to James A. Seddon, of Virginia: "Why do you persist in your attempt to deceive the North? You secessionists mean *fight*! You will keep right on with your treasonable schemes until you either whip us or we discipline you. I shall stay here until Congress adjourns on the 3d of March, because I cannot honorably resign from the Conference. Then I shall go home and help my people to get ready for the war in which you slaveholders intend to involve the republic!"

After the Conference I heard no more of Wadsworth until, among the first of the seventy-five thousand, he appeared in Washington with a full regiment of his neighbors from the Genesee Valley. They came so promptly, it was said, because they were armed and clothed by Wadsworth himself. I met him frequently afterward, always busy in caring for his regiment. He was appointed military governor of the District. One day in November he called at the Register's office on business. He wore the common soldier's blue overcoat and cap; his heavy boots, worn outside of his trousers, had a rich covering of red Virginia mud, and no one would have suspected that he was the owner of half a county of the fertile lands of the Genesee Valley. He invited me to dine with him. He said the carriage road to the governor's residence was slightly out of repair, and he would send saddle-horses for myself and a few other guests. I accepted the invitation.

On the day appointed the horses came with two orderlies. They were splendid animals or they could not have carried us through that bottomless mud from the end of the Long Bridge to our destination. The governor's residence was just such a tent as ten thousand soldiers in the same camp were provided with, only it was of a larger size. Our dinner had just the same material and number of courses as the dinner of these soldiers. Even the moderate quantity of excellent "old Jamaica" on our table was furnished to any soldier who really needed it. I have eaten many dinners and been made very miserable by some of them, but the experiences and memories of that one were and still are delightful. It was not difficult to understand why Wadsworth (he was then a brigadier) was living among and upon the same fare as his soldiers. No Scotch retainers better loved their chieftain than these men loved their general, and they proved their affection afterward in the bloody Wilderness.

It was after dark in that November night when we returned to Washington. Our host persisted in escorting us home, where we arrived without accident. A civil officer of high rank, a member of our party, insisted that we should call at his residence. We did so, and there we drank a loving-cup with the man we called the "Prince of Genesee."

I saw him only once more. I will not describe the interview, for I do not wish to revive unpleasant memories. It was in my own private office, when he was furious with indignation because he believed ten thousand loyal men and true had been sacrificed to inordinate vanity and professional jealousy, an opinion then generally entertained, which some afterward changed, but which I shall carry to my grave.

I loved James S. Wadsworth. Here is what I wrote of him when he fell in May, 1864: "In the Peace Conference or in the world there was never a purer or a more unselfish patriot. Those of us who were associated with him politically had learned to love and respect him. His adversaries admired his unflinching devotion to his country and his manly frankness and candor. He was the type of a true American, able, unselfish, prudent, unambitious, and good. Other pens will do justice to his memory, but I thought as I heard the last account of him alive, as he lay within the rebel lines, his face wearing that serenity which grew more beautiful the nearer death approached, that the good and true men of the nation would prize their government more highly when they remembered that it could only be maintained by such sacrifices."

MAJOR DANIEL McCOOK.

"Come and take a walk with me," said Secretary Chase, one May afternoon, after our dinner at the Rugby House, where we both then lived. "The First Regiment of Ohio Volunteers is in camp on Fourteenth Street, and I am going out to see them." I accepted his invitation. We reached the camp just as the evening parade was going on. When it was over their colonel made a short military speech to the regiment, in which he told them very plainly the purpose for which they had entered the service of their country and what they must do to qualify themselves for that service. The speech made a profound impression on my mind, for it was my first instruction in the art and purpose of war from the standpoint of the soldier.

Governor Chase was then invited to say a few words to the regiment. He declined to destroy the influence of the excellent speech of the colonel by any observations, but said that after the regiment was dismissed he would like to take every man by the hand, and he did so. We were then introduced to the officers. The officer in command was *Colonel* now *Major-General, Alexander McDowell McCook*.

A few days afterward, in his own office, Secretary Chase introduced me to a citizen of Ohio whose name he said was Major Daniel McCook, the father of the colonel of the First Ohio Regiment. The Secretary was not in a good frame of mind that morning. In fact, it was the only time I remember ever to have seen him when his temper appeared to have escaped the control of his judgment. He had just been describing how some Ohio regiments under the command of General Schenck, on a reconnoitring expedition to Vienna, Va., had been fired upon by the rebels from *a masked battery*, five men killed, and a number wounded and missing. The Secretary held in his hand a six-pound shot. His tall frame shook with indignation as he exclaimed, "There! there is a cannon-ball actually fired from a rebel cannon upon an Ohio regiment bearing the flag of their country!" We soon became so much accustomed to battles that a skirmish like that at Vienna did not attract much attention, and I did not hear the term "masked battery" again used during the war.

I invited Major McCook to my office, and he often called there afterward. He was a tall, erect, fine-looking man, who said he "had some boys who were going into the service, at all events such of them as were old enough." He was sixty-three years old—too old to get into the service in the regular way, but as he was in good health and felt as young as ever, he had come on to Washington to "see what Uncle Abe and the governor [Chase] could do for him." He said that he "could work in the commissary or the quartermaster's departments or in the hospitals. Anyway, he could not stay at home when the country wanted men. He wanted to do something for the country."

Daniel McCook did do something for the country. In the retreat from the first Bull Run he was taking care of the wounded as a volunteer nurse. *Charles Morris*, his youngest son save one, a boy of eighteen, a private in the First Ohio, was with his regiment covering the retreat of the army. Passing a field hospital, he stopped to assist his father with the wounded while his regiment marched on. He was surrounded by rebel cavalry. He disabled the officer in command and with his musket and bayonet kept the others at bay. In answer to his father's call to surrender to such inevitable odds, he replied that he *would never surrender to a rebel!* They shot him dead before his father's eyes.

Latimer A., the eldest son of Major Daniel McCook, served as a surgeon with John A. Logan's regiment. He was in the Western army, was wounded before Vicksburg, marched to the sea, was again wounded at Pocotaligo Bridge, and died a few years after the war of his wounds and exposure.

George W., the second son, served and lost his health in the war with Mexico. He studied law with Edwin M. Stanton, was attorney-general of Ohio, a brigadier-general in the War of the Rebellion, an efficient organizer of Ohio troops, but on account of infirm health was unable to take the field.

John J. McCook, at the age of nineteen, in 1842 died a midshipman in the naval service of his country, of a fever, off the coast of South America.

Robert L. McCook, the fourth son, by brilliant service rose to the command of a division as major-general in 1862. He was foully murdered by guerillas near Salem, in Alabama, while following his division in an ambulance, in which he lay prostrated by dysentery and a severe wound.

Alexander McDowell McCook served with distinction throughout the war, in which he rose to the rank of major-general. He is now a major-general in the regular army.

MAJOR DANIEL McCOOK.   309

Daniel McCook, Junior, the sixth son, was colonel of the Fifty-second Ohio; commander of a brigade in Sheridan's division; led the assault on Kenesaw Mountain, where he was mortally wounded. He was promoted to the rank of general of brigade for gallant service, and died in July, 1864, at the age of thirty years.

Edwin S. McCook, the seventh son, educated at Annapolis; captain in Logan's Thirty-first Illinois; with Logan through the Chattanooga and Atlanta campaigns, and to the sea; three times wounded; a brigadier and brevet major-general; survived the war; was acting governor of Dakota, where, while presiding at a public meeting, he was slain by an assassin.

As already stated, *Charles Morris*, the eighth son, was killed at Bull Run. *John J. McCook*, the ninth son, when the bolt of treason fell was sixteen years old. He enlisted in the Sixth Ohio cavalry; first lieutenant on the staff of General Crittenden in September, 1862; served through the campaigns in the West and with Grant in the last Potomac campaign; captain in 1863; was promoted to lieutenant-colonel for gallant service. He is now a lawyer in New York City, where in the autumn of 1892 he led the charge of the Presbyterians against Professor Briggs and the New York Seminary. John ·J. and Alexander are the only survivors of the family.

Major Daniel McCook, the father of this extraordinary family, was mortally wounded in a fight with the rebel General John Morgan, on his raid into Ohio, in July, 1863. His wife, the mother of these boys, was Martha Latimer, daughter of Abraham Latimer, of Washington, Pa.

GUSTAVUS VASA FOX.

Captain G. V. Fox had a good head and a mathematical brain, which he put to excellent practical uses, on a short, compact figure. He had been an officer in the navy and captain of a Pacific Mail steamer, and in 1861 was the business manager of a large factory in New England. He was connected by marriage with Secretary Montgomery Blair, and first attracted the notice of the President by his common-sense views on the subject of the reinforcement of Fort Sumter, which were contrary to those of the Navy Department. It was too late to make the trial. But the President made him an Assistant Secretary of the Navy, where his influence was excellent throughout the war.

Captain Fox was highly esteemed and freely consulted by the President, I think because of his strong common sense and freedom from prejudice. He never expressed an opinion, or, as I should better say, he never formed an opinion upon a subject until he had reduced it to the form of a mathematical proposition and, so far as practicable, proved all its details. *Then* he had an opinion and he was able to impart it to others. But for Captain Fox the *Monitor* would certainly not have been built in time for the fight with the *Merrimac*, and every one may imagine for himself what the consequences would have been had the *Merrimac* dropped anchor at the Long Bridge and thrown her shells into the Capitol, the Executive Mansion, and the Treasury, firing at will. I saw the captain frequently while he was engaged upon the subject and in almost daily consultation with the President. Once he said: "The proposition cannot be formulated. I can demonstrate many of its elements.

The vessel can be constructed; there is no difficulty about her stability or her steering. The principle of the raft is all right. But how she will behave in action pounded by hundred-pound shells nobody can tell. It is an experiment and nothing but an experiment. But I think it should be tried unless some one can point out defects in the plans of Captain Ericsson which I cannot discover."

The strong will of Abraham Lincoln had to be exerted—it was exerted, and the experiment was tried under the very eye of Captain Fox. When he returned from the scene of the conflict he seemed to be a changed man. He knew about when the battle would take place, and he left Washington to see it with a very anxious face. When he returned the care-worn expression had given place to one of restful satisfaction, and there was no longer any objection to building *Monitors*.

A young man, or rather a boy, from the Atlantic fleet one day presented to Captain Fox a note from "Dave Porter," as the captain usually denominated Commodore D. D. Porter, the substance of which was, "Cushing thinks he can sink the *Albemarle* and wants to try. I believe he can, so I send him to you."

"I was taken aback by the boyish appearance of Cushing," said Captain Fox, "but Green on the *Monitor* and some other boys had been doing good work, and I decided to examine him. 'Why,' I asked, 'do you think you can sink the rebel ram?'"

"'She is surrounded by a boom of logs about a hundred yards distant,' he said. 'I know that logs with the bark off, that have laid for a year in one of the Southern rivers, are covered with a slime which is very slippery. As the principal difficulty is to get at the *Albemarle*, I went up one night and examined the boom. The logs are so slippery that a boat with a keel of the proper shape will ride over them easily. I can get at her with a suitable boat.'

"'But how will you carry your torpedo?' I asked.

"'This way,' he replied, producing a small card on which he had drawn an ordinary cat-boat with a mast near the bow. He had hinged a spar to the bow which carried the torpedo on its end. When not in use this spar was drawn up so that it stood upright in contact with the mast. When ready to be used, the spar was lowered and the torpedo was to be exploded by a lanyard attached to the trigger of the lock."

"Don't you think it will require a cool man to go through that complicated performance?" asked the captain.

"Yes," he said. "A man must be cool to do anything worth doing. I think I can do it if I can get a boat."

"How do you expect to escape? The enemy will make the shore as light as day and hundreds of men will be firing upon you."

"I don't think I can tell beforehand what I will do. I propose to blow up the ram. We must take our chances of escape when the time comes. It may be best to jump overboard and swim for it. I have got a crew picked out and we are willing to take our chances."

The boy had worked out the problem, with the result that the chances were in favor of success. Captain Fox gave him an order on the navy-yard at Chester to have two boats built under his direction. He found two boats there which would answer the purpose. One was captured by the rebels, the other arrived safely in the river. How Cushing sunk the *Albemarle* and how he escaped he has himself told us, and the story is of such interest that I leave the reader to enjoy it and will not repeat any part of it here.

After the war the ram *Dunderberg* was sold to Russia. Captain Fox proposed to take her to the Baltic, and our Government made him the bearer of its congratulations to the new emperor. I asked the captain whether the voyage would not be one of danger.

"Not at all," he replied. "It will be much more comfortable than a voyage on an ocean steamer in midsummer. Instead of rising, falling, pitching, and rolling with the seas, the seas will quietly roll over the *Dunderberg* and the vessel will rest quietly on an even keel. Such a vessel is a raft that cannot be swamped." He offered to demonstrate the fact by tables of figures which were as inexplicable to me as the higher mathematics.

As he told me afterward, experience proved the correctness of his figures. He had a most comfortable voyage, and delivered the vessel to Russia, where he was received and entertained with all the honors.

Captain Fox took a leisurely journey through India and China. He was satisfied there was some good reason underlying the Chinese policy of the exclusion of foreigners. He believed he had ascertained that reason. It interested me as he gave it on his return, and as I have not seen it elsewhere, I repeat it on the chance that it may interest others.

In the interior provinces of China, he said, the adjustment of production to consumption was so close that in an average season the soil and the waters would just support the population. Not only was there no surplus, but every ounce of fertilizing material had to be saved, every superficial foot of soil be forced to yield its largest possible product, and the whole must be used with the most rigid economy.

He had actually seen in real life the original of the picture in our early school geographies, "A Chinese selling rats and puppies for pies." If by drought, tempest, or any other cause the crops were diminished, famine was inevitable. Famines were frequent and the deaths by starvation numbered inconceivable thousands. Any invasion of foreigners disturbed existing conditions and tended to increase the demand for and lessen the supply of food. The authorities therefore opposed foreigners as they did every other disturbing cause.

There were few officers connected with the Government during the war more intelligent, I am sure there were none more highly esteemed by the President, than Captain Fox. I do not know whether it was his habit to make notes. If it was, his note-books must contain a mine of valuable historical material.

BENJAMIN WADE.

Republicans never quite forgave Mr. Wade for his opposition to the renomination of Mr. Lincoln and the manifesto which he afterward signed with Henry Winter Davis. It will seem incredible to the present generation that General Fremont should have accepted a nomination which Mr. Chase refused, and then have had the assurance to write that if the Baltimore Convention nominated any one but Mr. Lincoln, he would not stand in the way; but if Mr. Lincoln was renominated "it would be fatal to the country to indorse a policy and renew a power which has cost us the lives of thousands of men and *needlessly* put the country on the road to bankruptcy." The nomination of General Fremont fell upon the country so dead that he probably had no friend who did not deeply regret that it had been made.

Ben Wade was a bluff, outspoken, earnest Republican who once happened to go wrong. I could forgive him for his error when I heard his exultation over the nomination of Governor Chase for chief justice. "In the early winter of 1861," he said, "when Chief Justice Taney was ill, I used to pray daily and earnestly that his life might be preserved until the inauguration of President Lincoln, who would appoint a Republican chief justice, but when I saw how complete his recovery was and how his life was prolonged, *I began to fear that I had overdone the business!*"

In this connection I must refer to what, though not intended for such a purpose, was a stroke of policy which would have excited the admiration of Richelieu. Upon the failure of the Fremont movement the restless element undertook to bring forward General Grant. They called a meeting in New York nominally to express the national gratitude to him, really to bring him out as a candidate, and supposed they made the incident cutting to the President by sending him an invitation to the meeting. Mr. Lincoln replied that he could not attend, but he wrote that he approved of "whatever might strengthen General Grant and the noble armies under his direction. . . .

He and his brave soldiers are now in the midst of their great trial, *and I trust that at your meeting you will so shape your good words that they may turn to men and guns moving to his and their support!*" This letter crushed the movement, though General Grant peremptorily refused to be made a candidate and reiterated the President's appeal for aid and support.

LINCOLN AS A WOOD-CHOPPER.

The President one day witnessed a singular scene from the Potomac front of the Treasury. The Virginia hills were covered with an original forest of noble chestnuts and other deciduous trees. They began to fall as if a resistless wave had swept over them, all in one direction, many acres of them at a time. To one who did not understand the cause it was almost frightful, and suggested an earthquake. As was not unusual, a colored messenger had brought the first information that the Sixth Maine, a regiment of lumbermen, would attack the forest on that day. They cut the trees until they were almost ready to fall, and then selecting those on the outside which would fall in the same direction, felled them at the same moment. As they struck the trees nearest them those also fell, and the whole forest went down like a row of bricks standing on end. A Treasury officer explained that the scene was the work of the Maine wood-choppers.

"I don't believe," said the President, "that there is a man in that regiment with longer arms than mine or who can swing an axe better than I can. By jings! I should like to change works with one of them. Sometimes I think that a private could run the engine better than I do! I would like to see all the soldiers in the rebel armies falling like those trees! and then I would like to see them all rise up as loyal men and stand upon their feet!" If this expression was blood-thirsty, it was the worst which I heard from his lips during the war.

FRANCIS E. SPINNER.

One of the best men in the civil service of the United States was the Treasurer, Francis E. Spinner. He was not a *many-sided* man. He had only one, his loyal side, which was so thick that it went clear through him. He was free and outspoken in his opinions. He sometimes used adjectives which were more emphatic and appropriate than they were select. I never regarded his expressions as at all profane.

One day he entered the Register's office very abruptly. He was literally furious. He threw a newspaper cutting upon my desk. "Read that," he exclaimed, "and see to what depths of infamy a Northern copperhead can descend. If the scoundrel who wrote that don't broil hereafter, it will be because the devil hasn't got enough hot iron to make a gridiron."

The article stated that Jeff. Davis was paid his salary in Confederate money, which was so depreciated that his twenty-five thousand was only worth fifteen hundred dollars, which was all he had to live on, but Lincoln would not take greenbacks because they were depreciated, and collected his twenty-five thousand a year in gold or gold certificates, while the soldiers had to accept greenbacks at a discount of more than fifty per cent!

The Treasurer wished me to have a statement made of the amounts shown by my books to have been paid Mr. Lincoln on account of salary. He was about to make a statement from his books, and he wished to publish my statement with his. I objected that we should dignify the scandal by noticing it, but he said he was getting letters every day inquiring about it and they made him sick. He could not kill the rascal, for he wrote anonymously, and we must therefore step on his lie.

Of course there was not a shadow of truth in the statement. The President's salary, like all others, was paid monthly by sending him a draft on the Treasury for the amount, deducting the internal revenue tax. These drafts he had not collected, but had left the money in the Treasury without interest until the loss of interest amounted, according to my recollection, to some five thousand dollars. The libel did operate to the profit of the President. His friends got from him written authority and afterward invested such amounts of his salary as he did not use in bonds of the United States bought at current rates in the open market.

This grand old man, Treasurer Spinner, died about two years ago. He was a long and patient sufferer from a painful disease which destroyed his eyesight long before his death. One of the choicest memorabilia in my possession is what I believe to be the last letter written by his own honest hand.

A TREASURY AUDITOR OF THE ANTIQUE PATTERN.

One of the auditors, a "hold-over" from some former administration, one day wished to read me an opinion which he had just completed. Evidently he was very proud of it, and I consented to listen to it at a considerable loss of time.

When it was decided that Captain Fox should attempt to reinforce Major Anderson in Fort Sumter, the commissary or quartermaster in New York had been ordered to purchase and load the vessel with supplies. That officer, aware that Major Anderson and his men had been living for a long time on very ancient army rations, had upon his own motion sent them some canned vegetables and fresh meats, small quantities of tobacco, cigars, and fluids that came in bottles, preserved fruits, and such other delicacies as he could think of; these extra articles amounting in all to some four or five hundred dollars. He had paid and claimed a credit for them in his monthly account upon which this auditor had to pass before the credits were allowed.

The first half of the opinion, which was thirty foolscap pages in length, was a lecture to the officer upon the necessity of conforming to the regulations and the imminent danger of departing from them. Each credit was then considered *in extenso*, with the final result that all the items were disallowed. After reading the opinion he asked what I thought of it.

"Have you any copies of the document?" I asked.

"No." But he intended to have copies made.

"Any memoranda or notes of it?"

"No." He had prepared it at his residence. He had written it off-hand and had made no notes.

"Are you quite certain that you have left no scraps of paper, no pencil-marks, nothing which could be associated or connected with the document?"

"I am," he said. "But why are you so particular about notes or memoranda?"

"Because," I said, "if I were in your place I should be very much ashamed of that document. I should put it into the nearest fire and watch it until it was consumed to the last word or period. I should be sure that I had picked up and destroyed every scrap of writing connected with it. I should then wash my hands thoroughly and pray the Almighty to forgive me the sin of writing it. Then I should have some hope of sleeping with a clear conscience."

Soon after he left my office. He never showed me another opinion. I thought from his appearance that he was not pleased with my criticisms. However, some months afterward it occurred to me to send to my files room for the account of the officer in New York for April, 1861. It was one containing the objectionable credits, and I was pleased to see that not one of them was disallowed.

ADAM GUROWSKI.

Among the many singular characters developed by the war in Washington, the most extraordinary, *me judice*, was Adam Gurowski. He was employed as a translator in the State Department. No one knew anything about his early history. He was supposed to be a Pole who had been obliged to leave Europe on account of his revolutionary proclivities. He spoke of crowned heads as familiar acquaintances, and claimed that he had taught Louis Napoleon and Cavour how to conspire. He was an amusing and interesting person, thoroughly truthful, but his judgment was so warped by prejudice as to be unreliable. He had an amazing facility for making acquaintances and discovering secrets, and wielded a trenchant pen. He hated slavery. I think in the course of the war he praised and blamed every man of any prominence on our side in the military and civil service. I find these notes of his which I preserved on account of their structure:

"The old brave warrior Scott watched at the door of the Union; his shadow made the infamous rats tremble and crawl off, and so Scott transmitted to Lincoln what could be saved during the treachery of Buchanan."

"Seward, Sumner, and the rest fear that Europe will recognize the secesh. I know there is no danger and I tell them so. Europe recognizes *faits accomplis*, and a great deal of blood will run before secesh becomes *un fait accompli*."

"April, 1861. *Consummatum est*. The crime in full blast; Sumter bombarded. Now the administration is startled; so is the brave old North. The President calls on the country for 75,000 men; telegram has spoken; they rise, they arm, they come. The excitement, the wrath, is terrible. Party lines burn, dissolved by excitement. Now the people is in fusion as bronze; if Lincoln and the leaders have mettle, they can cast such arms, moral, material, and legislative, as will at once destroy this rebellion."

Gurowski at the outset judged correctly of the length and magnitude of the struggle. In April, 1861, he wrote: "This war—war it will be and a terrible one, notwithstanding all the prophecies of Mr. Seward to the contrary—this war will generate new necessities and new formulas, it will bring forth new social, physical, and moral creations; so we are in the period of gestation. But democracy will not be destroyed; but destroyed will be the most infamous oligarchy ever known in history; oligarchy issued neither from the sword, nor the gown, nor the shop, but wombed, generated, cemented, and sustained by the traffic in man."

Was it not remarkable that this foreigner, whose views were so extreme that some called him crazy, should have judged the coming contest more accurately than the best American statesmen?

On the 6th of October, 1861, Gurowski saw and passed his judgment upon McClellan. "My enthusiasm for him," he wrote, "my faith is wholly extinct. It made me sick at heart to hear him, and to think that he is to decide over the destinies and blood of a free people. And he already an idol, incensed, worshipped before he has done anything whatever. He may have courage, so has almost every animal, but he has not the decision and the courage of a military leader and a captain."

On the 9th of November, 1862, he wrote: "Great and holy day! McClellan gone overboard. Better late than never. But this belated act of justice cannot atone for all the deadly disasters caused by this horrible vampire."

In July, 1863, when President Lincoln was pressing the pursuit of the rebel army, Gurowski wrote: "Lee retreats toward the Potomac. If they let him recross there, our shame is nameless." On the 16th he said: "Lee recrossed the Potomac! Thundering storms, rising waters, and about 150,000 men at his heels! Our brave soldiers again baffled, almost dishonored by know-nothing generalship. We have lost the occasion to crush three-fourths of the rebellion!"

"In that fated, cursed council of war which allowed Lee to escape, *my patriot Wadsworth* was the most decided, the most outspoken in favor of attacking Lee. Wadsworth never fails when honor and patriotism are to be sustained."

Does any critic ask why I have quoted these notes of Gurowski? It is because he did not hesitate to say what the masses of the American people thought, what their leaders knew but had not the courage to declare.

PERLEY P. PITKIN, A VOLUNTEER QUARTERMASTER.

It was at Montpelier, in the early fifties, during my first term in the State Senate, that a very long and awkward Vermonter came to my rooms and, introducing himself, consulted me about some act which seriously affected the town he represented. Had I judged by his apparel and appearance, I should have pronounced him *green*, but before the first interview was over I had discovered that he had a "heap of common sense," and knew perfectly what he did not want as well as what he wanted. I liked him, and though I have entirely forgotten what he wanted, I have no doubt, upon general principles, that I assisted him to the best of my ability.

In the autumn of 1861 he appeared one evening at my house in Washington, in uniform, accompanied by his son, a lad of some ten years. He had no business, he said; he called on me because I had assisted him once and he might have to call on me again. He then told me that he was quartermaster of the Second Vermont Regiment, which was then in camp, under Colonel Whiting, back of the ancient city of Alexandria, near Monson's Hill. He volunteered the statement that he didn't know much about the "regulations," but he expected to learn, and if he got into trouble he might want me to help him out —which, of course, I promised to do.

My next information about Quartermaster Pitkin was that he expected to be arrested on a charge of *stealing a steamboat* which was in the government service on the Potomac. Lieutenant-Colonel Stannard, who was afterward heard from at Gettysburg, gave me the facts, and said the regiment intended to stand by their quartermaster. Pitkin had just returned from Vermont with the horses which he had purchased for the mounted officers of the regiment, and had them in a stable in the outskirts of Alexandria. One night there was an alarm, the long roll was beaten, and the word went through the regiment that the terrible Mosby with his uncounted guerillas was about to pounce on the camp. Pitkin summoned his men, rushed his horses down to the dock and on board a steamboat which he found there, with steam up, waiting to carry some messenger to Washington. Being in uniform the engineer readily obeyed his orders to start the engine; some one went to the wheel, the boat was cast off and began to turn into the river, when the officer who was waiting for his dispatches succeeded in leaping on board and in great wrath wished to know what he was doing with his steamboat.

Pitkin replied that he "was taking a lot of the best horses in the country to a safe place where the rebels would not get them."

"But you have no right to take my boat! You are violating the regulations! You are liable to be courtmartialled and shot. Bring that boat back to the dock or I will complain of you and have you arrested. You will certainly be shot if you disobey."

"Oh! that's all right," coolly remarked the quartermaster. "They can shoot me if they want to, but *Mosby can't have them hosses!*"

Mosby did not get "them hosses." It turned out to be a false alarm, and being satisfied on that score, Pitkin ordered the steamboat back to the dock and surrendered possession to the legitimate officer. He was not court-martialled.

Pitkin came to my house several times, always accompanied by his son. Some time in the spring of Grant's battle summer of 1864, I saw that he wore the undress uniform of a colonel. I asked him about his promotion, to which he made some indefinite reply that he knew about wagons, and Grant had put him in charge of the army-wagon train. He did not tell me, what I learned later, that the army-wagon train consisted of *four thousand wagons*, and that his energy and ability had gained for him as high a position in the esteem of General Grant as General Amos Beckwith, another Green Mountain boy, had in that of General Sherman.

A surgeon brought my next report of Quartermaster Pitkin. It came just after Grant's continuous fighting for a week in the Wilderness, when that dreadful procession of ambulances, filled with the wounded, moved continuously for three days from the Sixth Street wharf to the hills north of Washington, never halting except to take in and discharge their helpless passengers. The wounded were brought to Belle Plain, on the Rappahannock, whence they were sent by steamers to Washington. All the steamers obtainable were making their trips as rapidly as possible, and yet so great was the multitude that thousands of wounded and dying men were lying in the fields, without shelter, awaiting their turn. Grant knew who the man was who would soonest get that suffering crowd into the hospitals, and he sent him from his other important duties to this indispensable one.

While these transfers were being made with all the energy possible to human hands, a fine, swift steamer came down from Washington. It was General Butler's dispatch-boat, with an officer on board carrying dispatches to the general. He had gone on his mission. Finding the steamboat at the wharf, Pitkin ordered his men to carry the wounded on board. The officer in charge stormed, raved, and threatened dire things if General Butler's boat was interfered with.

"Do you propose to have this boat do nothing for two days, with our men dying in the fields, when in that time she can make four trips to Washington?" demanded Pitkin.

The officer declared that he had nothing to do with the wounded. His orders were to lie at the dock until the messenger returned, and no man would move the boat except by his orders.

Pitkin called a sergeant and a file of men. "If that man," he said, pointing to the young officer, "attempts to interfere with the transfer of the wounded, you will put him under arrest and remove him!"

Then Pitkin went about his business. The steamboat made four trips to Washington before the return of the messenger, and when she carried him to the capital she carried another load of the wounded.

The young officer whose self-esteem had suffered in the transaction made complaint; a court of inquiry was ordered, which recommended that Pitkin should be tried by court-martial upon serious charges and specifications. These were prepared and submitted to General Grant for his approval. Nothing was heard from them for some time, and the young officer made inquiry of General Grant whether his attention had been called to them. The general replied that he had considered the case, and had decided that he would postpone its further consideration until *after the close of the war.*

Late in November, 1864, the governor of Vermont insisted that Pitkin must return to take the important office of quartermaster-general of the State, to which he had been unanimously elected by the legislature. Greatly to General Grant's regret Pitkin obeyed his governor and resigned his office. He held the new office to which he had been elected for the six following years and then declined a re-election. He was not tried by court-martial.

CHAPTER XXXI.

LAW AS A PROGRESSIVE SCIENCE—IS PROGRESS ALWAYS AN ADVANCE?—CIRCUMSTANTIAL EVIDENCE—THE BOORN CASE.

THE law is progressive. Progress is an element of all true science—very desirable when it is in the direction of an advance. It should be the care of the bar as well as the courts to see to it that the law does not experience what is sometimes called *apocatastasis*, or progress backward.

Recent occurrences, including decisions of courts once of high authority, have called this subject to the attention of thoughtful members of the bar. I will not name them further than to say that they suggest the possibility of securing, through evidence wholly circumstantial, a conviction for crimes which have not been committed. The danger arises from accepting circumstantial evidence of the *corpus delicti;* of the fact that a crime was committed as well as of the guilt of the person charged; and the violation of another *canon* of criminal evidence that circumstances consistent with any possible hypothesis of innocence are not admissible to prove guilt.

An incident which occurred when I was a student illustrates the caution of the courts of that time in accepting proof of the *corpus delicti*. A man was indicted in Franklin County, Vt., for the murder of his wife and child by drowning. In crossing a pond or lake in a leaky boat, the boat sank, the prisoner got ashore, but his wife and child were drowned. The rural community promptly decided that they were murdered. The necessary proof was supplied by *a dream*. Some neighbor dreamed that the shawls and detachable clothing of the victims had been concealed by the prisoner in a certain hollow tree, where they were found. As they must have been concealed by the prisoner, the fact was accepted as proof of his guilt.

The husband was indicted by the grand jury for murder. He was inadequately defended by a young attorney, and when the evidence of the dream was offered, *Benjamin H. Smalley*, who was sitting within the bar, volunteered to argue the objection to its admission. The Smalleys were a fearless race. It was another member of the family, *David A.*, who as judge of the Circuit Court of the United States, sitting in New York, convicted a wretch and caused him to be hung for piracy; and early in the spring of 1861, in a charge to the grand jury in the same city, defined the crime of treason in words that delighted loyal men and chilled the blood in the hearts of those who supposed they could commit the crime with impunity.

It must have been a powerful argument made on the spur of the moment which made such an impression upon the mind of a student that it has not been effaced by the lapse of forty years. The point of it was that neither the proof offered nor any that had been given was satisfactory evidence that a murder had been committed; and that the proof on that point must be positive and leave no doubt whatever of the fact of the crime. He cited as a precedent one of the most interesting cases which ever occurred, and on its force the evidence offered was excluded. Evidence of the prisoner's admissions secured his conviction, but his insanity rapidly developed and he died soon after the verdict.

The case cited by Mr. Smalley is known in Vermont as "the *Boorn case.*" The pamphlets in which it was reported are so scarce and the case is so instructive that I will give its substance.

In the year 1812 there resided in the town of Manchester, Vt., the two brothers Stephen and Jesse Boorn, and near them Russel Colvin, who had married their sister. All were in humble circumstances and supported their families by labor. All were of very ordinary capacity; Colvin a man of weak intellect, who was at times deranged. His family increased, his ability to maintain them diminished, and the obligation of supporting his wife and children in part fell upon the Boorns. This necessity led to bickerings and altercations, which became frequent and sometimes led to assaults upon the unfortunate Colvin. Two or three times he had disappeared, leaving his family to be wholly supported by the Boorns, but he had returned after absences, the longest of about nine months.

In May, 1812, Colvin again disappeared. Months and then years elapsed and he did not return. There were suspicions that he had met with foul play. Remarks were made by Stephen and Jesse Boorn which led the neighbors to believe that they were in some way connected with his disappearance.

Nearly seven years had passed after Colvin's last disappearance, when another member of the Boorn family, an uncle of Stephen and Jesse, *had a dream.*

In his dream Colvin came to his bedside and told him that he had been murdered; that if he would follow him he would lead him to the spot where his body was buried. This dream was repeated the conventional *three times*, and the place where the body was deposited was pointed out. It was a hole about four feet square, originally made for burying potatoes, on the site where a house had formerly stood; the hole having since been filled up. This pit was opened. It yielded a large jack-knife, a smaller one, and a button. Before they were shown to her, Mrs. Colvin described them minutely; and as soon as she saw them, declared that the large knife and the button belonged to her husband.

A marvellous circumstance then transpired. A lad with a spaniel dog, walking near the house of the father of the Boorns, observed a decaying stump, to which the dog endeavored to draw his attention by whining and running several times from the stump to his master. The dog then with his paws dug from beneath the stump a cluster of bones. Further investigation disclosed in the hollow cavity of the same stump two toe-nails which were supposed once to have been attached to a human foot. The doctors decided that the bones were human, though one of them thought otherwise.

About four years previously an amputated leg had been buried a few miles away. This was exhumed as a standard of comparison, when it was unanimously decided that the bones were not human. But it was concluded that the toe-nails were, and as the bones were somewhat broken, it was sagely decided that the body had been burned and the bones, not being consumed, had been cast into the stump, other bones being deposited with them for purposes of deception. It was then remembered that after Colvin's disappearance a barn belonging to the father of the Boorns had been accidentally consumed by fire. About the same time the Boorns had burned a log-heap in the vicinity. It was conjectured that the body, originally buried under the log-heap, had been then placed under the barn and there partially consumed.

Before these discoveries were made the rural community had almost unanimously decided that a murder had been perpetrated. It also transpired that on the day of Colvin's disappearance he had had a quarrel with the Boorns which might have ended in his murder. But as the evidence was wholly circumstantial it was determined to dismiss Jesse Boorn, who had been arrested, from any further examination. The inquiry had been adjourned from the 27th of April to the 1st day of May. In the mean time the search was continued and the discoveries adverted to had been made. Jesse was on the very point of being discharged, when with a trembling voice he said that "the first time he suspected that his brother Stephen had murdered Colvin was last winter, when Stephen told him that there had been a quarrel between himself and Colvin, and Colvin attempted to run away; that he struck him with a club or a stone on the back of his neck or head, which had fractured his skull and he supposed he was dead; that he could not tell what became of the body."

Stephen had removed to Lewis County, N. Y., a distance of nearly two hundred miles. An officer and two neighbors set out from Manchester, and, assisted by the people of Lewis County, surrounded the house of the supposed murderer, arrested him, put him in irons, tore him from his distressed family, and carried him to Manchester. He stoutly asserted his innocence and declared that he knew nothing about the murder of his brother-in-law. The prisoners were kept apart for a time, but finally were put into the same cell. Stephen denied the statements of Jesse with indignation. The examination was continued for many days. Every item of evidence was exaggerated and new facts were adduced. A son of Colvin testified that he saw his uncle Stephen knock his father down, when he was frightened and ran away. Jesse retracted his former statements and denied that Stephen ever told him that he had killed Colvin. But the community was of opinion that both prisoners were guilty, and they were committed for trial on the charge of murder, to be tried in the following September.

The prisoners were indicted by the grand jury, but the trial was deferred until the 26th of October. Stephen had maintained his innocence in the most solemn and impressive terms. In the long delay of the trial the people of the vicinity had free access to the prisoners, who were subjected to the influences which not infrequently control the opinions of the public. Belief in their guilt was universal. Every succeeding visitor advised them to confess as the only means of saving their lives. Good men knelt with them and prayed the Lord to lead them to confession; men in a little brief authority promised them the weight of their influence if they would confess. The black shadow of the gallows was ever before their eyes, only to be removed by confession. The rattle of their chains seemed to voice confession, the walls of their cells appeared to echo back the sound; even hope itself seemed bound up in the single word *confession!*

It was not strange that the weak minds of these inferior men lost their power of resistance and finally yielded. On the 27th of August Stephen called for pen, ink, and paper and in his cell wrote and signed his "confession." The miserable falsehood is before me. It is unnecessary to copy it in detail. Still, some of its expressions so clearly show the inexplicable workings of the mind that they ought to be presented. They had an altercation; Stephen called Colvin a little Tory. Colvin struck at him "with a piece of beech limb about two feet long." Stephen "caught it out of Colvin's hand, struck him a backhanded blow—there was a knot in it one inch long, which went in on the great cord on the back of Colvin's neck, close by the hair, broke off, and he fell." When he found Colvin was dead he put him in the corner of the fence by the cellar hole and put briars over him; in the night he dug a grave with a hoe, put him into it, covered him up and went home, crying. Long afterward he took up the bones and buried them under the stable floor of his father's barn. The next day the barn was burned. He went there, gathered up the few bones, and threw them into the river. There were a few little things that he gathered up and dropped into the hollow stump and kicked the dirt over them. "All these things I acknowledge before the world."

The trial came on in an excited community. The prisoners pleaded *not guilty.* Separate trials were denied them. Both repudiated their confessions and solemnly asserted that the admissions were extorted from their fears. An audience of six hundred people watched the trial. Every trifling circumstance was given in evidence, and as its substance had reached the jury, the prisoner's counsel permitted the written confession to be read. There could be but one result in such an excitement. Both prisoners were convicted of the crime of *murder*, and were sentenced "*to be hung by the neck until they were dead*" on the 28th of the following January.

The legislature was then in session at Montpelier, the State capital. Some of the good citizens of Manchester presented the petitions of the condemned prisoners for the commutation of the death-sentences to imprisonment for life. They were willing that the sentence of Jesse should be mitigated, but for Stephen they had no mercy. The legislature commuted the sentence of Jesse, but, by a vote of 97 against 42, left Stephen to the mercies of the hangman.

And hung he would have been but for an accident which should have covered that whole community with mortification. For many years there had been settled over a white congregation at West Rutland a colored clergyman, the Rev. Lemuel Haynes. From a very low origin in Connecticut, he had by his own exertions obtained an education, studied for the ministry, and become somewhat celebrated for his ability and fidelity in his Master's service. He had preached a sermon on "universal salvation," in answer to one by the Rev. Eli Ballou, which it was said had been oftener republished than any English book except the immortal allegory of John Bunyan. He had resigned his charge at West Rutland on account of his advanced age and come to Manchester to reside. But he had not ceased to visit the prisoner and comfort the mourner. He visited the jail in Manchester, saw

Jesse Boorn take his farewell of his brother and of his own family and depart to the State prison, there to spend the remainder of his life. He read the Scriptures to and prayed with the brother left to die. He insisted that the convict should be permitted to have a candle and other comforts. Here is what the venerable man wrote of him: "He said: 'Mr. Haynes, I see no way but I must die; everything works against me; but I am an innocent man; this you will know when I am dead. What will become of my poor wife and children?' I told him God would take care of them. He said: 'I don't want to die. If they would let me live even here some longer, perhaps something would happen which would convince the people of my innocence.' I was about to leave the prison when he asked, 'Will you pray with me?' He rose with heavy chains on his hands and legs, being chained down to the floor, and stood on his feet while I prayed."

And this good minister said to himself, "This poor creature may be an innocent man. I will try an experiment." In the next issue of the Rutland *Herald*, the nearest newspaper, appeared this advertisement:

"MURDER! Printers of newspapers throughout the United States are desired to publish that Stephen Boorn is sentenced to be executed for the murder of Russel Colvin, who has been absent about seven years. Any person who can give information of the said Colvin may save the life of an innocent man by making immediate communication. Colvin is about five feet five inches high, light complexion, light-colored hair, blue eyes, about forty years of age.

"MANCHESTER, VT., November 26th, 1819."

The minister was a poor man. He was sharply ridiculed for his folly in spending his money upon so

THE BOORN CASE. 337

foolish an advertisement. But he had not long to wait for his reward. The New York *Evening Post* published the advertisement as an item of interest on the 5th of December. On the 6th of December *Taber Chadwick*, a citizen of Shrewsbury, Monmouth Co., N. J., informed the editor of that paper *that the murdered Colvin was then living in that town*, weak in mind but in good bodily health. The *Post* published Mr. Chadwick's letter, and the information it comprised was not long in reaching the community which was so fierce in the punishment of crime that it had come very near taking the life of an innocent man. Even then many insisted that the story was a hoax which would end in the ridicule of the too confiding colored minister. One Whelpley, formerly of Manchester, but then of New York, who knew Colvin, went to New Jersey in quest of him. He returned and wrote to Manchester that "he had Colvin with him." Another acquaintance wrote to Manchester, "While I am writing Russel Colvin is before me." Even then the good people of Manchester were incredulous and laid wagers that the report was a deception.

But on the 22d of December, when the stage arrived at Bennington, where the court was in session, Mr. Whelpley was one of its passengers *and Russel Colvin was another*. The court suspended its session to look upon one who in a sense had been dead and was alive again. Colvin recognized and called several acquaintances by name.

"Toward evening," continues the narrative of the good minister, "Colvin reached Manchester. The cry was raised 'Colvin has come!' The stage was driven swiftly, and a signal given. All was bustle and confusion. The stage stopped at Captain Black's Inn. The village was all alive; all were running for the sight of the man whom all believed to be dead. The prison doors were unbolted and the news announced to Stephen that Colvin had come. The chains on his arms were taken off while those on his legs remained, so impatient was he to meet the one who came to bring him life. Colvin gazed upon the chains and asked, 'What is that for, Stephen?' The latter answered, 'Because they say I murdered you.' Russel replied, 'You never hurt me!'"

There is no occasion for pursuing the narrative of the excellent clergyman. I regard it as one of the most interesting in the annals of crime. The reverend author published it in the year 1820 as an appendix to his sermon entitled "The Prisoner Released. A sermon delivered at Manchester, Vt., Lord's day, January 9th, 1820, on the remarkable interposition of Divine Providence in the deliverance of Stephen and Jesse Boorn, who had been under sentence of death for the supposed murder of Russel Colvin."

The important difference between the Boorn case and the case now attracting attention is obvious. In the first what is termed in the law "*the corpus delicti*," the fact of the murder, was assumed; in the second case it is *proved*. But when the public is informed that the gravest suspicions against the accused rest upon her contradictory statements, we must be permitted to say that such statements are very unreliable, that the Boorn case shows how worthless they are when they rise to the dignity of complete confession of guilt. That they are contradictory proves that they are unstudied and ought to be regarded as an indication of innocence rather than as an evidence of criminality.

Notwithstanding the numerous and excellent maxims of criminal law the observance of which is supposed to insure the protection of innocent persons charged with the crime of murder, such innocent persons have been convicted and executed. Such an event as the taking of a human life to avenge a crime not committed is shocking to the moral sense. It will never again happen if judges will require positive proof of the *corpus delicti*, and after the crime is absolutely proved will follow the rule of law which disregards circumstances consistent with any hypothesis of innocence, and admits in evidence only those which are inconsistent with any theory except that of the guilt of the person charged with the crime.

CHAPTER XXXII.

Abraham Lincoln: A Study—His Origin and Early Life.

I shall undertake to write a sketch of Abraham Lincoln as he was known by me; to outline his portrait as it exists in my memory. From his first inauguration I can write from personal knowledge. His earlier life I must sketch from such materials as I have been able to collect from sources which I regard as authentic.

The Lincoln of my memory is a most attractive character and will form an instructive study for future generations. It is a subject for which my respect and my love increases with my years. If my outline shall attract the attention of the reader so that he shall fill it with all the facts and circumstances which may afterward fall under his notice, my whole object will be attained and I shall have discharged a duty to the memory of the man I loved.

I am not about to attempt another biography of Abraham Lincoln. I might do so without apology, for anything new and authentic concerning him will be welcomed by the American people. The number of those who can write of him from personal knowledge is rapidly diminishing; until for every good life of Washington there is an equally good one of Lincoln, there is little danger that the subject will be exhausted.

It would be well indeed for the youth of our time if they were as familiar with the facts of President Lincoln's life as their ancestors of the early years of the present century were with those of the life of Washington. Lives of Washington were published in country towns and exchanged by travelling peddlers for anything the farmer had to sell. Young orators in the district schools spoke their pieces from these books; they were read aloud in the family by the firelight. The name of Washington was venerated because his services were known.

I can read from my own memory words written upon it before I was eight years old: "In the History of Man we contemplate with particular satisfaction those Legislators, Heroes and Philosophers whose Wisdom, Valor and Virtue have contributed to the Happiness of the Human Species. We trace the Luminous Progress of those Excellent Beings with Secret Complacency. Our Emulation is roused while we behold them steadily pursue the Path of Rectitude in defiance of every Obstruction. We rejoice that we were of the same Species and thus Self-love becomes the Handmaid of Virtue." Such, capitals included, are the introductory observations to "Biographical Memoirs of the Illustrious Gen. George Washington," a book of one hundred and sixty pages, 24mo, published in 1813, in the mountain hamlet of Barnard, Vt., by Joseph Dix. It was published elsewhere many times. The volume is not much larger than the "New England Primer," which it resembles. It has done more to disseminate the knowledge of the great events in the life of "The Father of his Country" than the more pretentious volumes of John Marshall and Washington Irving.

The lives of Abraham Lincoln already published comprise all kinds, from the fairly good to those which are untruthful and misleading. The great work of Hay and Nicolay will always be indispensable to the student of that most important chapter of our history covered by his administration. But their volumes are rather a mine of materials than a deduction of facts, and require a more careful digest. The smaller life by Mr. Arnold is a charming biography, true as to its statements of fact. But Mr. Arnold was the associate and friend of Mr. Lincoln. How dearly he loved him his book discloses. The charm imparted to his pen by his affection is very delightful, but it sometimes leads one to distrust his impartiality.

Other lives of Lincoln may be passed without comment. He is an inadequate biographer of a great man who charges his mature age with the errors of his youth or is unable to appreciate his intellectual growth. No amount of protest will convince the impartial reader that the most reliable biographers of a public man are those who have abandoned his party and his principles and gone over into the camp of the enemy.

The writers who are responsible for the most erroneous views of the character of Abraham Lincoln are those who assert that he had a special pride in his humble origin and the poverty which repressed his early growth, and that he delighted in low and vulgar anecdote. *Their* ignorance is pitiable, inexcusable. He inherited a desponding temperament; his childhood except for his mother would have been cheerless; that mother died and left him desolate. There was little enough of sunshine in his youth. Up to the age of twenty-two his life had been a constant struggle against privation and poverty; he failed in every undertaking. His surveying instruments were sold by the sheriff on an execution for debt. He loved with all the intensity of his soul, and his love was returned by one who might have flooded his life with sunshine. She was stricken and died. He would not have been human if he had not become sad and melancholy. Despondency became almost his second nature. Great responsibilities were cast upon him which he would not evade, which he discharged with the most scrupulous fidelity. Where weaker men would have drowned their cares in dissipation, he sought a momentary escape from them in a humorous book or a sparkling story. That any form of vulgarity had any attraction for him, that he was proud of the poverty of his birth or early life, are statements never imposed upon any one who knew Abraham Lincoln.

His many-sided character cannot be estimated by ordinary rules. Men have usually attained eminence by the gradual development of qualities, sometimes promoted by advantages of position, the assistance of friends, and association with other men. Mr. Lincoln pre-eminently made himself, by intense thought, application, and good judgment. His intellectual growth was phenomenal. He reached celebrity almost at a bound. In the short space of six years the country attorney became the emancipator of a race, the preserver of the Republic, the greatest of Presidents, the foremost man of all his time. That study can scarcely fail to be profitable which gives us any better comprehension of such a character.

.   .   .   .

The ancestors of Abraham Lincoln were of Anglo-Saxon blood, enriched by years of New England culture which produced a stalwart race of men who had for several generations followed westward the advancing frontier. They had driven the Indians from the "dark and bloody ground," and, companions of Boone and the hunters of Kentucky, were clearing away the forests and planting the settlements which have since grown into great interior commonwealths.

Thomas Lincoln was an average representative of those early settlers. A boy of six years, he had seen his father shot dead by an Indian, whose triumphant yell was changed to a death-scream as his heart was pierced by a bullet from the rifle of the boy's brother. In such tragic scenes the Kentucky widow could give her son no education. Thomas grew to manhood a muscular, resolute, ignorant man, rough in speech but possessed of a kind and sympathetic heart. He was the protector of his widowed mother until he was twenty-eight years old. Then in the year 1806 he was married to Nancy Hanks. She was a Virginian by birth, but her blood like her name was English with a strong infusion from the veins of the New England Puritan. It is difficult to write of the mother of our great Lincoln without emotion. She was a beauty, forest-born, slight in person, a brunette with dark hair, soft hazel eyes, and a very musical voice. She was a woman of rare intellectual endowments, a strong will, and a most exemplary Christian character. In the ignorance and poverty of the infant settlement she had educated herself in all the duties of a frontier wife. A good old itinerant preacher had taught her to read and write and to draw comfort and inspiration from the Book of Books. Instructed by him at the age of twenty-three, she was a Dorcas full of good works and alms-deeds which she did.

Thomas Lincoln had no capacity for the accumulation of property and was infected with the nomadic spirit of the emigrant. In the forest of Hardin County, Ky., he built a log-cabin and thither carried his faithful wife with her slender outfit. There, on the 12th day of February, 1809, Abraham, their second child, was born. Even in that woodland solitude, where neighbors were few and scattered, Nancy Lincoln soon became celebrated. She taught other wives how to nurse the sick and to make their homes attractive to their husbands. Her log-cabin was no longer a cheerless, barn-like structure. Flowers blossomed around it, honeysuckles and vines climbed over it, and song-birds built their nests in its recesses. She was a model of wifely industry. No duty of the household was neglected. She had already taught her husband how to read and write, and had brought his rather coarse nature under her gentle, refining influence. With the birth of children a new sense of religious duty pervaded her soul. Her boy must know how to read and must be instructed in the Word of God. She gave him a daily lesson, while she was watched by an affectionate husband proud of his home, his wife, and his boy.

This family circle was too happy to remain long unbroken. When her son was nine years old, Nancy Lincoln sickened and died, at the early age of thirty-five. Other boys in solitary homes who have loved and lost their mothers will know by their own experience how desolate the life of young Lincoln was when his mother went out of it. What kindly heart will not beat more tenderly over the first recorded act of his life? The kind hands of neighbors had laid the mother to rest in her forest grave, with many tears but without a blessing or a prayer; for the nearest minister lived a hundred miles away. It grieved the heart of her son that this must be. And so it comes to pass that our first view of the motherless boy shows him in the act of making use, perhaps for the first time, of the art which his mother had taught him, in writing a letter to the travelling preacher whom she had known and esteemed, begging him to come and preach a sermon at her grave. Weeks later, riding a hundred miles through the pathless woods on horseback to reach the place, the preacher came. The father, daughter, and son, with the neighbors far and near, gathered in one of "God's first temples," and there beneath a spreading sycamore the preacher told the story and enforced the lesson of the pure and gentle life of Nancy Lincoln. It was not strange that true heart loved her until his dying day; that sitting in the Executive Mansion he should have said, "All that I am or hope to be I owe to my mother," or that when in his presence one spoke of strong sympathy with sorrow as a characteristic of the poor among the mountains, he replied, "I know from my own experience that it is just as strong in the forest and on the prairie."

It was from his father that Abraham Lincoln derived his lofty stature, giant frame, iron muscles, and elastic step, his long, sinewy arms and mighty strength. His mother gave him his temperament, melancholy yet not morose, his reverence for the word and works of God, and his sensitive conscience. The union of unlike parental forces invested him with a courage that knew no fear and a heart capacious enough for the sorrows of a race. His receptive nature, shut up in forest solitudes, was developed by association with men until it was filled with a human sympathy which made him a popular leader and bound other men to him with hooks of steel. His lofty integrity, love of justice, and hatred for all forms of tyranny and cruelty had the same origin.

By a second marriage, when his son was eleven years old, his father brought to his cabin another noble woman. She was a widow with three children, but with true impartiality she became for the son of Nancy Lincoln a second devoted mother. How well he loved her was proved by the last visit he made before leaving Springfield for Washington, in February, 1861. It was paid to her. She was seized with the spirit of prophecy. She embraced and kissed him, predicted his death by violence, and said that in this world she should never see him again.

It has been written by his biographers that the only books accessible to Lincoln in his youth were the Bible, "The Pilgrim's Progress," "The Poems of Burns," and "Weems' Life of Washington." No youth suffers any deprivation who has access to these volumes. Their influence upon young Lincoln was apparent in all his after-life. Except the instructions of his mother, the Bible more powerfully controlled the intellectual development of the son than all other causes combined. He memorized many of its chapters and had them perfectly at his command. Early in his professional life he learned that the most useful of all books to the public speaker is the Bible. After 1857 he seldom made a speech which did not comprise quotations from the Bible. The poems of the Ayrshire ploughman developed his poetic fancy, Bunyan's immortal dream taught him the force of figurative language, and the simple story of Parson Weems made him familiar with the noble qualities of Washington. In the poverty of his early life there were many deprivations, but the want of good books was not one of them.

The step-mother and the father encouraged their son to make use of every opportunity to learn. One of his teachers remembers him as his most eager and diligent scholar, arrayed in a buckskin suit with a cap made from the skin of a raccoon, coming with a worn-out arithmetic in his hands to begin his studies in the *higher branches*. But all the exertions of his parents could not give him a school attendance in all of more than a single year.

There are stories of his school life which gave promise of his future eminence. He was slow to anger; personal insult or ridicule could not provoke him, but no brute who attacked a weaker boy was safe from his punishment. Once he came upon six boys, each older than himself, who were drowning a kitten. He bounded upon them like a panther, and one after another the six went down under his blows. Then he released and fondled the poor kitten, and cried over it like a girl. He was ambitious to win a prize in a spelling-match. A poor girl was his only dangerous competitor. She hesitated over a letter which had she missed would have given the prize to Lincoln. Instantly he framed his lips into the form of the right letter; the blushing girl won the prize and the defeated boy was happy.

CHAPTER XXXIII.

ABRAHAM LINCOLN (CONTINUED)—HIS FAILURES—
THE FARM LABORER—THE FLAT-BOATMAN—
THE FIGHTER—THE MERCHANT—THE SUR-
VEYOR.

THE temptation is strong to linger over many of the incidents of his youth, but I must touch only upon those which perceptively influenced his career. At the age of nineteen he made a voyage to New Orleans on a flat-boat. Himself and the son of his employer constituted the officers and crew. On the voyage they were attacked by seven negroes who intended to capture the valuable cargo. Spurning all but the arms which nature had given him, Lincoln whipped the whole attacking party.

In New Orleans an event occurred which has been much distorted in many Lincoln biographies. He there attended a slave auction and saw a picture, never in this republic to be exhibited again. It was a young colored woman who stood on the auction block to be sold. Her limbs and bosom were bare. Traders in human flesh felt the density of her muscles as if she had been a quadruped. No doubt the young Kentuckian was disgusted, but there is no proof that this was his first object-lesson in human slavery, or that, as so often has been asserted, he turned to his companion and said, "If I ever get a chance to hit slavery, I will hit it hard." Such an expression from a flat-boatman would have been absurd. In its proper place I will give what his intimate friends suppose was the exhibition which converted him from an indifferent spectator of its horrors into a firm advocate of the abolition of slavery.

Nor am I able to find any proof of another event, by many supposed to have occurred about this time. It has been said that his fortune was told by a Voudoo woman, who said he was divinely commissioned to destroy slavery, which would cease to exist within a few years after he became President. I have never met with any reliable evidence in support of this statement.

After a second and uneventful voyage to New Orleans he assisted his father, who now removed a third time, to build a new log-cabin and to clear and fence another farm. This was in the year 1831, when, if ever, he earned the title of "The Railsplitter." For the benefit of those who have written and who believe that Mr. Lincoln was proud of and frequently adverted to this title as evidence of his humble origin, it is proper to say that the story has so slight a basis of truth that it might almost be called apocryphal. I do not find that he ever referred to it but once. At the State Convention in 1860, where he was to speak, two rails, adorned with banners and preceded by music, were brought into the hall. The declaration of the bearers that they were genuine created a wild enthusiasm. The statement that they were split by the hand of Lincoln made some reference to them necessary. It was made by Mr. Lincoln in these modest terms:

"Fellow-citizens! It is true that many, many years ago John Hanks and I made rails down on the

Sangamon. We made good, honest rails, but whether this is one of them, at this distance of time I am not able to say."

At the age of twenty-two Abraham Lincoln had no trade or occupation. He had tried several experiments, all of which were failures. He had been a farm hand, a ferryman, a flat-boatman. Then for a few months he was clerk in a country store and a superintendent of a flouring mill. He enlisted in the Black Hawk war, and his election as captain of his company gave him the supreme pleasure of his life. The war was a short one. He purchased and operated the county store. In this business he failed and was sold out by the sheriff. Then he studied surveying and became a land surveyor. In this occupation he did not succeed. His failure must have been complete, for his horse, his compass, and his instruments were sold upon an execution by the sheriff. One Bolin Greene, almost a stranger, purchased and sent his horse, compass, and instruments to him with a kindly message to " pay for them when he was able."

Incidents are related of what may be called the experimental period of Mr. Lincoln's life which deserve to be recorded. It was while he was doing business as a merchant that a farmer's wife made purchases from him which required weighing and computation. She had departed for her home some miles away when, upon a revision of the transaction, Lincoln became satisfied that he had overcharged his customer some thirty cents. Some merchants would have waited until the customer complained before reopening the transaction. Not so Abraham Lincoln. He walked the four miles, corrected the error, and then with a clear conscience went about his business. A new post-office was established and he was appointed postmaster. The income was so insignificant that he was not called on to pay the amount due to the Government until some years later when he was established as a lawyer in Springfield. A friend, who thought it would be inconvenient for him to pay the money on so short a notice, went to him with an offer to advance it. To his friend's surprise Mr. Lincoln produced from the drawer of his desk a package containing the identical coins to which the department was entitled. He had been very poor during the intervening years, but never poor enough to use one penny of the money which belonged to the United States.

We now touch the turning-point in Mr. Lincoln's career. The age of twenty-five is given by his biographer Mr. Arnold as the end of the unsuccessful portion of his life. Before this time he had failed in everything he had undertaken. But his life had not been altogether wasted. By the inflexible integrity of all his dealings he had fairly earned the name of "Honest Abe Lincoln." He had learned how to be *thorough*. His studies of grammar and logic were eventually to make him a celebrity in the world of letters. Much of his hard work in the past was to become invaluable to him when, as his friends declared, his "luck had turned" and he began to travel the highway of success.

An incident which exerted a powerful influence upon his professional success will close our sketch of the unsuccessful period of Abraham Lincoln's career. He was not a fighting man. But in those days a man of his stature would have been deemed a coward if he was not able to defend himself. He was the tallest and the strongest man in the township and he necessarily became the champion of New Salem. The nearest village had the name of Clary's Grove. This village had a champion, a good-natured giant of a fellow, by name John Armstrong.

The betting and bragging of the two villages over the merits of their respective champions had made it apparent that nothing but a fair, square fight would determine which was the better man. Personally the champions did not wish to fight, but the honor of their respective villages was involved and the contest became inevitable. The combatants did not go into training like the athletes of the modern science of self-defence, but the excitement ran high and the villages backed their respective favorites with money as well as their clamorous opinions. Neutral ground was selected and the day named for the fight. It came off in the presence of a great multitude, comprising the entire male population of the two villages. It was to be a rough-and-tumble combat, in which the first man who should "down" his adversary was to be the victor. There was but one rule. It was "no grasping or hitting below the belt, no weapons but those of nature."

In the first round Armstrong grasped the body of his adversary and converted the contest into a wrestling-match, in which he was supposed to be invincible. Lincoln appeared to be dazed and to give his whole strength to an effort to maintain his upright position. Armstrong put forth all his strength; he moved him from right to left, forward and backward, tried very hard to trip him, but all his struggles were useless. The tall figure of Lincoln was moved in every direction, but he stood upright as sturdy as an oak. The partisans of Armstrong yelled to him to make a rush, to down him before he could recover so as to make any attack. But he could not make any impression. Conscious of failure and overwhelmed by the clamor of his partisans, he grasped Lincoln far below the hips by what every one recognized as a foul attack. Even then he could not move him. Lincoln protested against the unfairness, but his protest was disregarded. Then for the first time he seemed to put forth his strength. His right arm shot out, his hand grappled Armstrong by the throat, broke his hold, and at the end of his extended arm shook him like a rat in the jaws of a terrier. The Clary's Grove boys saw that their champion was beaten, and attempted to break into the ring to assist him. But honest Jack, in spite of the grasp on his throat, shouted "No! Abe Lincoln has whipped me, fair and square! He is the best man that ever broke into this settlement, and if he will let up on me, the man that wants to whip him has first got to whip Armstrong." This manly expression ended the fight, to the satisfaction of both parties.

After this fight Lincoln never wanted a home. The energetic wife of Armstrong became his good angel; the children climbed upon his knees and kissed the sadness away from his melancholy face. I have sometimes thought that the fight with Armstrong may have been the turning-point in his career and that his success in life dates from its conclusion. At this time he was a vigorous man of about twenty-three years, not discouraged by his previous failures, although he was loaded with the debts he had incurred as a country merchant and a surveyor.

At the age of twenty-three he advocated the election to the presidency of Henry Clay. He then served through the Black Hawk war, was nominated for the legislature and defeated. At the age of twenty-five he was again nominated and this time he was elected. He was re-elected in 1836, 1838, and 1840, and in the last year was the candidate of his party for speaker. In the spring of 1837, having been admitted to the bar, he opened an office in Springfield with John T. Stuart as his partner, and notwithstanding the successful campaign in 1840 of "Tippecanoe and Tyler too," at its close he determined to withdraw from politics and devote himself to the practice of the law. We may therefore fix upon the year 1840 as the end of his mistakes and misfortunes, though his real successes began at a somewhat earlier period.

CHAPTER XXXIV.

ABRAHAM LINCOLN (CONTINUED)—HIS SUCCESSES—THE LAWYER—THE ADVOCATE—THE POPULAR MAN.

THE conspicuous element in the character of Mr. Lincoln was its intensity. The counsel of the preacher appears to have controlled his life. " Whatsoever thy hand findeth to do, do it with thy might," was for him not only a counsel, but a command. He studied grammar by committing the book to memory. A treatise on land-surveying fell into his hands by accident; it made him a surveyor. That he might be certain of the meaning of the word "demonstration," he solved the problems of Euclid. Although this intensity was the cause of much of his own unhappiness, we shall find in his later years that the English-speaking world is indebted to it for some of the gems of the language.

It is said of him that he loved Ann Rutledge with all the capacity of his soul, and that she was worthy of such a mighty love. She possessed personal beauty, and what was of greater value to the rising lawyer, a calm, equable temper and excellent judgment. She appreciated Lincoln and returned his love. How far her refining influence would have modified the impetuosity of his character, we can only imagine. It seemed for a time that the course of their love did run smooth. With the approval of all their friends, who saw how well they were suited to each other, they were about to be married, when after a very short illness she died. His grief for a time was uncontrollable. A tempest seemed to be raging within him. He sank into a kind of torpor from which it was difficult and dangerous to awake him. His friends feared for his sanity and his life. He rebelled against the injustice of the fate which had robbed him of a treasure which he valued more than life. Expressions which fell from him under the influence of this affliction have been treasured up in some memories and produced after his death as evidence of his disbelief in the Bible and his rejection of all the doctrines of Christianity.

Without capital or influential friends; impatient of a personal obligation which he could not discharge; burdened with debts incurred during his brief career as a merchant, he now came to the young city of Springfield to try his fortune in the profession of the law. He created the conditions of his own success. An honest lawyer is a desirable member of any community. The rugged integrity which had already given him a name speedily brought him clients, who knew that instead of promoting litigation he was a minister of peace who could be relied upon to give them good advice. In a new country, the ability to tell a good story goes far to secure what is called popularity. He cultivated his natural powers to this end, for the double purpose of diverting his hearers and occupying his own thoughts, until it made him celebrated. His popularity was as wide as his acquaintance. He had no rivals in his profession. Its members are quick to discover and appreciate one who is always just and honorable in his relations with them. He would not undertake an unjust cause. When he discovered that his client had deceived him he did not hesitate to abandon his case in open court. He was once prosecuting a claim for goods sold. He had proved every item by his own client, when, to his amazement, his adversary produced the written receipt of his client showing that every item had been paid for. He cross-examined the defendant far enough to make it clear that no explanation was possible, and then deliberately walked out of the court-room and over to the hotel. The judge, supposing that he had been called from the court for some purpose, sent a messenger for him to tell him that the court could not wait for him longer. "Tell his Honor that I cannot come," was the answer of the indignant lawyer; "my hands are dirty and I am washing them."

The most dramatic scene in his professional life, in which the advocate appears to the best advantage, was a trial for murder in which he showed his gratitude to the wife of Jack Armstrong. Armstrong was dead. His son, a young man of twenty, impatient of his mother's restraint and easily influenced in the wrong direction, had become associated with a party of reckless young men, the leader of whom was a vicious and dangerous criminal. This leader had provoked a fight in the night at a camp-meeting, in which one of the opposing party had been killed by a blow from a slung-shot or some similar weapon, which was found at the place of the murder.

To save himself, the leader charged the crime upon young Armstrong, and before the court of inquiry testified positively that he plainly saw him strike the fatal blow.

Armstrong was held for trial on the charge of murder. The testimony against him was positive. The murder was not only unprovoked, but the chief witness represented it as premeditated and vindictive. The public indignation increased. The country newspapers provided their weekly accretions. Every boyish fight, every circumstance or fact which tended to show his unruly disposition, was seized upon, magnified and multiplied, until young Armstrong was made out to be a fierce, blood-thirsty miscreant to whom murder was a recreation. It became the prevailing opinion that public justice could not wait for the slow forms of law. It was decided to hang him without the unnecessary delay and expense of a trial, and hung he would have been but for his secret and sudden removal by the sheriff to the jail in another county.

The calamity fell heavily upon the prisoner's widowed mother. Upon the little farm, the only property left by her husband, she had been able, by industry and the strictest economy, to keep her children together. She was now to see her neighbors turn away when they met her and avoid her house as though it was infected. The wise conclusion of the public was that the boy had not been properly brought up; if he had been he would not have committed the murder. Even the country attorney would not appear for her son unless she would mortgage her farm for his fees.

Upon this dark scene suddenly appeared the stalwart form of Lincoln. There is first a letter reproaching her for not calling on him when she was in trouble and volunteering to defend her son. It is followed by Lincoln in person. In a half-hour's examination he knows that the prisoner is innocent. Why cannot those who have great force of character always use it as he did? He went to the home of the sad widow and took her by the hand.

"Hannah!" he said, "your boy is innocent. He shall be made as clear of this charge as the sun in yonder sky."

It was like flooding her home with sunshine and filling her heart with joy. "I seemed to know then that my boy would be cleared," she said, "for Abram never deceived anybody."

Fortunately we have excellent reports of the trial that followed. I cite only those portions which illustrate Lincoln, and one source of my information is the Cleveland *Leader*. According to that account the prejudice against the accused was undiminished. Lincoln alone appeared confident of an acquittal. It was difficult to say which was the saddest face—that of the young man bleached by his imprisonment, appalled by constant fears of lynching, with a reckless enemy who was to swear his innocent life away, or the poor, pale, widowed mother whose son was to be tried for his life with every opinion settled in favor of his guilt. On one thing mother and son were agreed. Their only hope was in the tall, dark-faced man in whose deep-set eyes they read the message of hope and courage.

Of the six hundred people in the court-house, Lincoln appeared the most unconcerned. He had selected a young attorney to assist him, to whom all the preliminary work of the trial was intrusted. Lincoln seemed to take but little interest in the important work of selecting a jury. He sat by the table, his head resting upon his open hand, drawing portraits with a pencil. He interfered but once. A juror said he had not only formed an opinion, but he had said many times, what he believed, that Armstrong was guilty. Assuming that he would be excused, he was about leaving the box, when Lincoln arose. His tall form towered above the audience. " Was your father a justice of the peace down on the Sangamon?" he asked. The juror replied that he was. " We decline to excuse the juror," said Lincoln. " He is a fair man who will not go against his judgment," and this was the only interference with the selection of the jury.

The prosecuting attorney made a plain statement of a very simple case. He proved by reliable witnesses that two parties were engaged in the fight; that Armstrong belonged to one of them; that after it was over one man lay dead on the ground, his skull fractured, apparently by a slung-shot that lay near him; that some one said, " I saw Armstrong hit him;" that Armstrong appeared to be confused, but claimed that he did not hit the man; that as soon as he saw there was to be a fight he retreated, and was some distance away when he heard that a man had been killed. These witnesses were scarcely cross-examined. They were asked a few questions about the time of the *mêlée* and dismissed. They agreed about the time, which was also fixed by one of the regular exercises of the camp-meeting.

There was silence in the crowded court as the principal witness was sworn. He was a low-browed man of thirty with a hard, merciless face. His story was brief, but if true it was fatal. He had been in the company with Armstrong. The bottle had circulated freely. Armstrong was talkative. Said he would "do up" the man who was killed. He was outside the crowd during the *mêlée*. He saw Armstrong swing the shot, strike the head of his victim, who fell to the ground and never rose again. Asked how he could be so positive when the occurrence was in the evening, he said the parties stood in range between him and the full moon, which made the place almost as light as day. The moon had been a conspicuous figure in all his relations of the transaction.

"There has been bad blood and ill-feeling between Armstrong and yourself, has there not?"

"None whatever," the witness answered.

To the amazement of the counsel, court, and spectators, Lincoln dismissed the witness without another question. He knew better than to cross-examine a hostile witness.

The prosecution rested. Lincoln waived his opening argument and called four reputable, substantial farmers, the nearest neighbors, who had known Armstrong all his life. They all testified that although Armstrong was rather wild and irrepressible, he had never been charged with a wicked or malicious act.

"Why," said one, "he's Jack Armstrong's own boy. He's got no malice into him. He would share his last cent with anybody that was in want, and if he was cold would take off his coat and give it to him." The same witnesses proved that the worst enemy the prisoner had was the chief witness, who had often been heard to threaten him with violence.

"That," said Lincoln, "is our case."

Amazement filled the court. What could Lincoln be thinking of? The rope was tightening around the prisoner's neck. In the face of the positive, uncontradicted evidence, escape was impossible. Why did he not call the prisoner to deny the charge, or the mother to show the peaceable temper of the boy? He might at least have appealed to the sympathies of the jury. He had thrown away the boy's last chance of life. Thoughts like these pervaded all minds. The face of the widowed mother wore an expression of hopeless despair.

Lincoln saw it and it went to his heart. The court, for the moment, had suspended the trial. With grave courtesy the lawyer bent over the figure of the poor woman, offered her his arm and led her to an open window. Pointing to the sun, which had just passed the meridian, he whispered in her ear, "Hannah! before that sun sets your boy will be free!"

"O Abram! Abram! God bless you for those words! I don't see nor I don't ask how it can be. But I will hope, for you, Abram, I know would not deceive me!"

The prosecutor supposed he had a clear case. Upon the evidence the jury would have to convict. There was nothing to argue. Until some defence was suggested he said he would not occupy the time of the jury.

Every sound was hushed as Lincoln rose to plead for the prisoner. He went straight to the merits of the case. A few well-chosen words made every juror see that the whole case rested on the evidence of the principal witness—except that there was not a shred of proof of guilt. But for that, the prisoner was shown to be a generous, good-hearted boy. Reject that, and the jury must not only acquit, they must vindicate the prisoner. There was just enough of this to enable the advocate to rise to the command of the situation.

Then he began to describe the perjurer, calling on Almighty God to see him swear away the life of his associate, his friend. He showed how easy it was for an honest witness in the night time, in a crowd of angry men, to be mistaken; he referred to instances of innocent men condemned upon such uncertain evidence. Then when he had secured the close attention of every juror, when even the judge was leaning forward with his open hand to his ear to catch every word, he turned, extended his long arm and finger straight toward the witness, and in the sharp tones of a voice that pierced like a sword exclaimed: "But he cannot be mistaken; he is, he is sharp-eyed; he can see in the dark; he has the gift of second-sight. He saw, as he told you, the fatal blow struck, by the light of the moon, of the full moon—*two long hours before it rose above the eastern horizon.* Look for yourselves, gentlemen," he said, as he handed to the foreman the Almanac and Register in common use in that locality.

The change of opinion was electric. There was no doubt about the time when the blow was struck. Not guilty, was the thought in every heart. But the scene had not yet passed. In almost plaintive tones he described the home of his old friend, the boy's father; its open doors to him when he was a sad and lonely man; the boy that had climbed upon his knee and laid his curly head upon his shoulder; the bright-faced wife, almost a mother to him. "There she sits, gentlemen, a sad-faced, white-haired widow, awaiting your verdict which shall restore to her arms her son falsely accused.

"And the perjured accuser, what of him?" As well attempt to describe the flashes of lightning and the thunder-roll of the storm as to gather the burning words of scorn, invective, and crushing denunciation that fell from the lips of the eloquent advocate. It overwhelmed the witness with its terrible force. Human nature could not endure it. Ghastly with terror, his limbs trembling under him as he rose, he reeled toward the door, followed by that fearful finger, and almost sank to the floor when he was passing the prisoner, and the lawyer fiercely demanded: "Which of the two is the murderer?"

A swift acquittal followed. The widow fainted in the arms of her son. The applause that shook the building, the flight of the felon were witnesses of the power of the orator. The grateful woman undertook to explain how, and how soon, she could pay the lawyer's fee. Again he led her to the window and said, "The day is not yet ended and your son is free. I shall not charge you one cent, Hannah. Give me credit for what I have done on the debt I have owed you these many years."

To describe the man Lincoln, rather than to multiply anecdotes of him, I cannot do better than to give an account of him at this period of his life written by one of his contemporaries. At this time, he writes, the terms of court were held quarterly and usually lasted about two weeks. The terms were always seasons of great importance and much gayety in the little town that had the honor of being the county seat. Distinguished members of the bar from surrounding and even from distant counties, ex-judges and ex-members of Congress attended, and were personally, and many of them popularly, known to almost every adult, male and female, of the limited population. They came in by stages and on horseback. Among them, the one above all whose arrival was looked forward to with the most pleasurable anticipations, and whose possible absence—although he never was absent—was feared with the liveliest emotions of anxiety, was "Uncle Abe," as we all lovingly called him. Sometimes he was a day or two late, and then, as the Bloomington stage came in at sundown, the bench and bar, jurors and citizens, would gather in crowds at the hotel where he always put up, to give him a welcome if he should happily arrive, and to experience the keenest disappointment if he should not. If he arrived, as he alighted and stretched out both his long arms to shake hands with those nearest to him and with those who approached, his homely face, handsome in its broad and sunny smile, his voice touching in its kindly and cheerful accents, every one in his presence felt lighter and joyous in his heart. He brought happiness with him. He loved his fellowmen with all the strength of his great nature, and those who came in contact with him could not help reciprocating his love. His tenderness of the feelings of others was the extreme of sensitiveness.

I have written enough to serve my purpose. He was now established in his profession as its unquestioned leader. He had neither enemies nor rivals. He was the universal associate, counsellor, adviser, and friend. At this period in his career Abraham Lincoln was pre-eminently and for the first time a successful man.

CHAPTER XXXV.

ABRAHAM LINCOLN (CONTINUED)—THE ORATOR—
THE CANDIDATE—THE MAN OF THE PEOPLE.

IN the famous campaign of "Tippecanoe and Tyler too," of 1840, Mr. Lincoln advocated the election of Gen. W. H. Harrison, the successful candidate. In 1844 he was an earnest supporter of Henry Clay and was intensely disappointed by his defeat. In 1846 he was elected to the lower house of Congress and re-elected in 1848. He declined a re-election to Congress for the third time, and in 1850 returned to the practice of his profession.

He was influential in the legislature and politics of Illinois, an industrious and by no means a silent member of Congress. But when, in 1849, he declined a re-election to the House of Representatives and returned to his private and professional life, he had done almost nothing to make himself known outside of his State or to prove his superiority to many of his contemporaries. Had his life closed at the age of forty-five he would have left to his children a fair reputation, but the credit of no act which would have given him a place in history.

But in the year 1858, when he was past middle age, he suddenly rose above the political horizon and so challenged the public attention that he was taken out of private life and, without any intervening step, placed at the head of a great republic. Such an instance is almost without a parallel. I do not remember that it had happened to a really strong man since the days of Cincinnatus. I think we shall find its cause in the most significant event of Mr. Lincoln's career.

If I were attempting to write a biography, or even a connected account of his life, there are incidents in it which it would be necessary to describe but which are unimportant to my present purpose. Among these are his threatened duel with General Shields, his courtship and marriage, and several of his achievements in his profession. He appears to have had some skill as an inventor, and he took out letters patent for an invention to assist in the navigation of steamboats over rapids and shallows. But it cannot be said that any experience of his, earlier than 1858, had any special influence in his preparation for his subsequent career.

The decade which ended in 1858 covered the first aggressive campaign of the slave power. The old slave States had been content to abide by the compromises arranged from time to time, especially the Missouri compromise line, and had not attempted to extend slavery beyond it. But after slavery had secured the passage of the Fugitive Slave Act, during the Kansas controversy, its advocates arrogantly demanded the right to enter free territory with their slaves, in direct violation of the compact. The decision of the Supreme Court of the United States in the Dred Scott case gave to the institution almost all its demands. On the other hand, the friends of freedom had never claimed any right to interfere with slavery in the slave States or south of the compromise line. To that extent they conceded that the institution was intrenched in the Constitution as a permanent evil. The most extreme abolitionists had limited their efforts to the abolition of slavery in the District of Columbia and its exclusion from the Territories. No public man had ventured to attack it within its consecrated limits. Had its votaries been content to abide by the line to which they had once for a good consideration agreed, their institution would have never been disturbed except by themselves.

Mr. Lincoln by hard study had become a master of the art of profound thought. He knew the value of intellectual work and of facts irrespective of the source from which they were derived. We know that the great conclusions of his later life were reached by his own processes, without much assistance from others. We have an example of these processes in his first inaugural address, which he composed with no assistance beyond a copy of the Federal Constitution and a speech of Henry Clay's.

The advocates of slavery had committed the grave error of forcing its pretensions upon such minds as that of Mr. Lincoln. They had been successful in extorting new concessions from the people of the free States. Instead of appreciating that there was a point beyond which concession could not go, they made every success the pretext for a new aggression, until the halls of Congress became the theatre of a contest which annually became more angry and violent.

The subject being thus forced upon his attention before he left Congress, Mr. Lincoln saw in it an issue which touched the national life. When he returned to private life he became a close observer of the aggressions of slavery, never more extreme than from 1850 to 1857. He gave to the study of the subject in all its bearings all the strength of his powerful intellect. God made him a lover of justice, humanity, and freedom; an enemy, but a fair one, of the institution of human slavery. There is a letter written by him, August 24th, 1855, to his friend Joshua Speed, which reflects like a mirror the condition of his mind. He calls his friend's attention to a trip which they made together on a steamboat from Louisville to St. Louis in 1841. "There were on board ten or a dozen slaves shackled together with irons. That sight was a continual torment to me. I see something like it every time I touch the Ohio or any other slave border." He disliked slavery because it appeared to be cruel, oppressive, debasing to both master and slave. He loved freedom because it elevated the human race. It was the natural right of man, ordained by the Almighty and certain to triumph in his own good time.

But for the time his clear eye saw, and he knew in the depths of his soul, that freedom was fighting a losing battle. For years a solid South had stood like a rock demanding new concessions and in the end securing them from a divided North. Victorious in every skirmish, slavery was growing stronger, freedom weaker. A few more victories and slavery would be strong enough for the final struggle in which defeat would make ours a slave republic. After years of study he knew beyond a doubt where his party had erred, and he had wrought out in his own mind the lines upon which the battle for freedom could be won.

A mind accustomed to work out great problems

HIS STUDY OF SLAVERY.   371

unassisted becomes unconsciously secretive. It was more than a habit with Mr. Lincoln which constrained him, in the later years of his life, to study a subject in all its aspects and all its possible consequences; to solve all his doubts and reach all his conclusions, before he consulted or communicated with others. Aside from two letters, there was very little evidence that he was paying any attention to the subject of slavery for the first six years after he retired from Congress. But it is now known to those with whom he conversed freely, at the time the proclamation of emancipation was under consideration, that during these years he was a close observer of events, and that no fact or circumstance connected with the forward movement of the slave power escaped his notice. His familiarity with its details was remarked by every one with whom he talked on the subject. From the ratification of the treaty by which we acquired so large a part of Mexico, his memory was an encyclopedia of the facts of slavery in America.

I dwell upon this subject because I believe that Abraham Lincoln's greatest work for freedom was done long before he was elected President and at the very outset of his career as a statesman. It was that work which made him President. For the first time in our republic it put the controversy between human slavery and freedom upon its true ground, and launched against the peculiar institution the bolt of death.

In the first half of the year 1858 the Republicans of Illinois had by common consent determined that Mr. Lincoln should be their candidate for the Senate of the United States. In March, 1857, when Mr.

Buchanan was inaugurated, the fight for Kansas had almost reached the point of civil war. The Dred Scott decision, which virtually held the Missouri Compromise to be unconstitutional, was heralded by the slave power as decisive of the controversy. The trick of the Lecompton constitution was devised in the autumn. It submitted only a schedule on the subject of slavery to the people, so arranged that every vote, whether for or against the schedule, was a vote for slavery. Judge Douglas, whose senatorial term was about to expire, was a candidate for re-election. He had maintained, as the Dred Scott case held, that the Missouri Compromise was unconstitutional, but he would not defend the Lecompton fraud.

In announcing his hostility to the Lecompton constitution, Judge Douglas had declared that "he did not care whether slavery was voted up or voted down." His opposition to that fraud had made a split in his own party, and there were many Republicans who were in favor of returning him to the Senate, unopposed. This fact made him a most formidable candidate against any republican nominee and presented to the party a strong inducement not to make the abstract issue with slavery prominent in the campaign. Any other candidate than Mr. Lincoln would have temporized and treated slavery with extreme reserve.

As his habit was upon all occasions of importance, Mr. Lincoln made careful preparation for the nominating convention. To the body of Republicans who were to meet at Springfield on the 17th of June, 1858, he intended to give the results of ten years' careful study and observation of the political influence of slavery upon the republic. He well knew the force of words, and he selected those in which his conclusions should be announced. When the nomination was tendered to him, he accepted it in what has since come to be known as the "Divided House" speech, the most important of his life, possibly the most important in its consequences ever delivered in the republic, for it was the first which accurately stated the future of the struggle between freedom and slavery. He took his stand upon the great fact declared by our Saviour to the Scribes which came down from Jerusalem, "If a house be divided against itself that house cannot stand," and declared his own faith that "this Government cannot permanently endure half slave and half free."

The unexpected announcement of this bold prediction almost convulsed the Republican party. It came upon Mr. Lincoln's supporters like thunder from a cloudless sky. The leaders of the party were appalled. They declared that he had invited defeat; that he had destroyed his party; that he had made the issue one of life or death. They pressed him to explain or modify his statement so that it should not amount to a declaration of war against slavery, provided its advocates would restrict it within the limits to which they had once consented. But Mr. Lincoln scorned all subterfuge. He said that the statement that slavery could not exist unless it was aggressive was a fact proved by all human experience within the historic period. He said: "I had rather have this fact made prominent and discussed before the people at the cost of my defeat than to suppress it and secure my election. By it I will stand or fall."

What followed is familiar history. Judge Douglas seized the opportunity to show that the views of

Mr. Lincoln were more extreme and dangerous than those of the abolitionists; that they involved a war to the death with slavery. Mr. Lincoln did not flinch from their defence. He challenged his adversary to a public discussion. His challenge was accepted, and the debate instead of destroying the Republican party drew to it a majority of the voters of Illinois, and made Abraham Lincoln, although defeated by the legislature, the most conspicuous of its leaders.

There has never been in American history such a debate before the people as that of 1858 between Lincoln and Douglas. Both were great men, great enough to appreciate and respect each other. Its influence has not yet passed away. Not long after the Springfield convention, Mr. Douglas returned to Chicago, where he made a speech which was regarded as the supreme effort of his life. I have had an account of it from an intelligent gentleman who was one of the audience. Judge Douglas spoke of Mr. Lincoln as an amiable and good-hearted man, rather out of place in politics, and then proceeded with his argument in a tone of almost offensive superiority. Mr. Lincoln, who was present when Judge Douglas closed, was called on for a speech. He replied that the hour was late, too late for any reply to the great argument of Judge Douglas. But if the audience cared to come to the same place the following evening he would reply to Judge Douglas, and especially to his severe strictures upon the statement that this Government could not permanently endure half slave and half free. He would also answer his commendations of popular, or, as it used to be called, "*squatter* sovereignty."

The promised speech was delivered in the presence of a great audience. Like all his public addresses after June 17th, 1858, it was a great speech. Judge Douglas had charged him with making a carefully prepared address in favor of inviting the South to make war upon the North for the purpose of nationalizing slavery. He had reminded him that the Government had endured, half slave and half free, for more than eighty years, and that there was no reason why it should not endure in future!

In answer to the charge that his speech was *prepared*, Mr. Lincoln said: "I admit that it was. I am not a master of language; I have not a fine education; I am not capable of entering into a disquisition upon dialectics, as I believe you call it; but I do not believe my language bears any such construction as Judge Douglas puts upon it.

"He says I am in favor of making war by the North upon the South for the extinction of slavery; that I am also in favor of inviting (as he expresses it) the South to a war upon the North, for the purpose of nationalizing slavery. Now, it is singular enough, if you will carefully read that passage over, that I did not say that I was in favor of anything in it; I only said what I expected would take place. I made a prediction only. It may have been a foolish one, perhaps. I did not even say that I desired that slavery should be put in the course of ultimate extinction. *I do say so now*, however, so there need be no longer any difficulty about that."

Mr. Lincoln then announced another great truth. It was so self-evident that it is singular that it had not been announced and understood before. He said: "I am not, in the first place, unaware that this

Government has endured eighty-two years half slave and half free. I know that. I am tolerably well acquainted with the history of the country, and I know that it has endured eighty-two years half slave and half free. I *believe*—and that is what I meant to allude to there—*I believe it has endured because, during all that time, until the introduction of the Nebraska Bill,* THE PUBLIC MIND DID REST IN THE BELIEF THAT SLAVERY WAS IN THE COURSE OF ULTIMATE EXTINCTION. That was what gave us the rest that we had through that period of eighty-two years; at least I so believe. *I have always hated slavery, I think, as much as any abolitionist. I have been an old-time Whig. I have always hated it, but I have always been quiet about it until this new era of the introduction of the Nebraska Bill began,* because I believed that slavery was in the course of final extinction."

The italics are my own. This speech was a supplement to the speech of June 17th. Together they form the basis of Mr. Lincoln's platform in the great discussion. Slavery had been universally supposed to be in the course of extinction. It had changed front. It now claimed extension into the Territories and recognition in the free States as constitutional rights. These pretensions had been to a large extent sanctioned by the Supreme Court in the Dred Scott case. They had precipitated an irrepressible conflict for the control of the Government upon the single issue of the right or wrong of slavery. If slavery was just and right, then Judge Douglas ought to be sustained. If it was unjust and wrong, he ought to be voted down. This view of the situation, the result of long and careful study by a powerful intellect, touched the life of the republic. In comparison with it the success of candidates appeared to him insignificant and contemptible. He compelled his adversary to assume the defence of the institution on the ground that it was just and right and not inconsistent with the theory of a free republican government.

Senator Douglas was a statesman of great ability, quick of apprehension and adroit in argument. He had had great experience in debate, in which he had never before encountered his superior. Mr. Lincoln's equipment was his clear conception of the subject, acquired by study and profound thought operating upon a mind intolerant of every form of wrong and injustice. They were worthy adversaries and they sincerely respected each other.

The student will find no chapter in American history which he will read with greater profit than the story of this debate. It illustrates the value of preparation in all public discussions. There are many who measure the ability of a speaker by his readiness and facility of speech upon all subjects and all occasions. Such men may be brilliant, but they are always superficial. There was great force in an observation attributed to the celebrated Dr. Nott, of Union College, Schenectady. He said that "he did not so much object to extempory speaking as he did to *extemporary thinking.*" There was no extemporary thought or speech on the part of Mr. Lincoln in this debate. It was instructive as well as entertaining. It furnished to its auditors material for thought. It drew crowds of plain citizens, which increased at every session and were largest at the close. Its study even now is an intellectual feast.

In it Mr. Lincoln always appears as the leader. He held his adversary inflexibly to the issue of the right or wrong of slavery. He represented freedom as noble, merciful, just, and true; he held slavery up to public reprobation in words of burning eloquence as cruel, brutal, unjust, and inhuman, and the people cried, "Amen."

Mr. Lincoln was defeated as a candidate for the Senate and Judge Douglas was elected. But this now famous debate had consequences of infinitely greater moment than the election of a Senator. It not only drew to Mr. Lincoln the support of a majority of the voters of Illinois; it marked out the lines upon which the future battle of slavery against freedom was to be fought. It established his title to the leadership of the army of freedom, as the most powerful and acceptable public speaker of his time. The people came to respect him as a statesman; to love him as one of themselves. Henceforth, wherever he was to be announced as a speaker, multitudes were to listen to him as the champion of freedom, the great orator of his time.

CHAPTER XXXVI.

ABRAHAM LINCOLN (CONTINUED)—HIS ELECTION —HIS PREPARATION AND HIS PROMISES.

THE debate with Senator Douglas closed at Alton, Ill., on the 15th of October, 1858. Mr. Lincoln had made (including those in the debate) more than fifty speeches in the campaign. The first was unanswerable, and every successive speech appeared to be more convincing and powerful than its predecessor. Their strength was in their simplicity. Their conclusions were soon to be condensed into the platform of a national Republican party.

In the early autumn of the following year, 1859, the contest was transferred to Ohio, where the Democrats had nominated Mr. Pugh as their candidate for governor, and Senator Douglas had been secured to advocate his election. The Ohio Republicans sent to Mr. Lincoln the Macedonian cry, "Come over and help us!"

He came; he made two speeches, the first at Columbus, the other at Cincinnati. The speech at Columbus was a review. It concerned the past and the present. It exposed the insidious dangers of Mr. Douglas' favorite doctrine of Popular Sovereignty, and the exposure destroyed it. He showed how the Democratic doctrines were changing the negro from a man into an animal. "You are prepared," he said to the Democrats, "to deal with the negro as with the brute. One or two more turns of the screw and you will support or submit to the slave trade, revived with all its horrors; a slave code enforced in our Territories; a new Dred Scott decision to bring slavery into the very heart of the free North."

At Cincinnati, after announcing to the Democrats that they might be beaten in the next presidential campaign with Mr. Douglas as their candidate, but they must take him, for under any other candidate they would inevitably be defeated, he outlined the Republican platform of the future. The reader will not fail to note the modesty, simplicity, and the power of his words: " In order to beat our opponents, I think we want and must have a national policy in regard to the institution of slavery, that acknowledges and deals with that institution *as being wrong.*" "We must not interfere with slavery in the States where it exists, because the Constitution forbids it, and the general welfare does not require us to do so. We must not withhold an efficient fugitive slave law, because the Constitution requires us (as I understand it) not to withhold such a law. *But we must prevent the outspreading of the institution* because neither the Constitution nor the general welfare requires us to extend it. We must prevent the revival of the African slave trade and the enacting by Congress of a territorial slave code. We must prevent each of these things being done by either Congresses or courts. The people of these United States are the rightful masters of both Congresses and courts, not to overthrow the Constitution, but to overthrow the men who pervert the Constitution."

"To do these things we must employ instrumentalities. We must hold conventions; we must adopt platforms; we must nominate candidates; we must carry elections. In all these things, I think, we ought to keep in view our real purpose, and in none do anything that stands adverse to our purpose."

The telegraph carried the Ohio speeches to Kansas. They were answered by an invitation of the people to visit the new State, and a desire to see the man upon whom the people looked as the finisher, if not the author of their faith. He accepted their invitation. His journey through the young commonwealth was an unbroken procession. On foot, on horseback, in carriages and improvised vehicles, from distant farms the people came. Aged grandsire, sturdy boy, sunburned youth, blushing school-girl, maid and matron, united their voices in a continuous song of popular approval of the man who had done so much to make Kansas prosperous and free.

Meantime his fame had travelled eastward. Fortunately for the country he came to deliver an address in the great hall of the Cooper Institute in New York, in February, 1860. The hearts of the invitation committee sank in their bosoms when an awkward, ill-dressed, unassuming man announced himself as Abraham Lincoln, and expressed his doubts whether he could say anything to interest the people of a great city. A Sunday intervened. He went to hear Mr. Beecher. After the sermon the preacher introduced him to leading members of his congregation, who made swift discovery that he was no ordinary man.

There was magic enough in his name to fill the Cooper Institute with eager listeners. Bryant, the great poet, presided. Mr. Lincoln's address was long and it had none of the stirring eloquence of abolitionists of the Wendell Phillips school. It had little of the expected Western humor—it was profoundly argumentative. But the approval of the audience was unanimous and enthusiastic, and the most competent critics promptly pronounced it the most powerful contribution ever made to the literature of the slave question, and recognized the fact that it was the production of a great orator, competent to lead the army of freedom in a contest for the control of the republic.

Invitations to the New England cities were numerous from those who knew that he would touch the conscience of his hearers with the fire of his own enthusiasm. His lecture course was brief, his lectures four in number, but each one left a delighted audience and an ineffaceable impression upon the popular mind.

It is practically demonstrable that the speech in the Cooper Institute made Mr. Lincoln President of the United States. The Republican National Convention was held at Chicago on the 16th of May, 1860. Mr. Seward was the strongest candidate; Governor Chase, Mr. Cameron, and Judge Bates, of Missouri, each had their friends. But for the impression made by Mr. Lincoln's addresses in the East, the delegates from New York and New England would have unanimously supported Mr. Seward to the end. As it was, Mr. Seward would have been nominated if the vote had been taken immediately on the adoption of the platform. It was not, and the delay to him was fatal.

The balloting began on the morning of Friday, the 18th. No man ever surpassed Mr. Lincoln in the warm attachment of his friends. The delegation from

Illinois was solid and prepared to do anything honorable for their candidate. Knowing how closely he was in touch with the popular heart, it was said that they had packed the galleries with men who were to lead the applause for him. If this work was done it was superfluous. The delegates were touched with an enthusiasm for Lincoln that was infectious. There were four hundred and sixty-five votes in the convention, of which on the first ballot Mr. Seward received $173\frac{1}{2}$ and Mr. Lincoln 102. On the second ballot, Vermont, as she has done on many other occasions, led the triumphal march. Her delegates had voted for Mr. Collamer on the first ballot. The chairman, when Vermont was called on the second, announced her "ten votes for Abraham Lincoln." On this ballot Mr. Lincoln's vote was one hundred and eighty-one, or only three and a half votes less than Mr. Seward's one hundred and eighty-four and one half. On the third ballot Mr. Lincoln came within two of a majority. Before the vote was announced Mr. Carter, of Ohio, announced a change in the delegation from that State of four votes to Mr. Lincoln, which gave him the nomination.

Success in a national convention is always announced with applause. But no candidate was ever greeted with more vociferous evidences of approval than Mr. Lincoln. The ringing cheers of the delegates and the spectators, the shouts of the greater multitude in the streets, the music of many bands, the firing of cannon, created an uproar which delayed the announcement of the vote. On the final count there were three hundred and fifty-four votes for Mr. Lincoln. On motion of Mr. Evarts, the tried friend of Mr. Seward, the nomination was made unanimous; the convention took a recess until the afternoon, when the work of the convention was completed by the nomination of Mr. Hamlin for the second place on the ticket.

No one who took an active part in the campaign could have doubted the affection of the people for Mr. Lincoln or the wisdom of his nomination. The people are quick to discover in a candidate the qualities they value. Abraham Lincoln was no stranger in any section of the free States. As I have elsewhere written, "His name was an inspiration. It was everywhere the same. In the crowded city or at the country cross-roads; up in the mountain hamlets or out on the Western prairies; among the fishermen of the Atlantic and the miners of the Pacific coast, the political orator was heard with quiet consideration until he spoke the name of Lincoln. At that name, cheers such as never welcomed king or conqueror supplied his peroration." His unsoiled integrity; his kindness of heart; his sympathies broad enough for all forms of sorrow and misfortune; his earnest sincerity; his aversion to cant and pretence in the quadrangular contest which followed, secured to him his election, where Mr. Seward or Governor Chase or Mr. Cameron or Judge Bates would have been defeated. His nomination was one of the many providences which have contributed to the preservation of the republic.

It would be premature here to advert to the singular felicity and power with which Mr. Lincoln expressed his ideas. But as a perfect document of its kind, as well as a refutation of the wicked charge of infidelity which has been made against him, I here present his letter accepting this nomination:

"I accept the nomination tendered me by the convention. The declaration of principles and sentiments which accompanies your letter meets my approval, and it shall be my care not to violate or disregard it in any part. Imploring the assistance of Divine Providence and with due regard to the views and feelings of all who were represented in the convention, to the rights of all the States and Territories and people of the nation, to the inviolability of the Constitution, and the perpetual union, harmony, and prosperity of all, I am most happy to co-operate for the practical success of the principles declared by the convention."

Mr. Lincoln preserved his unbroken tranquillity of mind from his nomination until his election. His position was known; it required no explanation. He was opposed to slavery upon principle; he believed any increase of its power to be detrimental. But it had been established in the slave States by law and recognized by the Constitution. There it was a local institution, with which the Federal Government had no concern. He believed in the power and the duty of Congress to exclude slavery from the Territories by positive law, and he was ready to co-operate with all who were willing to labor to that end.

He was opposed by Mr. Douglas, the advocate of the doctrine of popular sovereignty, or the exclusive control by their legislatures of slavery in the Territories; by Mr. Breckenridge, the candidate of the Democrats, who asserted the duty and power of Congress to protect slavery in the Territories, and by Mr. Bell, the candidate of those who had no opinions on the subject of slavery. He firmly believed in his own election, he did nothing to divert the people from his support, and he was not disappointed. He received every electoral vote of the free States save four in New Jersey cast for Douglas; one hundred and eighty in all, or a majority in the electoral college of fifty-seven. Mr. Douglas received twelve, Mr. Breckenridge seventy-two, and Mr. Bell thirty-nine electoral votes. Of the popular vote Mr. Lincoln received 1,857,610; Mr. Douglas, 1,365,976; Breckenridge, 847,953; and Bell, 590,631.

Mr. Lincoln was not disturbed by the important events which followed his election and preceded his inauguration. Nor do I wish now to recall one single event in that disgraceful chapter of official weakness, of malignity, depravity, and actual treason. Mr. Lincoln had no difficulty in the selection of his Cabinet. Mr. Seward, Governor Chase, Messrs. Cameron, Bates, and Montgomery Blair had been the defeated candidates in the Chicago convention. They were therefore the principal favorites of his party, and their selection as members of his official family would secure the party support. One place in the Cabinet he would have given to the South; but no one would accept it in whom he could repose confidence, and he would not appoint any man to office whom he could not trust. One of the remaining places went to Indiana in fulfilment of a pledge which, unknown to him, his friends in the nominating convention had given to the delegates from that State, and with which he now rather unwillingly complied; the other to an acquaintance accidentally made on his New England lecture tour.

He had many visitors, who were received with perfect cordiality, but learned nothing of his future purposes. Toward the end of January, with the assistance of a copy of the Federal Constitution and a speech made by Henry Clay, he composed his first inaugural address, that official paper, for the power, eloquence, and beauty of which I have no words of adequate commendation, and he was then ready to abandon all private and personal interests and devote himself wholly and unreservedly to the service of his country.

He paid his last visit to one whom he loved as if she had been his own mother. His parting with her was the close of his private life. Henceforth he was to live for his country. He then prepared to commence his journey to the capital, where he was to enter upon his great official career.

Historians have written, artists have commemorated, and massive arches and columns have preserved the story of triumphal marches, imperial processions, and royal entries into great capitals; but history records no journey like that of the President-elect from Springfield to Washington. He had thus announced his faith: "I know that there is a God who hates slavery and injustice. If he has a place and work for me—and I think he has—I am ready; I know that I am right because liberty is right. Christ teaches it, and Christ is God." Never was farewell more touching than his to his Springfield neighbors: "To this people I owe all that I am; here I have lived more than a quarter of a century; here my children were born and here one of them lies buried. I go to perform a task more difficult than that which devolved upon Washington. Unless the great God who sustained him shall be with me and aid me, I shall fail. But if the same Omniscient Hand and Almighty Arm that directed him shall guide and support me, I shall not fail; I shall succeed. To him I commend you all. I ask that with equal faith you shall invoke his wisdom and guidance for me."

Then on the 11th of February he began that journey the record of which will be read with interest in distant centuries. At every city or considerable town he said something worthy to be remembered. At Tolono he said that the clouds were dark, but the sun was shining behind them. At Indianapolis he declared that the gates of hell could not prevail against a people united to defend their country. At Cincinnati, where were many Kentuckians, he told them that he must follow the great examples of Washington, Jefferson, and Madison, and again referring to the great task he had undertaken, he said: "I turn then and look to the great American people and to God, who has never forsaken them, for support." At Steubenville he declared that he should enforce the right of the majority to rule, and that if his policy was wrong they could turn him out at the end of four years. At Pittsburg he referred to the distracted condition of the country and announced his unswerving fidelity to the Constitution. At Cleveland he said that his heart was glad because all parties had united in his reception, and added: "If we do not unite now to save the good old ship of the Union on this voyage, no one will ever pilot her on another." At Buffalo, Rochester, Syracuse, Utica, Albany, Troy, Hudson, Poughkeepsie, Peekskill, New York City, Jersey City, and Newark, in various forms he repeated his confidence in the loyal people and his trust in God to preserve an united republic. At Trenton he told, out of Weems' life of Washington, the story of the depression of the loyal people when Washington crossed the Delaware and revived their hopes by the victory over the Hessians: a story learned in his boyhood. At Philadelphia the mayor had referred to the great Declaration and the Constitution, which had been made in Independence Hall. Mr. Lincoln seemed to be treading the mountain heights of eloquence when he replied: "All my political warfare has been in favor of the teachings that came forth from these sacred walls. May my right hand forget its cunning and my tongue cleave to the roof of my mouth if I ever prove false to those teachings." We know now the solemn sincerity of his assertion that sooner than give up the promise of liberty to all men made by that Declaration he *would be assassinated*. He predicted that there would be no bloodshed in the near future, unless the necessity was forced upon the Government, and then it would be shed in self-defence. Thus he pledged himself to the great Declaration and the Constitution, and with the solemnity of a prophet of old promised to live, and if it were the pleasure of Almighty God to die, by their immortal principles.

Where is there a word-picture more powerful or beautiful than that he drew at Harrisburg, the last upon this journey? It was the natal day of Washington. From Independence Hall with its crowded memories his hand had flung the Stars and Stripes to the golden rays of the morning sun. He thanked the commonwealth for its friendship to him, for its loyalty to the republic. He praised her military, and hoped it would never shed fraternal blood. The picture was brilliant in an atmosphere of freedom; there was on it no spot of rebellion, no stain of secession.

It was worthy of the time, of the country, and of the master-hand of Abraham Lincoln.

Left to his own inclinations, Mr. Lincoln would have left Harrisburg in the morning of February 23d, and have passed through Baltimore about midday, where, unless providentially protected, he would have fallen by the hand of hired assassins who lay in wait for him. He listened to good counsels; left Harrisburg about six o'clock in the evening, arrived in Philadelphia, crossed the city in a carriage, and entered a sleeping-car for Washington about twelve o'clock at night. Except a Scotch cap which he usually wore on the cars at night, he was undisguised. He was accompanied by Mr. Lamon, who was to be his marshal. His mind was so completely at rest that he fell asleep before the train left Baltimore and slept until it arrived at Washington. At the station he was met by Mr. Seward and Mr. Washburn, and unannounced, unheralded, almost unattended, Abraham Lincoln entered the capital of the republic he was divinely appointed to preserve.

Washington was a disloyal city. There had been weeks when loyal men and women could not walk its streets without insult. The horde of soldiers of fortune from Maryland and Virginia, attracted thither by the promise of revolution and the hope of plunder, and angry because both were postponed, dominated the city. The count of the electoral vote on the 13th of February had brought a delegation of active loyal men from the North and West, who defended themselves and for a few days had driven the drunken, gambling crew into their dens and holes. But the enfeebled administration, the audacity of the traitors, the lack of any defensive organization for the

Union, had so emboldened the gang that they had again assumed the offensive, and nothing appeared to restrain them but the threat of General Scott to manure the hills of Arlington with fragments of their bodies, blown from his cannon, if they dared to lay hands upon loyal men or their property. But the insignificance of his force was coming to be known, the States were seceding, the rebels growing bolder, and on the 23d of February the city was shrouded to loyal eyes in gloom and despondency.

No apartments had been engaged, no preparations were made for the reception of the President-elect. Accompanied by Mr. Seward and Mr. E. B. Washburn, he descended from an ordinary carriage at the ladies' entrance to Willard's, waited like a common traveller in the reception-room until rooms were assigned for his use, and then his friends left him. But he was not permitted to enjoy his seclusion. Twenty-four hours had not elapsed before the country knew that it had elected a President and that his name was Abraham Lincoln.

The discovery was produced by the "Peace Conference," as it was called, which was then in session in the hall of Willard's hotel. That conference had made a formal call upon the outgoing President at the instance of its delegates from the slave States. At the request of the delegates from the free North it voted to call upon the incoming President, who said he would be happy to receive its members in the evening of the day of his arrival.

In the Conference were influential men from the South, who became afterward prominent in the councils of secession. Among them were ex-President Tyler, William C. Rives, James A. Seddon,

Geo. M. Davis, General Zollicoffer, and others. These gentlemen anticipated a rare evening's entertainment. They expected to meet a "rail-splitter," a boor who would not open his lips without exposing his ignorance; a buffoon with a ready stock of vulgar wit; a clown whose antics would amuse them and mortify the Republicans. As they were successively presented they formed a circle about him, and each was held there by some inexplicable attraction. They saw a tall, powerful man whose grand face overlooked them all; whose voice was kindly, who greeted every one with dignity and a courteous propriety of expression which surprised his friends. Two or three of them experimented with questions which involved a slight contemptuous disrespect. Then his stature seemed to grow loftier and there was a ring to his voice and a flash from his eyes which discouraged a repetition of the experiment. Except for these answers his theme was the Constitution. That instrument was the safeguard of the republic. It was a great charter of liberty, framed by wise and prudent men, which bound the conscience of every citizen. He was about to renew his oath to obey and enforce it. It would not be obeyed and enforced until all its provisions and the laws passed by Congress were enforced in every State and Territory of the Union. If he became President the Constitution and laws would be so enforced to the utmost extent of his power!

Three well-defined types of expression were visible upon the faces of his auditors as these earnest words fell upon their ears. That of the secessionists was profound astonishment and disappointment. The more able Southerners evinced their regret for having misjudged him; the faces of the Northern loyal men were ablaze with a patriotic exultation which was almost irrepressible. There were a few Southern men whose opinions found expression in the declaration by one of them, "If those are your principles, Mr. Lincoln, I am with you to the end!"

On our way to our apartments after the close of the reception, an experienced and very able Southern statesman said: "The South is unfortunate; we have been deceived in Mr. Lincoln. We have been told and we believed that he was a reckless, ignorant man, unfit for the presidency, easily controlled by bad men. What I have seen to-night convinces me that he is a strong man who will have a strong administration."

If ten disciplined regiments of infantry had suddenly appeared on Pennsylvania Avenue, marching to the War Office to reinforce the few soldiers of General Scott, they would not have so inspired the hearts of loyal men with courage and confidence as did this timely, statesmanlike, bold announcement by Abraham Lincoln of his purpose to enforce, as well as obey, the Constitution and the laws. Flashed over the wires to the remotest portions of the free States, it aroused loyal men out of their despondency and thrilled their breasts with a new hope. The Almighty had called him to a great work, and the loyal country knew that Abraham Lincoln was ready.

CHAPTER XXXVII.

ABRAHAM LINCOLN: THE DIPLOMATIST — THE MILITARY STRATEGIST — THE MASTER OF ENGLISH PROSE — THE STATESMAN — THE GREAT PRESIDENT.

WHO shall write the history of the administration of our great President? Not one who knew the true-hearted man, who was so patient, so apt to teach, so gentle to others, that he inspired in one who came in contact with him an undying love which could not fail to find expression in his pen. By and by, in another century, when all those who saw his face when it did shine as the sun are no longer to be called as his witnesses, let the man be found who is his equal in prose composition, who is as just as Solomon, as wise as Solon, as great a soldier as Wellington, the Tacitus of his time; and let him be assigned to that duty. I will be content if I can describe some of the incidents which made us so honor and love Abraham Lincoln.

From the dome of the Capitol the statue of Liberty looked upon a great spectacle on the bright morning of March 4th, 1861. From the Executive Mansion to the Capitol gate, the avenue and its buildings on either side, from basement to roof; the grounds on the Potomac front; the many seats provided on the eastern side, the great square of the Columbus statue, and the windows of the Capitol—all the space was occupied by American citizens. They were orderly.

HIS INAUGRATION.

There were a few policemen present—they were in citizen's dress. A single field battery, the only one in Washington, was so concealed on the street fronting the old Capitol that only the few who were in the secret knew that even this slight preparation had been made to suppress any attempt at rebellion.

A small hollow square formed by the engineers of the regular army, inclosing an open carriage in which rode the aged, enervated, outgoing President, moved like a machine from the White House to Willard's Hotel. There a tall and stalwart figure, with an earnest face and firm step, entered the carriage, and the procession moved down the avenue to the Capitol, which was entered at the Senate door. After a brief delay for the exercises in the Senate chamber, another procession was formed and marched to the principal eastern exit. First came the stalwart figure, arm in arm with a senator. The venerable chief justice and associated justices of the United States, the diplomatic corps in full dress, senators, and high officers of the army and navy followed them. They advanced well to the front, where a table had been placed. On their right and left and in front of them, in silent expectation, was the largest audience that ever witnessed an inauguration. Then, clear as the tones of a silver bell, the voice of the most knightly man in all the land seemed to fill the invigorating air, reaching the most distant auditor, when the gallant Senator Baker said: "Fellow-citizens, I introduce to you Abraham Lincoln, the President-elect of the United States of America."

His first inaugural address was then delivered. From its opening words to its beautiful closing paragraph, the assembled thousands listened with an expectation almost painful in its intensity to every word of this remarkable paper. This had been the first silent inauguration since the foundation of the Government. When the President-elect first appeared to enter the carriage at his hotel, there was an attempt to applaud, but it was not successful. His long ride down the avenue, his entrance to the Senate chamber, his appearance before his great audience called forth almost no applause. His protest that he had no purpose to interfere with slavery, his reference to the Chicago platform, drew the attention of his audience more closely; his statement that he took the official oath with no mental reservations raised upon many faces a look of hopeful anticipation which grew more earnest when he declared his opinion that under the Constitution the Union of the States was perpetual—it was perilously near breaking into sound as he enlarged upon this topic—then he paused, and with face and hands uplifted, as if he was looking far into the unknown future, with a voice in which there was no trace of hesitation or uncertainty, he declared his own purpose to use the power confided to him by the Constitution to *hold, occupy, and possess the places and property of the United States, and to collect the duties and imposts,* and then all the barriers of doubt were swept away and every loyal breast gave forth a shout of thanksgiving which shook the ground and rent the air like a pæan of victory and freedom sung by loyal millions over the irrevocable doom of rebellion. The remaining paragraphs of this remarkable paper were heard with increasing evidences of loyal approval, and its close was indescribably pathetic. It was like the concentrated yearnings of a mother over a wayward child.

HIS OATH OF OFFICE.

With his left hand upon the open Bible, his right raised toward heaven, the solemn, earnest voice repeated slowly with distinct enunciation, after the venerable chief justice, the words of the oath to defend the Constitution: "I do solemnly swear that I will faithfully execute the office of President of the United States and will, to the best of my ability, preserve, protect, and defend the Constitution of the United States, so help me God."

Thus Abraham Lincoln became President of a republic from which seven States had attempted to secede, at an hour when it was infested by treason and threatened with armed rebellion. The telegraph flashed his great inaugural to the remotest corners of the country, but it was many days before its power or the plain declaration of its policy was appreciated. The country was not prepared for such a document. The more it was studied the more unanswerable it was felt to be. It was new in the elegance of its composition, but its principles were those which had long been advocated by its author. Still there was a force in its pointed truths which captivated the judgment, although there were some loyal Democrats who did not yield to its conclusions until the blow of treason fell.

In the rapid survey of the acts for which President Lincoln is to be justly credited or held responsible, to which this article is restricted, the reader should understand, at the outset and once for all, that for about three years in his judgment certain propositions had been firmly established and were no longer open to argument or question. One of these was that the slave power had determined to make slavery lawful everywhere within the republic, and nothing would prevent that consummation but the destruction of that power. In its success he knew the free States would never acquiesce until they were conquered. He conscientiously believed that slavery was a cruel injustice to the slave, a menace of increasing strength to the republic. By the clear light of his matured judgment he saw that for him the path of duty was the path of honor; he must obey the Constitution and enforce the laws; he must repress rebellion and destroy treason. If slavery and armed rebellion must both perish in the conflict he could not be held responsible at the bar of justice or his own conscience, and it would still be true that "all they that take the sword shall perish with the sword."

It was most fortunate for himself and for the country that Mr. Lincoln had constantly in his mind this standard of judgment, which determined for him what he should and what he should not do. For he had an extremely sensitive conscience and no capacity to avoid trouble or escape responsibility. Other Presidents had acquiesced in questionable precedents on the ground that they were established by department officers who were alone responsible for their continued application. He never in such or any other case permitted another to perform a duty which was imposed upon him by the law. If he had not been able by certain and fixed principles to determine questions of difficulty, anxiety and care would have worn out his life before the close of the second year of his term. In our judgment of his acts, then, we must never lose sight of his convictions. He knew that slavery was aiming at the domination of the republic and would fight before it would yield;

therefore in his mind slavery was doomed to extinction.

His inaugural address was denounced by the disloyal press as warlike and uncompromising. Seven States had formed a confederate government. One of its first acts was to dispatch envoys to Washington to negotiate for "a peaceful adjustment of the questions growing out of their political separation." The prompt decision of the President to deny them recognition was communicated to the envoys by Secretary Seward, on the 15th of March. On the 21st, Mr. A. H. Stephens, Vice-President of the Confederacy, in a speech in Savannah, Ga., fully justified the conclusions of President Lincoln by publicly declaring that the "*foundations of our new government are laid; its corner-stone rests upon the great truth that the negro is not equal to the white man; that slavery, subordination to the superior race, is his natural and moral condition. This our new government is the first in the history of the world based upon this great physical, philosophical, and moral truth.*" In a later speech Mr. Stephens declared that "the South was warring for political and social existence;" that "the most important feature in it [the Federal Constitution] was the obligation to return fugitive slaves;" that he would never surrender this obligation, "though every valley from here to the Potomac should run with Southern blood and every hill-top be bleached with Southern bones." He predicted that "in less than three years Lincoln and his Cabinet would come to the gallows or the guillotine, as those did who led the French to war," and all the people of the South shouted "Amen!" The envenomed suggestions of the Southern press, to fire into the loyal forts brittle cylinders filled with stinging snakes, tarantulas, centipedes, and scorpions, might be disregarded as silly, but Mr. Stephens was a statesman who spoke for slavery with authority.

President Lincoln neither predicted results nor attempted to change the lines of a conflict fixed by powers beyond his control. He had said that it was his duty to collect the revenues, enforce the laws, and occupy and possess the places and property of the Government. To this present duty he gave himself and used all the available resources of the country. At the head of each department he placed the best man he could select and restricted him only by one direction: to use all its powers to aid in the work to which he was called and had undertaken to execute. He prepared to reinforce Fort Sumter. But it was too late. The flag of Sumter fell before the trial could be made. Then the slave power struck the blow and fired the opening gun of rebellious war. Before its crime-infected roar had reached all the loyal States, as the flag of Sumter fell, the loyal lightning followed the sound, calling seventy-five thousand loyal men into the field, and the Congress to meet in extraordinary session. A million would have answered " Ready" to the call of Abraham Lincoln. Four days later he proclaimed a blockade of the Southern ports, and with favoring winds a hundred ships sailed to enforce it. High above the din of preparation came another call for forty-two thousand men to serve as infantry or cavalry, for *three years or during the war*, for an increase of twenty-three thousand men for the regular army, and eighteen thousand seamen for the same three years' term.

President Lincoln was no autocrat. He had called a force sufficient to maintain the *status quo*. Now it was his duty to consult Congress. A great wave of loyalty was rolling down from the free North. The nations saw the uprising of a great people, such as never shook the foundations of the earth before. It transcended description. It was more than life to live in such a time and to witness it. Lincoln saw it, and on the first day when Congress met and could affirm his act he answered it by another call for *four hundred thousand men and four hundred millions of money.*

Men born since the war, or, if before, were of those who stayed at home and resolved that the war was a failure, have criticised the President because he failed to appreciate the magnitude of the conflict and to call for a larger number of men to suppress the rebellion. Those who lived at the time or can intelligently read its history know better. The country had been at peace for almost fifty years (for in such gigantic events the brush with feeble Mexico should not count). Treason in high places had done its worst to exhaust the loyal North and to strengthen slavery with Northern resources. In such a country at such a time these labors of President Lincoln during the four first months of his administration are full proof that he rose above the highest level of his duty and earned his title of the great President of a free people.

There was no concealment of the policy of the President and his administration. He defined it in his letter to Mr. Greeley in August, 1862. "I would save the Union," he said; "I would save it in the shortest way under the Constitution." Such was his estimate of his duty. By it he measured every act which occurred to himself or was suggested by others. Was it right? Would it tend to suppress the rebellion and save the Union? If it would, he pressed it into instant service with all the strength he could command. If it would not, arguments in its favor made no more impression than if addressed to a granite rock. Was the man proposed the man who in that place would make it strongest for the Union? If yes, he received the appointment, no matter if he had spoken contemptuously and was the enemy of Abraham Lincoln. If nay, there was not influence enough in the nation to secure his appointment.

Aggressive war would tend to save the Union by destroying its enemies. Therefore it must be waged. But war entailed sorrow, misery, death, which wounded his great heart, and therefore no labor or sacrifice of his must be spared to diminish its miseries. This war was to be waged between citizens of the same country, brothers almost; therefore there must be no unnecessary ferocity, no vengeance in it, and for those who laid down their arms no punishment, no hard conditions.

Let us briefly sketch a few of the principal acts of his official term and ascertain whether or not they conform to this outline of his policy.

He wept hot tears for the men who fell in the first battle of Bull Run, and his heart bled for the wounded and the suffering; but he saw in the defeat only a necessary discipline by the Almighty of those who had exaggerated the strength of the Northern army and under-estimated the work it had to do. Not for one moment did he lose faith in the result, but he rose to the full appreciation of the danger and prepared his country for the new sacrifices it demanded.

In November, 1861, Captain Wilkes, of the U. S. steamer *San Jacinto*, took Mason and Slidell, the Confederate envoys, out of the British mail steamer *Trent*, on the high seas, and permitted her to continue her voyage. England demanded and the President ordered their surrender. Captain Wilkes could only have justified the seizure by bringing the steamer into port and securing her legal condemnation. Failing to do this, his act became a trespass *ab initio*, and so incapable of justification. Mr. Seward made this point clear by a diplomatic letter to Lord Lyons, the British minister, covering many pages of manuscript. Mr. Lincoln made it equally clear in the compact sentence, "Captain Wilkes had no authority to turn his quarter-deck into a court of admiralty."

From the fall of Sumter many strong men constantly pressed the President to strike the death-blow of slavery by a proclamation of emancipation. His answer was: "I will do it when it will best promote the national cause, and not until it will most help to save the Union." Early in August, 1862, he had substantially decided to issue this proclamation, and he again put off the day. Then Mr. Greeley wrote his querulous letter almost charging the President with cowardice and bad faith. The President replied in a remarkable and unanswerable model of official dignity, argumentative force, and English composition.

The colored people, who were most interested, did not share in Mr. Greeley's impatience. They had learned in whatsoever opinion *Massa Linkum* was, therewith to be content. A colored man brought to a Treasury officer in August, 1862, the news of the postponement of the proclamation. His words were "Massa Linkum thinks it best to wait until we win a victory, so the rebs won't think it is a *brutal* fulmen." "And you colored people must be greatly disappointed," said the officer. "Oh, no, sir!" was his cheerful, satisfied reply. "O' course Massa Linkum knows best when we should be made free." He did know best. On the 22d day of September, 1862, when the shattered legions of rebellion were fleeing from their bloody defeat at Antietam, he issued the proclamation. It was no *brutum fulmen*. The loyal people gave him audience unto this word, *emancipation;* and they lifted up their voices and said, "Away with such a monster from the earth! It is not fit that he should live." And as they cried out, slavery fell by the hand of Abraham Lincoln!

It was in this year 1862 that the letters from the President to the generals of his armies began to appear, which commonly closed with the remark, "This is what I think and not an order," but which so arrested the attention of military authorities. Masters of military science, skilled leaders of great armies in the field, read those letters now and exclaim: "This man was greater than any general then in command! He was a military strategist, the greatest of his time!"

Notable was his strong common sense which gave Fox to the navy and drew Sherman from his retirement to the command of armies. He restrained pretentious inexperience and brushed away the absurd hostility and contempt of the regular for the volunteer service in the army and navy; he bestowed the Christian and the Sanitary commissions upon the armies; gave the *Monitor* and armored vessels to the navy and improved arms to both branches of the service.

The literary world has had no superior to Abraham Lincoln in the composition of English prose. His farewell to his Springfield neighbors; his speeches at Trenton and at Independence Hall in Philadelphia; the closing paragraph of the first and the whole of the second inaugural address; the speech at Gettysburg; his letters to Mrs. Bixby and to Horace Greeley will not suffer by comparison with any English prose which had been theretofore written. A competent critic who has written an appreciative volume on the English prose of the present century properly selects the long letter of August 26th, 1863, to James C. Conkling as an unexcelled example of English prose.

I have said that he would appoint the best man for a place although he was his enemy. The quality which in this respect controlled him has been called his magnanimity. He seems to have been incapable, in such a case, of taking into account anything but qualifications for the place. General McClellan, who with singular impropriety had asserted that he was divinely appointed to save the country and had undertaken to instruct the President how to discharge his duties, had not hesitated to make imputations against him which were insulting. Yet he gave McClellan the command at Antietam, against the remonstrances of his Cabinet, because he believed that, as matters then stood, McClellan's appointment was the best he could make. Mr. Stanton in a domineering manner had appropriated a position in an important lawsuit to which Mr. Lincoln was entitled, and he felt the slight keenly at the time. He did not remember the incident when he made Mr. Stanton the great War Secretary and a member of his Cabinet. Mr. Chase had ridiculed his peculiarities, and resigned without excuse in a manner which was almost contemptuous. In the very hour of his resignation, when any but a great man would have resented the act, he decided to make Mr. Chase Chief Justice of the United States. Chase and Stanton stood by his dying bed. Sincere, intense grief silenced the voice of one; the other exclaimed, "There lies the greatest ruler of men the world ever saw!"

What man so sensitive, so compassionate, so tender, was ever so sorely tried? His children, and especially in his later life, were the objects that filled up the measure of his domestic life. There was something terrible in his speechless, cheerless grief when he lost them. His sorrow over Ellsworth, Baker, and other near friends found some relief in tears. His fear lest some great calamity might fall upon some life through his neglect took many hours from the rest so necessary to his wearied body. He seldom approved the death-sentence of a court-martial, and never until he knew all the facts and that the culprit deserved to die. "You will destroy the discipline of the army if you continue these pardons," remonstrated a high officer. "You must get along some way, for I cannot help doing it," was his noble, his beautiful reply. How speaking was every feature of his face when the captain was pleading for the sleeping sentinel! how quick his resolution himself to go and save him! How tender that interview, when none but God was present, and he talked with the boy "about his mother, and how she looked and how he ought never to cause her a sorrow or a tear," and so changed the mountain boy into a hero and then gave him his life! Who can read that letter to the Boston mother of five sons, who all "had died gloriously on the field of battle for their country" —nay, who has ever had one clear, unobstructed view of the inner life of Abraham Lincoln, and does not know that he was gentle as the beloved disciple and that a tenderer heart than his never beat in a human bosom?

That he was a *statesman* is now proved by almost every act of his administration for which he was responsible and which bears the impress of his own hand. No member of his Cabinet or of either house of Congress had at all times a clearer view of the situation or of what measures were practicable to suppress the rebellion and restore the Union. Surely no man had a clearer view than his of the cause of the Civil War and of the necessity of removing that cause in order to a lasting peace. His position as a wise, prudent, far-seeing statesman stands unquestioned in the history of his time.

He was a *diplomatist.* He influenced a Cabinet composed of able men of pronounced and conflicting opinions to act as a harmonious whole. The great powers would willingly have witnessed the fall of the republic. But our ship of State had a skilful pilot and an able captain. Lord Lyons and Drouyn de l'Huys met their equal in Mr. Seward, and Mr. Lincoln was never disturbed by the machinations of Louis Napoleon or the injudicious threats of Earl Russell.

He was a *military strategist.* Had his clear and

wise suggestions been followed as they should have been, the army of General Lee would not have recrossed the Potomac after Antietam nor after Gettysburg. His letter of October 13th, 1862, to General McClellan is pronounced by competent military critics as a masterpiece, which recognized and dealt with every alternative, and which, properly executed, would have ended the war in that year. His suggestions to the generals in command were always wise and prudent, and remarkable for their grasp of all the details of the situation.

He was a *master of English composition*. His two inaugural messages, his address at Gettysburg, and his letter to James C. Conkling of August 26th, 1863, have placed him at the very head of the English writers of the nineteenth century.

He was a *great President*. Before we conclude this brief and inadequate sketch, another of his qualities must be considered.

CHAPTER XXXVIII.

ABRAHAM LINCOLN—THE MAN FULL OF FAITH AND POWER.

IT remains to speak of the most attractive and altogether the grandest quality in the noble character of Abraham Lincoln: his simple, constant, undoubting Christian faith. To those who are familiar with his history or his words, any discussion of this trait will seem unnecessary. But there is a necessity for it which may as well be dealt with now as at any future time.

Only bold, bad men assert that there is no God—no future life. The statement is so shocking that most men hesitate to make it. The *free-thinkers*, as they call themselves, compromise with their sensibilities by admitting that there is a God, to whom they deny all useful attributes, and a future life, which they say is free from all responsibility.

Shades of professed belief among these people are unimportant. To all intents and purposes they are infidels and the world so regards them. They believe that they have no souls to be saved, but are laid in the grave like sheep. They are, as Paul declares, of all men most miserable. They love to insist that those whom the world delights to honor are as destitute of faith as themselves. It seems to comfort them to show that others are as miserable as themselves. They persist in the claim that Abraham

Lincon was an infidel. They know that faith in the God of the Bible has been comforting to millions; that it has always made men better as well as happier; that where that belief is not, there are the dark places of the earth. They know that men love the memory of Lincoln because of his faith in God. Yet they would drag him down to their own level, although it should distress and shock the world.

Except the proprietors of this calumny of his disbelief in the Bible and revealed religion, no man has sought to stain the memory of Lincoln. His revilers are few; they can be counted on the fingers of a single hand. They are all infidels of course; coarse-grained men, in whom the animal strongly predominates. With a strange perversity they profess to admire the man while they wound his friends and cover his name with obloquy. One of them, who is harmless because he is so vile, is a common scold. Others, whose association he admitted out of his kindness of heart, are moved by the habit of the guest who publishes what he imperfectly gathered at the table of his host, will be remembered only for their scandals and be forgotten with them; and another defies the opinions of good men and finds great satisfaction in the misuse of his intellect by extolling infidel writers and (to use his own expression) in "pitching into" Moses, our Saviour, and the religious faith of our greatest American.

Abraham Lincoln an infidel? It is time that this foul libel, which crawls in dark places like a noisome reptile, had the life stamped out of it by the steel-clad heel of God's eternal truth. Whether in that furnace of affliction through which he passed when pure Ann Rutledge died, when his friends feared for his reason, there were not hours of despondency when he cried out, "There is no God! no future, no justice," I neither know nor care. What I do know, what any one may know, is that he was afterward clothed and in his right mind, and then and ever afterward there was no more doubt of his sublime faith in an all-wise, omnipotent God and in the Bible than there was of his honesty or his existence.

There were men, and some of them still live, to whom his own expressions of his firm, undoubting faith are among their dearest memories of Abraham Lincoln. But they would despise themselves if they should oppose their personal testimony to the hearsay brain-dribble of these infidels and their witnesses. Nor would it be quite dignified to follow the example of Mr. Greeley, who commenced his refutation of a libel by remarking to the libeller: "You lie! You know you lie!" The witness I shall call will be unimpeachable; the world will accept his evidence against all the infidels who have been of all men most miserable since Nebuchadnezzar did eat grass as oxen and his nails were grown as bird's claws. My witness is *Abraham Lincoln!* Although it may involve some repetition, I shall bring togther his own statements of his views of the Deity, Christianity, and the Bible.

On the 11th of February, 1861, Abraham Lincoln left his home and private life on his way to the capital to undertake a great public trust, under circumstances of appalling difficulty. He knew and said that the duty was greater than had been imposed upon Washington or any man since his time. He said: "He [Washington] never could have succeeded except for the aid of Divine Providence. I feel that

I cannot succeed without the same divine aid which sustained him, and on the same Almighty Being I place my reliance for support; and I hope you, my friends, will all pray that I may receive that divine assistance without which I cannot succeed, but with which success is certain." *)

Was Abraham Lincoln a pretender? No traitor, copperhead, or infidel ever made that accusation. Then he believed in and trusted Almighty God and in the efficacy of the prayers of his neighbors.

At Cincinnati on the same journey he said: "I cannot but turn and look for the support without which it will be impossible for me to perform that great task. I turn, then, and look to the great American people, *and to that God who has never forsaken them.*"

At Albany he said that he still had "confidence that the Almighty, the Maker of the Universe, will bring us through this as he has through all the other difficulties of our country."

At Newark, N. J., on the 21st of February, he said to the mayor: "With regard to the great work of which you speak, I will say that I bring to it a heart filled with love for my country and an honest desire to do what is right. I am sure, however, that I have not the ability to do anything unaided of God, and that without his support and that of this free, happy, and intelligent people, no man can succeed in doing that, the importance of which we all comprehend."

In Independence Hall, after a patriotic reference to the memories of the place and the statement that he would be assassinated sooner than give up the promise of liberty to all men comprised in the great

Declaration there signed, he concluded thus: "I have said nothing but what I am willing to live by and, if it be the pleasure of Almighty God, to die by."

So much before he became President. But the Pickthanks of infidelity will say that these extracts do not prove that he had any faith in the Christian religion or in organized systems of Christianity. The doubting Thomases on that subject may be referred to the sentence in his first inaugural address in which he said that "intelligence, patriotism, Christianity, and a firm reliance on Him who has never yet forsaken this favored land are still competent to adjust in the best way our present difficulty."

His first message to Congress, on the 5th of July, 1861, after a complete statement of his views of the national duty, closes with these words:

"And having thus chosen our course, without guile and with pure purpose, let us renew our trust in God and go forward without fear and with manly hearts."

His message to the first regular session of Congress in December closed with this paragraph:

"The struggle of to-day is not altogether for to-day: it is for a vast future also. With a reliance on Providence, all the more firm and earnest, let us proceed in the great task which events have devolved upon us."

On the 13th of September, 1862, a deputation representing the religious denominations of Chicago presented a memorial requesting him to issue the proclamation of emancipation at once. To this memorial he made a very temperate reply, and arguments pro and con followed. If he entertained the contempt of the infidel for Christian organization and work, here was an excellent opportunity to express it. Instead of doing so he said:

"I have not decided against a proclamation of liberty to the slaves, but hold the matter under advisement. And I can assure you that the subject is on my mind, by day and by night, more than any other. *Whatever shall appear to be God's will, I will do.*"

On the opening day of the year 1863 he did proclaim liberty throughout all the land unto all the inhabitants thereof. And he said: "Upon this act, sincerely believed to be an act of of justice . . . I invoke the considerate judgment of mankind and the gracious favor of Almighty God."

On the 24th of September, 1862, referring to his announcement of his purpose to issue the emancipation proclamation, he said to his fellow-citizens who serenaded him in the Executive Mansion: "What I did, I did after a very full deliberation and under a very heavy and solemn sense of responsibility. I can only trust in God I have made no mistake."

On the 16th of November, 1862, by an order over his own signature, he enjoined upon the officers and men of the army and navy "the orderly observance of the Sabbath," and added: "The importance for man and beast of the prescribed weekly rest, the sacred rights of Christian soldiers and sailors, a becoming deference to the best sentiments of a Christian people and a due regard for the divine will, demand that Sunday labor be reduced to the measure of strict necessity. The discipline and character of the national forces should not suffer nor the cause they defend be imperilled by the profanation of the day or name of the Most High." He also adopted the words of Washington in a similar order issued in 1776.

April 10th, 1862, after the bloody battle of Pittsburg Landing, because "it has pleased Almighty God to vouchsafe signal victories to the land and naval forces," he recommended to the people of the United States, at their next weekly meeting, that "they especially acknowledge and render thanks to our Heavenly Father for these inestimable blessings; that they implore spiritual consolation in behalf of all who have been brought into affliction by the casualties and calamities of sedition and civil war, and that they reverently invoke the divine guidance for our national counsels," to the restoration of harmony and peace.

In December, in his message to the third session of the Thirty-seventh Congress, he said:

"We know how to save the Union. The world knows we do know how to save it. In giving freedom to the slave we assure freedom to the free. Other means may succeed; this could not, cannot fail. The way is plain, peaceful, generous, just; a way which, if followed, the world will forever applaud and God must forever bless."

July 4th, 1863, after Gettysburg, the President in a proclamation of six lines announced the great success to the cause of the Union, and "especially desires that on this day He whose will, not ours, should ever be done, be everywhere remembered and reverenced with profoundest gratitude."

On the 19th of November, dropping from his lips like lilies, the entranced world received the golden words of the Gettysburg address, and knew that the brave men who there gave their lives that the nation might live had "not died in vain; that this nation under God shall have a new birth of freedom, and that government of the people, by the people, and for the people shall not perish from the earth."

On July 15th, in view of the victories and losses and domestic afflictions which had followed them, he said it was "meet and right to recognize and confess the presence of the Almighty Father and the power of his hand." He called on the people, "in the form approved by their own consciences, to render the homage due to the Divine Majesty for the wonderful things he has done in the nation's behalf, and invoke the influence of his holy Spirit to subdue the anger which has sustained a needless and cruel rebellion; to change the hearts of the insurgents; to guide the counsels of the Government with wisdom adequate to so great an emergency, and to lead the whole nation through paths of repentance and submission to the divine will back to union and fraternal peace."

On the 3d of October, 1863, Abraham Lincoln, in a thanksgiving proclamation, declared that the bounties we enjoyed could "not fail to penetrate and soften even the heart which is habitually insensible to the ever-watchful providence of Almighty God. . . . No human counsel hath devised nor hath any mortal hand worked out these great things. They are the gracious gifts of the Most High God, who, while dealing with us in anger for our sins, hath nevertheless remembered mercy."

He therefore "set apart a day of thanksgiving and prayer to our beneficent Father, who dwelleth in the heavens, and recommends to the people that they may commend to his tender care the widows, orphans, mourners, and sufferers, and implore the Almighty Hand to heal the wounds of the nation."

In the letter to J. C. Conkling of August, 1863, justly reproduced by an eminent British authority in the world of letters as one of the best specimens of English prose of the current century, he said in conclusion: "Let us apply the means, never doubting that a just God, in his own good time, will give us a rightful result."

Invited, but being unable to preside over a meeting of the Christian Commission in Washington on the day it was held, Mr. Lincoln declined in a letter in which he said: " I cannot withhold my approval of the meeting and its worthy objects. Whatever shall be, sincerely and in God's name, devised for the good of the soldiers and seamen, can scarcely fail to be blessed, and whatever . . . shall strengthen our reliance on the Supreme Being for the final triumph of the right cannot but be well for us all."

"The birthday of Washington and the Christian Sabbath coinciding this year, and suggesting together the highest interests of this life and of that to come, is most propitious for the meeting proposed."

He said: "For their conduct during this war God bless the women of America." At the close of the bloody week in the Wilderness, on the 9th of May, 1864, he said of it: "Enough is known to claim our special gratitude to God. While what remains undone demands our prayers to and reliance on him (without whom effort is vain), I recommend that all patriots do unite in common thanksgiving and prayer to Almighty God."

Congress had adopted a resolution for a day of fasting and prayer. President Lincoln appointed it on the first Thursday in August. He calls upon all who are in the service of the Government and all citizens to unite with him "to confess and repent of their sins; to implore the compassion and forgiveness of the Almighty, that he may enlighten the nation to know and to do his will; that he might quicken the consciences of those in rebellion to lay down their arms, that peace may be established throughout our borders." Mr. Lincoln writes that he "cordially concurs with Congress in the penitential and pious sentiments expressed in the resolutions, and heartily approves the devotional design and purpose thereof."

On the 3d of September, 1864, the successes of Sherman and his army and the other victories called forth from Abraham Lincoln another proclamation of "devout acknowledgment to the Supreme Being, in whose hands are the destinies of nations, of thanksgiving for his mercy, and that prayer be made for divine protection to our brave soldiers and for comfort from the Father of Mercies to the sick, the wounded, and the prisoners, and that he will continue to uphold the Government."

The thanksgiving proclamation of October 20th, 1864, was of a similar tenor. His address on November 10th, in answer to a serenade, contained that golden sentence, "So long as I have been here I have not willingly planted a thorn in any man's bosom," and he said: "I am duly grateful, as I trust, to Almighty God for having directed my countrymen to a right conclusion."

To that Boston mother of "five sons who have died gloriously on the field of battle" he wrote among other comforting words: "I pray that our Heavenly Father may assuage the anguish of your bereavement and leave you only the cherished memory of the loved and lost."

To Mrs. Gurney, the excellent Quakeress, he wrote: "It has been your purpose to strengthen my reliance in God. I am much indebted to the good Christian people of the country for their constant prayer and consolation, and to none of them more than to yourself. The purposes of the Almighty are perfect and must prevail. We hoped for a termination of this terrible war long before this, but God knows best and has ruled otherwise. We shall yet acknowledge his wisdom and our own errors. Meanwhile we must work earnestly. Surely he intends some great good to follow this mighty convulsion which no mortal could make and no mortal could stay. . . . I hope still to receive for my country and myself your earnest prayers to our Father in heaven."

To the Presbyterians who had presented him with resolutions of approval he said: "From the beginning I saw that the issues of the great struggle depended on the divine interposition and favor. Relying as I do upon the Almighty Power, with support which I receive from Christian men, I shall not hesitate to use all the means at my control to secure the termination of the rebellion, and with hope for success."

To the Methodists he said: "It is no fault in others that the Methodist Church sends more soldiers to the field, more nurses to the hospitals, and more prayers to heaven than any other. God bless the Methodist Church. Bless all the churches; and blessed be God, who in this our great trial gives us the churches."

To the Baptists he said he had "great cause of gratitude for the support so unanimously given by all the Christian denominations of the country."

It only remains to cite two additional evidences under his own hand of the faith of Abraham Lincoln. One is the second inaugural message, a composition so beautiful in itself, so irresistible in its demonstration of his Christian faith that it deserves to be engraved upon the memory of every American citizen. To quote an extract from it would be to emasculate a document in which there is no superfluous word. As in the pathetic beauty of its composition this address has no superior, so in its faith in the Bible and the just providences of God it will stand forever as a permanent witness of the Christian faith of its great author.

Mr. Lincoln has left the world in no doubt about his opinion of the Bible. The reason why his speeches and writings are so admirable is because of the influence of the Bible which pervades them. Here is his opinion of the Book of Books, first publicly given to the colored men of Baltimore who presented him with a copy of one of its best editions:

"In regard to the great Book, I have only to say *that it is the best gift which God has ever given to man. All the good from the Saviour of the world is communicated to us through this Book. But for this Book we could not know right from wrong. All those things desirable to man are contained in it. I return you sincere thanks for this very elegant copy of this great Book of God which you present.*"

If Abraham Lincoln had foreseen that in the latter times there would be men to give heed to seducing spirits and speak lies of his Christian faith, he could not have given stronger proof of it than he has in these declarations and in his daily life and conversation. He has left no point uncovered. He believed in an all-powerful, all-wise, merciful God who rewards the good and punishes the wicked; who hears and answers prayer; who is forgiving to the penitent and compassionate to the sorrowing; who hates slavery and all forms of cruelty; who no more resembles the good-for-nothing Deity of Paine and Voltaire than the wooden god of the Fiji Islander. His creed comprised immortality and a future life of conscience and responsibility. He not only accepted but he welcomed the Bible as the revelation of God's will, and he united with all the thinking men who have made frequent use of its inspired pages, in the opinion that it is the greatest of all books, "the best gift which God has ever given to man." He esteemed it primarily because it revealed "the Saviour of the world." His use of the Bible appears in his best writings; the second inaugural address shows how well he knew it. He was under a constant sense of his responsibility to his God; he favored and assisted all forms of Christian organization and work; he thanked God for the churches—for *all* the churches. It strengthened him to know that good men and good women remembered him in their prayers. On one subject his faith amounted to conviction: the suppression of the rebellion, the restoration of the Unon, were certain because they had been decreed by Almighty God. No public man has left on record so many and such conclusive proofs of his belief in the Bible and in the teachings of the Bible, comprising in these teachings all the details common to Christian systems and churches.

His libellers say that Mr. Lincoln never attended religious exercises or united with any church. Omission to unite with a church is no evidence of a want of Christian faith. The influences are numerous which restrain many good men from uniting with a church; too numerous to be mentioned here. But it would be singular, indeed, if such a man had not set the good example to others of attendance on some religious services on the Sabbath day when not prevented by unavoidable duties. Therefore its treasury records will show that from March, 1861, when he came to Washington, until the close of his life, more than four years afterward, he was a pew-holder and a reverent worshipper in the Presbyterian church on New York Avenue, between Thirteenth and Fourteenth Streets, of which the Rev. P. D. Gurley, D.D., was the pastor. That he was a regular attendant there on Sabbath mornings is a fact known to a very large congregation of residents of and visitors to the capital; to none better than to the writer. Dr. Gurley, his beloved pastor, who had been his comforter in many sorrowful hours, was on his knees by the President's bedside in audible prayer when invisible saints and angels bore his great soul to the God in whom he trusted.

Voltaire and Paine are the standards by which the free-thinkers love to compare Mr. Lincoln. It is possible that their disciples may discover in some infrequented corner of their writings evidence that Voltaire and Paine believed in some kind of immortality and in a God for which they had but little use. But men are the architects of their own reputation. These gentlemen have made theirs. They have made the world accept them as deists, scoffers at religion, contemners of all Christian organization and work; who abhorred churches; who rejected the Bible and all divine revelation. They are supposed to have been *infidels* of a blind and senseless perversity in refusing belief in anything Christian. To compare Abraham Lincoln with such men is wicked—as wicked as blasphemy. He was as far apart from them as the east is from the west; as far superior to them as the heaven is high above the earth.

Farther proof would be wasted. None but those who wish to deceive themselves in the face of his words, his acts, and his daily life will believe that Mr. Lincoln was a deist, an infidel, or a disciple of Paine and Voltaire. If they will not accept his own evidence, if they hear not Moses and the prophets, neither will they be persuaded though one rose from the dead.

Should it become necessary to resort to the description of hearsay evidence upon which the charges of infidelity are exclusively founded, those who love the fame of Lincoln will find themselves compassed about with a great cloud of witnesses, who, lest their testimony might be lost, have entered it upon a permanent record. Newton Bateman, in 1861 the Superintendent of Public Instruction in Illinois; Dr. Holland, Noah Brooks, Schuyler Colfax, General Wadsworth, H.C. Deming, of Connecticut, Sojourner Truth, and the Rev. Drs. J. C. Thompson, Bellows, and Vinton, and a multitude of others have left on record material evidence.

The extract which follows is scarcely an exception to my purpose to restrict the evidence of Mr. Lincoln's view of Christianity to his own statements. Isaac N. Arnold was no stranger to me. He possessed some of Mr. Lincoln's best qualities; for example, his kindness of heart and amiability. No man knew Mr. Lincoln more appreciatively than Mr. Arnold. He had known him from the time he came to the bar; had been many times associated with him as counsel, and they had been close friends. Mr. Arnold had "wintered and summered" with him and was consulted by him frequently while he was President. I know of no man who enjoyed his confidence more thoroughly, who had studied his character more profoundly, or who could speak more accurately of his religious views than Mr. Arnold. Yet I would not call him as a witness if he had not furnished the proof of his own conclusions.

" Mr. Arnold says of him what his writings prove: "He knew the Bible by heart. There was not a clergyman to be found so familiar with it as he. Scarcely a speech or paper prepared by him but contains apt allusions and striking illustrations from the sacred book." "No more reverent Christian than he ever sat in the executive chair, not excepting Washington. He was by nature religious; full of religious sentiment. It is not claimed that he was orthodox. For creeds and dogmas he cared little. But in the great fundamental principles of the Christian religion he was a firm believer. Belief in the existence of God; in the immortality of the soul; in the Bible as the revelation of God to man; in the efficacy and duty of prayer; in reverence toward the Almighty and in love and charity to man, was the basis of his religion." "

" After referring to some of the written proofs of Mr. Lincoln's views above cited and his letter to his sick father written in January, 1851, Mr. Arnold gives the creed of the President in his own words:

"I have never united myself to any church, because I found difficulty in giving my assent, without mental reservation, to the long and complicated statements of Christian doctrine which characterize their articles of belief and confessions of faith. When any church will inscribe over its altar, as its sole qualification for membership, the Saviour's condensed statement of the substance of both law and gospel (the golden rule), that church shall I join with all my heart and soul."

"When," continues Mr. Arnold, "the unbeliever shall convince the people that this man, whose life was straightforward, truthful, clear, and honest, was a sham and a hypocrite, then, but not before, may he make the world doubt his Christianity."

It is to be regretted that the germs of the falsehood of Mr. Lincoln's infidelity cannot be annihilated once for all. But it is difficult to destroy such a falsehood. Remains of the poison will survive and occasionally find some diseased brain where they may rest, multiply, and create an offensive local suppuration. But it cannot spread among the American people. A public service of his country and almighty God, guided by the gospels of our Saviour, which began in his letter to his sick father in 1851 and ended with his last proclamation for a national thanksgiving, has so enshrined the memory of Lincoln in the hearts of his countrymen that it can neither be clouded by falsehood nor defaced by time.

The attentive reader of the letters, documents, and reported speeches of Mr. Lincoln will be impressed with the compactness, force, and beauty of his sentences. Immediately after his death the extreme rarity of his autograph notes and letters became noticeable.

Except those of an official character, they are scarcer and more difficult to procure than those of any other President, not excepting Washington. The finish of his prose and the scarcity of his unofficial autographs are both evidences of the depth and thoroughness of his character. He never spoke from a manuscript, yet he never wrote, spoke, or thought extemporaneously. To remove his doubts about a word he solved all the problems of Euclid. His mastery of the whole subject of slavery was equalled by none of its votaries. It was his custom, reclining in a quiet room, to repeat the different forms of expressing the same idea. It has been said that he wrote the Gettysburg address with a lead-pencil on the cars riding to the battle-field. Possibly—and yet it would not follow that he had not expended as much time and thought over its few lines as Mr. Everett had upon his ornate oration.

Abraham Lincoln was great because he was an honest, thorough, faithful Christian man. He was the man whom God raised up to save the Union and to set before the world a great example. To us who were his witnesses, he was a man called and assigned to a mighty work, thoroughly conscious that he was God's instrument to do that work; to the last hour of the republic he should serve as an example of the highest type of the statesman, patriot, citizen, in a government of the people. I have written this sketch, not as an attempt at his biography, but as a witness to the truth and to commend his life to the study of my countrymen.

Was he our greatest American? Was he greater than Washington? I do not know. Such inquiries do not concern me. What I do know is that they lived at different times, under different conditions, and were endowed with different qualities. They were both great men. But they are neither rivals nor competitors in American history nor in the American heart. The noble form, majestic presence, and patriotic example of Washington have lost none of their force upon the American mind by the lapse of one hundred years. The strong face of Lincoln grows more beautiful, his rich voice more musical, his perfect sentences more powerful as they are seen and heard only in our memories. Hand in hand and side by side Washington *and* Lincoln will grow in influence and power as they recede into the past. One will always be known as the Father, the other as the Saviour, of his country; and so long as patriotism, integrity, and virtue are honored among men, so long shall the memories of both be venerated and that of our Lincoln be tenderly loved.

THE END.

INDEX.

Adirondack fishing days, 148
Adirondack Woods, Vandalism in, 159; Importance to water-supply of Hudson valley, 160; Necessity for protection of, 163
Albemarle, the ram, Sinking of, 311
Allen, Gen. Ethan, his daughter enters a convent, 79
Allen, Fanny, the beautiful American Nun, 83
Armory, Burning of, in Savannah, 260
Armstrong, Jack, his fight with Lincoln, 353
Artist, An American, and his Scotch wife, 141
Auditor, Opinion of a "holdover," 318

Bar supper, The annual, 205, 219
Barn-Burners, The New York, 12
Banks, A skilful fraud on Vermont, 29; A way to swindle with fraudulent notes, 54; State effect of National Currency Act on, 96
Bank swindler, How to know a, 26

Bang, a favorite Irish setter, 178, 181
Barber, Edward D., the poet of Free Soil, 206
Barn and other swallows, 111
Barney, Valentine and Elisha, 277
Bear, how I lost one in the Adirondacks, 144
Beckwith, Gen. Amos, Sherman's Quartermaster, 255
Bench and bar, Early, of Vermont, 18
Bennett, Milo L., a Vermont judge, 200
Bible, Mr. Lincoln's opinion of the, 421
Birds, Notes on, 101, 106
Blair, Francis P., letter on Lincoln's death, 243
Book chase, The, 279
Book thieves, their work, 295
Book-account, Action of, 209
Boorn case, The, 330
Bradley, William C., Mr. Van Buren's opinion of, 15
Bramble, Hiram, his wife and his trials, 170, 174, 176
British captain, A disappointed, 254
Bronx River, its diminution, 166

Bryant, W. C., on Diminution of Streams, 167
Bucking the tiger in Nevada, 135
Buffalo Convention, 1848, Call for, 16
Bulwagga Bay, Duck-shooting in, 182
Burlington, her misfortunes, 201

Cabinet officers, Lincoln's reason for their selection, 386
Cartier, Jacques, his men cured of scurvy by an Indian, 196
Case, A celebrated, 200
Catholicism, Fanny Allen's conversion to, 88
Chase, Secretary, his policy, 90
Champlain, Autumn on, 169; Game on, 185
China, "La Chine," supposed to be by Cartier's men, 196
Chipman, George, a side judge and a gentleman, 206
Chipman, Daniel, an early Vermont lawyer, 22
Client, A grateful, 53
Circumstantial evidence, Dangers of, 330
Cold River and its trout in 1846, 148
Collamer, Hon. J., assists in Bank Act, 98
College graduate, A, mining in Nevada, 129
Colored people following Sherman's army, 267
Colored pilot on the Savannah River, 204

Comanche Indians, how best disposed of, 118
Contempt of court goes unpunished, 214
Contrast, The, the first American play, 287
Crow family, The, habits of, 102
Cushing, Lieut., sinks the *Albemarle*, 311
Cooper Institute speech, Lincoln's, 381
Conkling, J. C., Lincoln's letter to, 405

Dams on Adirondack rivers, their injury, 163
Deer, Floating for, 141
Democratic Convention in Vermont in 1848, 4
Dialects, Canuck-French and Yankee, 169
Douglas, debate with Lincoln, 374
Duck-shooting in East Creek, 175
Dunderberg, The ram, sold to Russia, 313

Eagle, The white-headed, a robber, 225
East Creek, Duck-shooting in, 175
Emancipation Proclamation, The, 403
Engineering taught by swallows, 113
Essex Junction, its miseries, 202

INDEX. 431

Faro, A game of, and its results, 136
Fires, Forest, and their injuries, 163
Fisher, Fort, Second attack on, 249
Floodwood, The Vermont, 47
Forests destroyed for charcoal, 160
Fox, Capt. G. V., his character, 107
Free Soil Party, Origin of, 1
Free Soil Courier, Publication of, 9

Gambler, A Western, 126
Geary, General, his division in Savannah, 132
Goesbriand, Bishop, of Vermont, his cathedral, 81, 89
Greaser, a Mexican, A chase for, 117
Greenbacks, their first issue, 95
Green River Station, a tenderfoot, 116
Greeley, Horace, The President's letter to, 404
Grizzly Gulch under Lynch law, 132
Gurowski, Adam, his notes, 320
Gurley, Rev. P. D., Lincoln's pastor, 420

Hall, Mr. and Mrs., their spiritualism, 70
Harrington, Theophilus, on title to a slave, 21
Hatteras Inlet, Fishing in, 263

Haynes, Rev. Lemuel, a colored minister, 335
Hog Island, Teaching school on, 269–273
Hough, Prof. John, his criticism, 285
Hudson River, its diminution from forest destruction, 165
Hypnotism, Experiences in, 70

Indian medical remedies, 196
Inaugural address, Lincoln's, 396
Italy, Destruction of forests in, 166

Judges, Early Vermont, 19
Judges, Wooden side, 44

Keyes, Elias, Anecdote of, 20

Law, a progressive science, 328
Law and order at a discount in a mining country, 130
Lecompton fraud, 372
Lincoln, Abraham, Notes on the day of his death, 236; Effect of his death in New York, 242; Blair, F. P., letter on, 243; Clears a steamer for Savannah, 247; How he reinforced Grant, 315; A woodchopper, 316; His origin and early life, 340; His ancestors, 344; His books, 347; His failures, 349; Was he a rail-splitter? 350; His fight with Armstrong, 353; His success as a lawyer, 356; Defends

INDEX.

young Armstrong, 358; His popularity, 365; A popular speaker, 367; His letter to Joshua Speed, 370; His study of slavery, 377; Opposes Lecompton fraud, 372; His "Divided House" speech, 375; His debate with Douglas, 374; His reply to Douglas in Chicago, 375; His speeches in Ohio in 1859, 379; Speeches in Kansas and in Cooper Institute, New York, 381; Nominated for the Presidency, 383; His election, 356; His first inaugural, 387; Farewell to Springfield, 388; Arrives in Washington, 390; Receives the Peace Conference, 391; Delivers his first inaugural, 395; Takes the oath of office, 397; His pardons, 406; His prose composition, 406; His Christian faith, 409; His opinion of the Bible, 421; His attendance at Dr. Gurley's church, 421

Lindenwald, A day at, in 1848, 14

Long Lake in 1846, 139

Lynch law, An execution by, 123

McCook family, The fighting, 306

Maeck, Jacob, attorney, 199

Magazines, Early, in Vermont, 284

Malaria in Tuscany which swallows avoid, 166

Medicine, the "Ecolectic" school, 191

Militia Act of the Third House, 49

Minister and his boys in the forest, 140

Miracle, A Vermont, 81

Monte, A game of, 128

Moosalamoo Bank charter, 37

Moose Creek, Floating for deer in, 145

Mosby "can't have them hosses," 325

Murder in a mining-camp, 126; Statistics of, 137

Murderer, Swift punishment of a, 136

Needham, Horatio, 206

New England, Diminution of rivers in, 160

New York, ill-treatment of Croton water-shed, 168

Niles, Nathaniel, his Sapphic ode, 287

Official influence, Value of, 231

Omaha railroad station, An incident in, 114

Osborne, W., Murder of, 128

Ospreys and their habits, 223

Otter Creek, Little, incidents, 169

Owls and their peculiarities, 221

Pacific Railroad travel, Early, 114

Pamphlets, their short lives, 289

INDEX. 433

Partridge, common name of ruffed grouse, 105
Peace Conference calls on President Lincoln, 392
Phelps, Hon. Samuel S., Mr. Webster's opinion of, 18
Phelps, Edward J., a Vermont lawyer, 80
Pierpont Brothers, Robert and John, 18, 206
Pigeon, The passenger, its disappearance, 107
Pitkin, Perley P., a Vermont quartermaster, 323
Pliny, Medical remedies of, 194
Porpoises, how do they communicate? 264
Presents to Treasury officers, 228
Privilege, The quack's, 190
Profits of office, 234
P........ who "made all the noise," 206

Quack, A typical, 189
Quacks and quackery, 186

Railroad engineering taught by birds, 113
Ramon, Jesus, a Mexican Greaser, 117
Railroads, Early, in Vermont, 198
Robinson, Rowland, his books, 169
Rushlow, Captain, one of my scholars, 278

Sabattis, Mitchell, Adirondack guide, 141, 146, 156

28

"Sanders' Indian Wars," its rarity, 282
Savannah in winter and in war, 246, 260
"Scrap" in a Nevada faro game, 135
Scientific navigation by a coasting captain, 251
School-teaching on Hog Island, 272
Seymour, "Squire" Horatio, father of the bar, 206
Sherman and his army in Savannah, 259
Slavery, changes in its policy, 376; The corner-stone of the Confederacy, 399
Smalley family, The, 329
Snipe, English, their habits, 180, 196
Speed, Joshua, Lincoln's letter to, 370
Spinner, Francis E., his character, 317
Spiritualism and its mediums, 70
Spooner, Judah Paddock, first Vermont printer, 287
Stage held up by robbers, 132
Stanley, Marcus Cicero, detective, 55
Stolen drawings of old masters, 296
Suffolk Bank and its president, 27
Swallows, their habits, 109
Switzerland, Destruction of forests in, 166
Swanton, Teaching school in, 276

INDEX.

Teal, blue-winged and green-winged, Flight of, 175
Telegraphic message, A peculiar, 114, 120
Third House, The, in Vermont, 33, 49, 51
Thompson, John, organizes First National Bank, 99
"Ti" Creek, Shooting in, 181
Tiger, Bucking the, in Nevada, 135
Tilden, Samuel J., a Barn-Burner, 15
Treasury, U. S., condition in 1861, 90; Experiences in, 228
Trent case, The, 403
Tunnel, A new railroad, 103
Tuscany, Destruction of forests in, 166
Tyler, Royal, author of "The Contrast," 287

Unique books do not exist, 292

Unlicensed sale of liquors, 211
Valentine, Basil, his last will, 194
Van Buren, Martin and John, 11
Vermont, Early bench and bar of, 18
Vernon, Mount, Washington's plan of, 294

Wade, Ben, opposes Lincoln's renomination, 314
Wadsworth, Gen. James S., 303, 322
Washington in March '861, 390
Washington, George, sale of his books, etc., 290, 293, 341
Wetherby, Alonzo, an Adirondack guide, 141
Wilson, Thomas ~~~~~~~, 54, 67
Yale graduate, a miner and judge in Nevada, 130, 136

www.ingramcontent.com/pod-product-compliance
Lightning Source LLC
Chambersburg PA
CBHW022148300426
44115CB00006B/392